American Immigrants and Their Generations

Marcus Lee Hansen. "What the son wishes to forget the grandson wishes to remember." (University of Illinois Archives)

American Immigrants and Their Generations

Studies and Commentaries on the Hansen Thesis after Fifty Years

Edited by

Peter Kivisto and Dag Blanck

UNIVERSITY OF ILLINOIS PRESS
Urbana and Chicago

This book is printed on acid-free paper.

Publication of this work was supported in part by grants from Augustana College, Rock Island, Illinois, from the Augustana Historical Society, and from the Swenson Swedish Immigration Research Center.

Library of Congress Cataloging-in-Publication Data

American immigrants and their generations : studies and commentaries
on the Hansen thesis after fifty years / edited by Peter Kivisto and
Dag Blanck.
   p. cm.
   "Essays in this book stem from a conference arranged by the
Swenson Swedish Immigration Research Center at Augustana College.
Rock Island, Illinois in April 1987"—Pref.
  ISBN 0-252-01689-0
   1. Hansen, Marcus Lee, 1892–1938—Congresses. 2. Immigrants—
United States—Historiography—Congresses. 3. United States—
Emigration and immigration—Historiography—Congresses.
4. Ethnicity—United States—Historiography—Congresses.
5. Immigrants—United States—History—Congresses. 6. United
States—Emigration and immigration—History—Congresses.
7. Ethnicity—United States—History—Congresses. I. Kivisto,
Peter, 1948– . II. Blanck, Dag. III. Swenson Swedish Immigration
Research Center.
E175.5.H3A44 1990
305.8'00973—dc20
                             89-5206
                               CIP

Contents

Contents

Preface

From the time we began to think about a small conference that would provide a retrospective examination of Marcus Lee Hansen's "The Problem of the Third Generation" essay up to the present, we have benefited from the assistance of numerous individuals and from the generosity of several organizations which provided timely and much needed financial support. Our initial idea was to invite a distinguished scholar to present an address at Augustana fifty years after Hansen delivered his famous speech to the members of the Augustana Historical Society. However, we quickly discovered that there was widespread interest in a larger conference that would be designed to both reflect upon the contributions of Hansen to the study of immigrants and their generations and on the implications of scholarly developments that have transpired since Hansen's death. To that end, we invited a number of prominent scholars—historians and social scientists—to Augustana College in the spring of 1987. A memorable exchange of ideas ensued, the results of which are contained in this collection.

In addition to the scholars who have contributed articles to this volume, we have benefited from the advice, the comments, and the encouragement of many other individuals, including Arthur Mann, Oscar Handlin, Herbert Gans, Robert Harney, and John Bodnar. We would like to single out for special thanks Rudy Vecoli, Harald Runblom, and Werner Sollors.

Closer to home, countless people both on and off the Augustana campus helped us along the way. We are especially indebted to Victoria Oliver, John Caldwell, Kermit Westerberg, Perry Mason, Michael Smith, Andy Terronez, Harold Sundelius, Jane Telleen, Jill Seaholm, Mary-Beth Walker-Van Tress, Elizabeth Dochterman-Walsh, and Glen Brolander. We could not have accomplished this project without their labor and good will.

The conference at which these essays were first presented was made possible by generous grants from the Illinois Humanities Council, the Iowa Humanities Board, the Swedish Council of America, and the

Augustana Humanities Fund. We would like to especially thank Jane Hood, former director of the Illinois Humanities Council, for her enthusiastic support thoughout. Costs associated with the publication of this volume were partially offset by the financial assistance of the Augustana Historical Society, the Augustana Faculty Research Fund, and the Swenson Swedish Immigration Research Center.

Richard Wentworth, director of the University of Illinois Press, attended the conference, and since then has been most supportive and sympathetic. He and the members of the Press's staff, especially Harriet Stockanes and Mary Giles, have made the sometimes arduous tasks associated with putting together a collection such as this a remarkably pleasant experience.

Special recognition must go to the Augustana Historical Society, which for fifty years has shown a great commitment to the third generation thesis, and to the Swenson Swedish Immigration Research Center, which took the initiative for the whole project.

Ethnicity and the Problem
of Generations in American History

The discussions in this volume constitute an attempt to explore the shifting significance of ethnicity in America predicated on historical change and generational succession.

Three years before the passage of the immigration restriction legislation of 1924, the historian Arthur Schlesinger, Sr., suggested a research agenda intended to serve as a coda for establishing "the significance of immigration in American history." Writing in the *American Journal of Sociology*, the official organ of the Chicago School of sociology, he proposed that scholars devote attention to two interrelated themes: "the influence of immigration upon American life and institutions," and "the influence of America on the everchanging composite population."[1] Although a number of historians during the interwar period would, indeed, expend considerable intellectual energy in pursuing this agenda, with notable instances including Carl F. Wittke, George M. Stephenson, and Theodore C. Blegen, the most significant figure during this period was certainly Marcus Lee Hansen.[2]

Despite his untimely death in 1938 at the age of forty-five, with much of his life work before him, Hansen has been widely acclaimed as the most astute and profound observer of the Atlantic migration. Nathan Glazer, for example, characterized him in the early 1950s as "the greatest student of American immigration," while Moses Rischin has depicted him as "America's first transethnic historian," the first to "conceptualize, legitimate, and give stature and universality to the ethnic dimension in American life."[3] This scholarly reputation is based largely on Hansen's monumental research work that focused on the process of immigration from Europe to America. Thanks to Schlesinger, what became his two most important books were published posthumously: *The Immigrant in American History* and *The Atlantic Migration* (the latter being the recipient of the 1940 Pulitzer Prize for History).[4]

However, as Rischin has suggested, Hansen was also, especially during the final years of his life, "an advocate and evangelist" concerned with the long-term fates of ethnic groups and cultures. As two essays written at the end of his life amply attest, he was a "brooding cultural historian."[5] The first of these is the essay that became the focal point for the discussions presented herein, while the second is a little-known address—Hansen's last before his death—delivered just ten days after the Augustana speech. Entitled "Who Shall Inherit America?," it was presented to a group of social reformers at the annual meeting of the National Conference of Social Work in Indianapolis.[6] In both instances, Hansen's primary concern was not with the past, but with the future of ethnicity. "Who Shall Inherit Ameica?" has previously only appeared in single-spaced typescript form in *Interpreter Releases* (July 6, 1937). Both it and "The Problem of the Third Generation" are included in the Appendix of this volume.

The Augustana address was published by the Augustana Historical Society the year after its delivery. However, as Philip Gleason indicates in his essay in this volume, it was not widely read until 1952, when Glazer (who, in an instance of intellectual serendipity, stumbled onto it as it gathered dust on the shelves of the New York Public Library) had the piece reprinted in *Commentary*. Since that time, it has become, as Oscar Handlin's introduction in that magazine suggested, a classic essay in immigration history.[7]

The significance of Hansen's address, as sociologist Richard Alba has written, lies in the fact that it calls attention to the issue of ethnic identity—to the subjective dimension of the ethnic phenomenon.[8] As such, it is the precursor to the ever-expanding body of scholarship concerned with explicating the form and content of the ethnic experience. It also is one of the first expressions of the theme of generations as a sociohistorical problem in the study of ethnicity.

It is rather remarkable that such a seminal essay for scholars of ethnicity would have the origins that this one did. Hansen's speech, presented on May 15, 1937, was addressed not to a group of academics, but to a literate lay audience interested in the preservation of their ethnic heritage. Specifically, Hansen had been asked to address the membership of the Augustana Historical Society in Rock Island at their annual meeting. The society, founded in 1930, was composed of Swedish Americans, with the membership being affiliated, to great extent, with the Lutheran Augustana Synod. This context is important because it has an obvious bearing on the style and tone of Hansen's work: discursive and suggestive rather than rigorously analytic and bolstered by compelling empirical data.

It is not surprising, therefore, that commentators have chosen to read the essay in rather different ways. It is worth mentioning several recurring and distinguishable approaches to the thesis because they have come to serve as the interpretive filters through which we view "The Problem of the Third Generation Immigrant." In the first instance, repeated efforts have been made to test empirically a literal reading of the argument, with John Appel's study of the American Jewish Historical Society being perhaps the most explicit example.[9] Not surprisingly, such studies have generally concluded that Hansen's "law of third generation return" is not borne out by the evidence. Generational differences are much more complex and varied than the simple notion of second generation flight and third generation return would suggest. Indeed, Hansen was aware of this. He knew, for instance, that his Rock Island audience was composed primarily of first and second generation Swedish Americans, but he contended that they were "third generation in spirit."

This might be what Margaret Mead had in mind when she viewed this notion metaphorically, contending that we are all third generation. In her book, *And Keep Your Powder Dry*, Mead indicates no awareness of Hansen, but her intent clearly parallels that contained in Hansen's "in spirit" phrase.[10] This second way of reading the essay has by no means been the most common, but the fact that it continues to be an option can be seen in Werner Sollors's fascinating attempt to present the essay as a redemption story rooted in American literary tradition. He argues that the rhetoric of generations is essentially moral rather than analytical. Hansen seeks to "delineate(e) a moral map" in which the language of generations is used to construct a bipolar symbolization of good and evil. The second generation is seen as "deficient" as opposed to the "wholesome" third, which is seen as the redeemer capable of remedying the apostasy of the second.[11]

A third approach originated with Will Herberg's reformulation that was designed to understand changes in religious affiliation and religiosity in the United States. His proposal to fuse Hansen's thesis to Ruby Jo Reeves Kennedy's "triple melting pot" argument found its way into the work of Gerhard Lenski, which in turn, stimulated a great deal of research in the sociology of religion.[12]

Finally, in attempting to make sense of the resurgence of ethnicity in America during the past two decades, Hansen's work, read loosely for its appreciation of the variability of ethnicity, was taken to be a precursor to discussions of "the ethnic revival," "emergent ethnicity," "the new ethnicity," "symbolic ethnicity," and similar concepts.[13] Its virtue was taken to be its sensitivity to the situationally conditioned character of ethnicity.

The first three essays in this volume look at Hansen's work from the perspective of the intervening half-century. John Higham's contribution illustrates the gulf between Hansen's brand of historical writ-

ing and that of contemporary social historians. Although Higham
thinks it neither possible nor advisable to go back to Hansen, he does
think that important lessons can be learned and new directions pursued
that would overcome some of the deficiencies of structuralist histories.
Specifically, he observes that Hansen's immigration history contains
both an explicit protagonist—the solitary individual—and a clear sense
of historical direction, predicated on a view that tended to equate
process with progress. Although this perspective can, and indeed has,
been criticized, Higham thinks there is something worth saving: narrative history. Comparing Hansen's writings to the work of John Bodnar, especially his highly influential synthetic work *The Transplanted*,
Higham suggests that the latter might benefit from a consideration of
a new kind of narrative history appropriate to the perspective of social
historians.

In a different vein, Thomas Archdeacon looks specifically at Hansen's analysis of generational change. He attempts to decompose and
reconstruct an abstract model based on Hansen's thesis, but accounting
for a variety of critical historical variables missing in Hansen's singular
focus on the internal dynamics of generational change. He suggests
that generations must be linked to other variables such as ethnicity,
social status, and societal tolerance. While disputing Hansen's claim
to universality, Archdeacon offers a series of propositions that would
indicate when to expect a heightened ethnic interest and under what
circumstances it would be expected to wane.

Moses Rischin borrows from the *annales* historians to treat ethnicity as *mentalité*. In his meditation on the complexity and ambiguity
surrounding the place of ethnicity in the forging of an American identity, Rischin ranges over long periods of time to include treatments of
the eighteenth-century French immigrant Michael-Guillaume Jean de
Crèvecoeur [Hector St. John] and speculations about the dilemmas
attendant upon efforts to create the "new man" to Richard Rodriquez's
sensitive and painful account of what it means to come to terms with
one's ethnicity in the late twentieth century.

The next five chapters extrapolate from Hansen's thesis by examining its usefulness in understanding various ethnic, religious, and
cultural groups, including Catholics, Jews, Swedes, blacks, and Slavs.
Philip Gleason is concerned with the linkage between ethnicity and
religion. He focuses on the reception of the Hansen thesis during the
1950s (paying particular attention to its reformulation by Herberg)
and seeks to comprehend why Jewish intellectuals during the period
were so drawn to the argument, while Catholics and Protestants appeared not to be. Next, Glazer returns to the essay that he was responsible for introducing to a larger audience in the 1950s. Noting

that Hansen's depiction of generational change is cast in psychological terms, Glazer uses the Jewish-American case to argue that this "fertile hypothesis" needs to be refined by indicating the manner in which generation interacts with historical change. He calls for being more attuned to the historical specificity of factors shaping the life experiences of generations. Then, H. Arnold Barton's essay returns to Hansen and to the setting of the Augustana address. In attempting to answer the question, How much did Hansen know about the Swedes in America?, he again returns to Hansen's very simple formulation, suggesting both the virtues and the limitations of the thesis.

Stanford M. Lyman introduces in general terms the relationship between race and ethnicity, and in more specific terms Hansen's treatment of blacks in America. He inquires into Hansen's somewhat curious use of Margaret Mitchell's *Gone With the Wind* in the advancement of his thesis. Reviewing Hansen's treatment of blacks in America's immigrant experience, Lyman proceeds to explore the issue of third generation interest among American blacks via an analysis of William Wells Brown's novel, *Clotel; or, The President's Daughter: A Narrative of Slave Life in the United States* (1853). This section concludes with Victor Greene's essay, which takes seriously Arthur Schlesinger, Sr.'s call for looking at the reciprocal interplay of American and ethnic cultures. Greene examines the pervasive influence of the international folk-dance movement and "old-time" music, especially as it was popularized by such performers as "Whoopee John" Wilfarhrt, Lawrence Welk, and Frankie Yankovic. In rich detail he indicates the irony of the situation: as the second generation immigrants were becoming Americanized, American culture was becoming ethnicized.

The final contribution, by intellectual historian Fred Matthews, returns to some of the themes introduced by Higham while opening up a wider intellectual horizon by placing Hansen into context. His essay provides a portrait of the interpretive shifts in American scholarship concerning the topic of ethnicity during a half-century period beginning in 1930. In contending that a paradigm that focused on process yielded to one that stressed structure, Matthews attempts to locate Hansen's work within the larger currents of scholarly discourse, concluding that Hansen ultimately remained an adherent of the process model and, indeed, did not question the assumption that process implied progress. He seeks to illustrate how these assumptions were subsequently questioned, first in the work of Handlin, a transitional figure, and later in such influential popular works as Michael Novak's *The Rise of the Unmeltable Ethnics*.

As was expected, in opening up new vistas for inquiring into the lives of immigrants and their offspring in America, and in locating the contribution of Marcus Lee Hansen to that quest, a number of conflicting perspectives are articulated in this volume. An introduction is not an appropriate place to attempt to resolve or to adjudicate these differing perspectives, but it is useful to note some of the more obvious points of disagreement among our contributors. First, epistemological questions arise in four of the essays that seek to determine how best to construe generations. Glazer, and in richer detail, Archdeacon seek to link generational change to historical change, and in so doing argue for periodizing generational analysis. In contrast, Lyman, and in a more limited way, Rischin, seek to view generations as mental constructs.

Second, a variety of assessments are evident in addressing the question concerning the applicability of Hansen's generational thesis. Rischin is the contributor most inclined to treat the notion of third generational interest as having universal application, while Greene appears at least implicitly to argue that it is a flawed argument that does not apply in any circumstances. Between these two extremes, Barton raises questions about whether Hansen really understood Swedish Americans and their presumed "interest" in ethnicity, while Gleason suggests that Herberg's rendering of Hansen's "law" turns out to depict Jews correctly at mid-century, but does not provide an accurate characterization of Catholics in America during the same period. A third issue involves Hansen and race. Hansen's reference to *Gone With the Wind* is discussed in two essays: Barton seems to think that this reference indicates Hansen's impartiality, whereas Lyman treats it as an illustration of Hansen's difficulties in coming to grips with locating Afro-Americans in the overall history of immigration.

Finally, there is at the very least uncertainty about the novelty of Hansen's focus on the third generation. Rischin contends that Hansen "minted" the term *third generation immigrant*, but its novelty is not so obvious in Greene or Barton. As indicated earlier, Margaret Mead used the term without any obvious awareness of Hansen's essay. This might suggest that issues related to the third generation had a more pervasive impact than Rischin would imply. It is clear, as Greene's essay amply attests, that the interwar period witnessed a rather widespread concern about the "problems of the second generation." Whether or not this attention paid to conflict between the immigrant generation and their descendants extended to include the third and subsequent generations is a matter that needs further explanation.

Taken together, these essays amply indicate that a half-century after Hansen's speech, ethnicity in America remains a perplexing, enigmatic topic. They also indicate that Hansen's "problem" not only evokes considerable discussion and debate, but also provides a starting point for treating generations in history and the history of generations.

NOTES

1. Arthur Schlesinger, "The Significance of Immigration in American History," *American Journal of Sociology* 27 (January 1921):71.

2. O. Fritiof Ander, "Four Historians of Immigration," in *In the Trek of the Immigrants: Essays Presented to Carl Wittke,* ed. O. Fritiof Ander (Rock Island: Augustana College Library, 1964), pp. 17–32.

3. Nathan Glazer, "America's Ethnic Pattern: 'Melting Pot' or 'Nation of Nations'?" *Commentary* 15 (April 1953):407; Moses Rischin, "Marcus Lee Hansen: America's First Transethnic Historian," in *Uprooted Americans: Essays to Honor Oscar Handlin,* ed. Richard Bushman, Neil Harris, David Rothman, Barbara Miller Solomon, and Stephan Thernstrom (Boston: Little, Brown, 1979), p. 322.

4. Marcus Lee Hansen, *The Immigrant in American History,* ed. Arthur M. Schlesinger (Cambridge: Harvard University Press, 1940) and *The Atlantic Migration, 1607-1860: A History of the Continuing Settlement of the United States,* ed. Arthur M. Schlesinger (Cambridge: Harvard University Press, 1940).

5. Rischin, "Marcus Lee Hansen," p. 323.

6. Marcus Lee Hansen, "Who Shall Inherit America?," *Interpreter Releases* 14 (July 6, 1937):231.

7. Oscar Handlin, "A Classic Essay in Immigrant History," *Commentary* 14 (November 1952):492.

8. Richard Alba, "Ethnic Identity Among American Whites." Paper presented at the annual meeting of the American Sociological Association, Chicago, 1987, p. 38.

9. John Appel, "Hansen's Third Generation 'Law' and the Origins of the American Jewish Historical Society," *Jewish Social Studies* 23 (January 1961):3–20. See also, Bernard Lazowitz and Louis Rowitz, "The Three-Generations Hypothesis," *American Journal of Sociology* 69 (March 1964):529–38; Vladimir Nahirny and Joshua Fishman, "American Immigrant Groups: Ethnic Identification and the Problem of Generations," *Sociological Review* 13 (November 1965):311–26; and Harold Abramson, "The Religioethnic Factor and the American Experience," *Ethnicity* 2 (July 1975):165–77.

10. Margaret Mead, *And Keep Your Powder Dry: An Anthropologist Looks at America* (New York: William Morrow, 1942).

11. Werner Sollors, *Beyond Ethnicity: Consent and Descent in American Culture* (New York: Oxford University Press, 1986), pp. 214–21.

12. Will Herberg, *Protestant-Catholic-Jew: An Essay in American Religious Sociology* (Garden City: Doubleday, 1955). Ruby Joe Reeves Kennedy "Single or Triple Melting Pot?: Intermarriage Trends in New Haven, 1870–1940," *American Journal of Sociology* 49 (January 1944):331–39; Gerhard Lenski *The Religious Factor* (Garden City: Doubleday, 1961).

13. See, for example, Herbert Gans, "Symbolic Ethnicity: The Future of Ethnic Groups and Cultures in American," *Ethnic and Racial Studies* 2 (January 1979):1–20; William Douglass and Stanford Lyman, "L'ethnie: Structure, processus et saillance," *Cahiers Internationale de Sociologie* 61 (July-December 1976); and William Yancey, Eugene P. Ericksen, and Richard Juliani, "Emergent Ethnicity," *American Sociological Review* 41 (June 1976):391–403.

PART ONE

Hansen's "Law" After Fifty Years

From Process to Structure: Formulations of American Immigration History

A symposium on Marcus Lee Hansen would surely be incomplete if it dealt only with the prescient address given at Augustana College half a century ago. Hansen's elusive third generation did not figure in the history produced during his short career, and it has played almost no part in the history his successors have written. Hansen's most substantial legacy consists of his principal historical works. They too deserve our attention.

Yet the question, What is living in Hansen's historical work?, is not easy to answer. In spite of Moses Rischin's sensitive and appreciative essay about Hansen in 1979[1] few people read him any more. Hansen is vaguely remembered as our first major immigration historian, a man of fine breadth and supple vision, but the books he wrote in the 1930s are too distant to engage us. Since the 1960s, young scholars have discovered their models, positive and negative, largely in historians who have flourished in the period since World War II. Hansen speaks to us from another era, when everything was a great deal simpler. One can not expect his work to provide a large body of reliable knowledge, or even many concrete insights, on which to build today. But Hansen's very distance puts the problems of our own time in a useful perspective. The simplicity of Hansen's conceptual universe, although it cannot be entirely recaptured, helps in coping with complexities we now want to overcome.

The attractive simplicity of Hansen's best-known books, *The Atlantic Migration* (1940) and *The Immigrant in American History* (1940), arises partly from having a single, distinct, uncomplicated protagonist. Like his mentor Frederick Jackson Turner, Hansen made the unencumbered, migratory individual the fundamental reality of his history. In sharp contrast to historians today, Hansen dismissed the role of government, downplayed the church, ignored the family, and paid scant attention to ethnic differences. In announcing his theme at the opening of *The Atlantic Migration*, Hansen declared, "The European of 1815 or 1914 left the Old World and settled in the New usually as an individual." In earlier long-distance migrations, "the individual had been a cog in a mechanism greater than himself." In the nineteenth-century exodus from Europe, however, "A human atom wrenched itself from an old society and attached itself to a new."[2] Describing the myriad circumstances of the immigrants' departures and the varied origins from which they sprang, Hansen sought not to distinguish one strain from another, not to compare classes or nationalities or generations, but rather to convey a common process. Here and even more in his boldly interpretive essays, *The Immigrant in American History*, Hansen wrote primarily about the immigrant as a prototypical individual: a person whose motives for leaving home "were unusually mixed," who had "an innate aversion to the wilderness," but who was withal "a capitalist at heart." To *the* immigrant, the essays freely attributed much influence on other features of American history.

Hansen's history may not seem an obvious testimonial to American individualism, for it broke decisively with the celebration of particular individuals so evident in the work of the filiopietistic historians who wrote for the immigrant historical societies. Their books concentrated on notable individuals—the heroes and avatars whom each ethnic group proudly claimed.[3] Hansen focussed instead on the anonymous commoner—European, to be sure, and rural in background, but a mythic individual in his or her implicit separation from any collective body and detachment from any institutional matrix.

Following in Hansen's footsteps, Oscar Handlin in 1951 still treated the immigrant as a type. Armed with a new sociological sophistication, however, Handlin did not envision a detached individual, "a human atom." Handlin's immigrant differed from Hansen's in becoming an individual through a painful uprooting from the collective solidarity of a warmly sustaining community. From the Chicago School of urban sociology, which flourished between the wars, Handlin learned how to make the breakdown of communities and the tensions within individuals the theme of a history of people in motion.[4]

A more decisive shift from the scholarship of Hansen's day to our own came with the appearance in the 1960s of a "new social history." At first it was said to be new because of its relish for "problem-solving," its quantitative bent, and its affinity with the social sciences. Yet none of these characteristics touched the heart of the enterprise. At bottom, the new social history abandoned the individual as a unit of analysis. It turned instead to substantial, collective bodies: groups, classes, organizations, and institutions. Historians now wanted to know how different social species have maintained and defined themselves, what resources each brings to a situation, and what collective strategy it adopts. Instead of the immigrant, we now encounter Italian families, Polish coal miners, Jewish Zionists, German Lutherans, and Finnish socialists, to name just a few. These are the protagonists in the new social history. They make Hansen's generalized immigrant look insubstantial and unconvincing.

The new social history produced a mighty outpouring of social description and analysis; but the gain in concreteness did not yield a greater coherence. An enormous fragmentation ensued. Burrowing into records of a favorite community or cohort, innumerable young scholars pressed questions suggested by some theory or personal affiliation. Immigrants were scrutinized as industrial workers, as women, as voters, as ethnics or church members, as school children, criminals, and leaders. Specialists in immigration history, labor history, religious history, family history, women's history, electoral history, urban history, and educational history studied overlapping facets of a common population but did so within separate networks. Each network developed its own scholarly journal, its own energizing question, its own agenda, and to some extent its own language. Often these groups were entirely out of touch with one another; concepts that interested one set of scholars were rarely articulated with the problems that interested other sets.[5]

By the 1980s, the need for a new synthesis could no longer be ignored. Somehow social historians would have to find a subject—specifically a protagonist—large enough to embrace, or mediate among, the confusing multiplicity of groups and identities standing before us and thus to reconstitute the focus that the prototypical, individual immigrant had supplied for Marcus Lee Hansen.

Along with a strategic focus, historical synthesis requires an encompassing pattern. Here Hansen's best work exemplifies a second kind of simplicity, complementing his fixation on a single protagonist. His practice was to follow a movement through time and space; the pattern in which he cast that movement was one of progress. His most nearly finished book, *The Atlantic Migration*, engages the immigrant in a dramatic narrative: a story of travail and hope in moving toward a promised land.

By giving a narrative form and a progressive bent to his key work, Hansen adopted a pattern that was common among the leading social historians of his era. Like Carl Bridenbaugh and Arthur M. Schlesinger, Sr., Hansen described a flow of experience. These interwar historians treated social change as an accumulation of responses that countless individuals made, bit by bit, to new conditions. Their works fell naturally into a narrative form, although it was sometimes hard to see the protagonist (often the "common man" or the American people).

Images of movement ran through their pages. It is hardly accidental that Hansen found his great theme in the actual process of migration rather than the creation of a social order in America. In Hansen's day even the leading social scientists in the United States were preoccupied with process and little inclined to investigate the supposedly misleading "rigidities" of structure.[6]

The inclination of scholars during the interwar period to see history advancing toward some large, humane goal encouraged and supported their confidence in knowledge as a guide to social change. Progressive scholars looked to history as a direction-finder, a means of probing deep currents in human affairs and thus linking the past to the present and future. If history can demonstrate that the object of study has moved persistently—albeit painfully and ambiguously—in a particular direction, can it not prepare us to meet the attendant difficulties?[7] Some such faith surely guided Hansen's narrative of the Atlantic migration to an upbeat conclusion. Hansen's confidence that history has a partially discernible, even predictable, direction must have provided the assurance with which he sketched the succession of generations in America, telling the third generation of Swedish Americans in 1937 that they stood at a precious but transitory juncture between an immigrant past and a future of complete amalgamation.[8]

The new social history has addressed issues of form and purpose in historical writing without relying either on narrative or on a belief in progress. The protagonist, although now appearing in a bewildering variety of shapes and forms, remains. What social history has lost is the progressive design. Rebelling against narrative, most social historians since the 1960s have sought meaning outside of the old framework of incremental progressive change. In place of direction, the new social history fixes attention on constraint and resistance. Instead of following a narrative, it explores persistent relationships. Structure has superseded process as the underlying configuration of historical thought. The result is a "motionless" history in which people are perceived as caught in a system or contained within a discontinuous moment.[9] Obviously, in much of our historiography today the rigidifying tendency of structure is flexed and softened, just as the flow of process in Hansen's time was usually restricted by some sense of institutional limits. Nevertheless, the shift from one paradigm to the other has altered profoundly the cast of American social, cultural, and intellectual history.

These contrasts between the scholarship of fifty years ago and today may be illustrated by comparing The Atlantic Migration with the most recent and advanced study of the same subject. While Hansen's book covers the entire immigration from northern and western

Europe to 1860, John Bodnar's *The Transplanted* (1985) encompasses immigration from all parts of the world to American industrial towns and cities in the century after 1830.[10] In opening up a phase of history then largely unexplored, Hansen based his account of the nineteenth century primarily on his own indefatigible researches. Fifty years later, surveying a span of time reaching into the twentieth century and a wider range of ethnic origins, Bodnar entered a field crowded with hundreds of studies produced in many different countries. He was able, as Hansen was not, to draw on a generation of intensive scholarship. Still, the crucial divergence between the two books is not in their sources but in their assumptions and aims. Hansen shaped a creative synthesis from the ideas available to him as a progressive historian. Bodnar has woven another pattern from ideas that the new social history has authorized.

In identifying a protagonist large enough and central enough for the big picture he wanted to create, Bodnar vaulted across one of the most troublesome conceptual barriers that had grown up in this part of American social history in recent years. The study of workers in the industrial era and the study of immigrants in urban America took off simultaneously in the late 1960s. Centering essentially on the same people—the immigrant masses who comprised so much of the industrial labor force—the two inquiries nevertheless flourished in separate academic networks. The study of workers engaged historians of American labor. They concentrated on the formation of class consciousness. Immigrant studies attracted a different set of historians, specialists in demography, emigration, and the history of immigrant communities in the United States. These scholars have usually been most interested in the maintenance or loss of a particular ethnic identity. One group focussed on the workplace, the other on distinctive ethnic locales such as churches and immigrant neighborhoods.

Some labor historians, however, began in the 1970s to widen their purview from the history of labor protests and organizations to a broader study of ideas, life-styles, and communities. Bodnar, although trained as an immigration historian, quickly followed the example of the labor historians in connecting the economic pressures of the workplace with the world of home and family. Blending the two perspectives, he identified a composite population as his protagonist—an immigrant working class.

In Bodnar's telling, the immigrant working class deserves our respect not for the heroic initiatives of its venture into a new world or the embattled pride of its struggles there, but rather for its stubbornly conservative adaptation to forces it could not control. Swept up in the immense upheaval that capitalism created, Bodnar's immigrants accepted the economic changes they could not prevent while using the private sphere of family and kinship to maintain the stability, security, and tradition they valued. Theirs was a "mediating culture" with "modest goals . . . devoid of extremely radical or liberal impulses."[11] By coping practically with day-to-day exigencies, they sustained an enduring dignity. In effect, Bodnar gives up the labor historians' search for a radical class consciousness and the ethnic historians' fascination with unique group cultures. In his hands, ethnicity becomes simply a collective strategy for blunting the force of social change.

In contrast to Hansen's mythic individual, then, Bodnar offers a mythic collectivity—amorphous, intricately divided in many ways, but well suited to the over-all design of the new social history. The striking feature of Bodnar's "transplanted" is how little their activity impacts on the world outside their own sphere. Continually in motion, fractured into a myriad separated communities and urged in a dozen different directions, they seem to turn like figurines on a music box, revolving in place.

The contrast with Hansen's design strikes us at the very outset of the two books, even in the epigraph each author chose. *The Atlantic Migration* opens with a stirring quotation from an American magazine of 1852 describing "the process of settlement and naturalization" as a "flood of emigration . . . from every isle and continent, under the whole heaven. . . . There has been nothing like it in appearance since the encampments of the Roman empire, or the tents of the crusaders." Thus the historian locates his story against a background of earlier stories of dramatic change. Bodnar, however, chooses a quotation from a contemporary statement of historical theory: "A social interpretation of history places ideas, events and behavior as well as institutions in the larger context of the overall social system."[12] Bodnar's text then starts with a dense section, characteristically entitled "The Structure of Emigration." It argues that emigrants moved within established social relationships and institutions and that individual self-interest played only a minor role in their decisions. Instead of acclaiming the newness and distinctiveness of the immigrants' experience, Bodnar sees a painful, repetitive adaptation to unwanted changes.

The same contrast between a dramatic moment in time and a gray, impersonal continuum marks the close of the two books. Hansen's narrative ends with the interruption of immigration by the American Civil War and the dawning of a new day. "When the war ended," he concludes, "ideals had changed. All who lived in America, alien-born and native-born, were resolved to become one people."[13] Bodnar has no ending. His book just stops, since the immigrant experience for him was not a "linear progression," but rather an endless struggle of little people to maintain some order and stability in their lives. To be sure, there is good reason in historical reality for terminating a survey of immigration at the onset of the Great Depression. Thereafter the world of the immigrants was drastically transformed. But Bodnar gives no hint of the impending upheaval: continuity is his theme.

Do we have here another framework of meaning in place of the progression and predictability that the new social history has renounced? Bodnar makes clear that we do. In finding a lesson in history outside of the old paradigm of incremental, progressive change, Bodnar sees history as cautionary and connective. It teaches the unreliability of everything big, impersonal, and powerful. By conveying the hard lessons our forebears learned, history reveals the basic continuities that persist through changing circumstances; it preserves the "fragile link between the generations."[14] To expand the point somewhat, one can say that the new social history wants to strengthen social identities by elucidating what has survival value in a chaotic, unsatisfactory world.

The objective is hard to fault—but even harder to attain, especially within the terms that the new social history has prescribed. Ironically, the search for what was constant or recurrent during a bygone era can make the rupture between then and now seem devastating. So much that Bodnar describes—the strong communal feeling, the tight-knit family life, the crowded urban neighborhoods, the closeness to Old World experience—has not survived among most descendants of the nineteenth-century immigration. Their transplanted ethnic heritage has become symbolic, if preserved at all.[15] Their class position has changed dramatically. Their abandoned neighborhoods have fallen into other hands. By largely ignoring development, the new social history leaves us with the disturbing spectacle of ancestors who clung unflinchingly to commitments that a feckless progeny has inexplicably surrendered. Without recovering some idea of the direction of history, historians cannot say much about the problem of "survival"—that is, the adaptation of traditions—in our own time.

I believe that the project of recapturing for the new social history some of the larger purposes of the old social history deserves our best thought and effort. We cannot go back to the confident, although sometimes also wistful, idea of progress that oriented Hansen. We cannot assume that an overarching direction, whether it be progress or decline or cyclical recurrence, channels the course of modern times. But we can—indeed we must—look at the history of the last century with an eye for trends. When studies of this sort become available, the achievement of the new social history in making structure visible should no longer obscure the flow of process. A clearer definition of successive periods and their causal epicenters should come into view.

To regain Marcus Hansen's concern with the direction of American immigration history, without losing a more developed understanding of groups and institutions, scholars will have to probe more deeply into both social categories that have entangled labor and immigration historians in a common endeavor. Working out a developmental relationship between class and ethnicity means taking neither for granted as a fixed entity. Their relationship may change because the ethnic groups realign, or because the classes alter, or because both structures move in dissimilar ways. Scholars need to look on both sides of the equation.

To complicate matters still further, significant change in the ethnic-class relationship can come either from the larger social structure or within particular ethnic groups. Each ethnic group is likely to have its own class hierarchy that is partly based upon but only imperfectly reproduces the class system of the dominant society. Ethnicity and class, in other words, are not only the boundaries and segmentations of minorities. They are also organizing principles of the larger social order, separating and connecting all of its members according to the priorities of that society and changing as the whole society evolves. To understand class and ethnicity in these dynamic terms is to integrate the story of the immigrants into the development of American society.

This is a far more ambitious undertaking than I can attempt here. My object is simply to delineate the problem and sketch a partial approach to it. To do so it will be necessary to define some terms and summarize a little more the conceptual strategies that have guided research to date.

Following Jon Elster, I define *class* as a broad stratum of society, the members of which make use of an interlocking endowment of power, skill, and property. (The specifically Marxian definition of class as determined by one's relation to the means of production overlooks the many historical situations in which possession of political power or cultural capital has preceded the accumulation of property.) Thus classes, as Max Weber pointed out, are "phenomena of the distribution of power within a community." They are not themselves communities, Weber tells us, but "represent possible, and frequent, bases for communal action."[16] It would be more accurate to say that a class can become a community under conditions that foster a persistent sense of mutuality and belonging. Ethnic groups, however, are essentially communities because they embody a diffuse awareness of mutual interdependence and connectedness over an extended period. An ethnic group resembles a family in sharing a presumption of common origin and a sense of obligation to all who display the marks of that origin. Thus *ethnicity*, although it often articulates and advances material

interests, centers in tradition.[17] Class, on the other hand, is grounded
in present interests although it may invoke tradition. An ethnic group
may become concentrated in a particular class, even to the point of
monopolizing the class interest. Alternatively, the ethnic tie may bind
together people of different classes. In either case, ethnicity maintains
an inheritance from the past that should (in principle) belong to an
occupationally diverse population, whereas class concerns the alloca-
tion of more or less tangible resources between different ranks of people.

In the tangle of historical circumstance, differences between class
and ethnicity are far from absolute. Rhetorically, however, they inhabit
separate realms of discourse that are hard to move between. Infusing
contemporary scholarly discourse is an assumption that class is powerful because it is material and that ethnicity is precious because it is
cultural. Today, most people who write about ethnicity celebrate it.
Behind the affirmations, however, lurks an implicit sense that ethnic
institutions and attachments are vulnerable unless politicized by a nationalist movement.[18] This sense that ethnic groups are precious but
all too feeble in the United States helps to explain why social historians
do not ordinarily offer them as causes of wider historical developments.
Scholars who write about classes, on the other hand, unhesitatingly
attribute extensive causal influence to them. These scholars see class
as always powerful in history, ethnicity only intermittently so. In
much academic discourse today, class works as an engine of history.
Ethnic groups appear as the flowers of history, although sometimes
also as fuel in the locomotive of class. Treating class and ethnicity as
fully comparable allegiances, sometimes autonomous and sometimes
cunningly intertwined, will require a more ambivalent and realistic
attitude toward both.

To that end, two highly charged concepts related to ethnicity—
nationalism and race—need scrutiny. A nation is simply an ethnic
group (sometimes a federation of ethnic groups) that claims sover-
eignty, or at least guarantees, of its cultural autonomy. Nationalism
is therefore an especially strong form of ethnic feeling that demands
the creation or control of a state or otherwise subjects identity to a
political test. Race, like language and religion, serves as a marker of
ethnic relatedness, but not necessarily or consistently. A race becomes
an ethnic group only if perceived as such in a race-conscious society.
In North America, race has been a peculiarly rigid and invidious principle of ethnic categorization.[19]

The close linkage postulated here between ethnicity, nationality,
and race violates the existing division of labor in historical scholarship.
In discourse about the United States, ethnicity is often treated as the

domain of immigrants and their descendants. Indians and blacks belong to separated groups of specialists, who sometimes insist that the special statuses imposed on these racial minorities make a mockery of any comprehensive scheme of ethnic classification. A racial minority, we are told, is not an ethnic group. It is formed by pure oppression, not by any internalized belief that the group shares a distinctive culture or identity.[20]

The objection to treating a race as an ethnic group, although understandable as a reaction against the idealization of ethnicity in so much current scholarship, needlessly vitiates any broadly comparative study. No ethnic group is self-created; nor does any such group escape assignment to some social location that may be advantageous but is frequently the reverse. All ethnic groups come into being through the perceptions of outsiders as well as the responses of those perceived, and this cultural interaction always occurs in a context of differential power and potential domination. The subordination of some racial minorities presents an extreme case on an ethnic continuum.

Recognizing the primarily cultural basis of race and ethnicity and the primarily economic structure of class helps to sort out the main strategies scholars have employed in correlating these two dimensions of the social order. One approach to the relation between class and ethnicity is rooted in class analysis. It interprets ethnicity as a reinforcement of, or complication within, the pattern of class struggle. A second approach assigns preeminent importance in history to culture and therefore subordinates class to ethnicity. A third approach envisages class and ethnicity as separate but possibly convergent determinants of social location and social change.

The first position assumes that class operates at a deeper explanatory level than race or ethnicity because it refers directly to an inequality in material circumstances, whereas race and ethnicity are ideological inventions. Following this approach, a sparkling essay by Barbara J. Fields argues that ideas about race, powerful although they have been, do not refer clearly to an objective reality and therefore are less stable and predictable than we often imagine. Developing a broader version of the same argument, Stephen J. Steinberg, a sociologist, construes all of the inequalities between races and ethnic groups in America as the outcome of differences in power and wealth rather than culture.[21]

How then does one explain the volcanic force or imbedded persistence of ethnic sentiments in situations that would seem more appropriately addressed through class alignments? The materialist argument has been refined to interpret such situations as special variants or complications within an underlying economic conflict. For example, a theory of "internal colonialism" accounts for sharp and persistent ethnic conflict as an outgrowth of differential economic exploitation. A somewhat similar theory of "segmentation" of the labor market since World War I into primary and secondary jobs finds employers responsible for keeping the working class divided along ethnic lines. A variant known as the "split labor market theory" shifts much of the blame on to the white working class.[22] More influential among historians has been the "cultural Marxism" of Herbert Gutman and other labor historians, who have found in the ethnic heritages of American workers certain cultural resources that sustained resistance to employers.[23]

Here the predominance of class over ethnicity becomes much attenuated. One result of cultural Marxism is a growing uncertainty among Marxist scholars over questions of causation.[24] Yet the underlying interest of labor historians in the roots of class struggle has perpetuated the ultimately privileged status that Marxism of any kind grants to class as the basic structural reality of capitalist society. Cultural Marxism deals effectively with ethnic sentiments that feed into class formations, but not with ethnic sentiments that supersede or disrupt such formations.

All class-based theories stand in sharp opposition to ethnicity-based theories in which cultural differences are seen as more important than material circumstances. From an ethnic perspective, the heritage that people bring into a new situation tends to determine its outcome. Thomas Sowell has offered perhaps the most explicit formulation of cultural determinism. Arguing that European domination of the world was a consequence of superior knowledge and technology, Sowell goes on to show that the unequal achievement of American ethnic groups can also be attributed to their respective cultural endowments.[25] Thus ethnicity rather than class may appear to be the engine of history, although it is doubtful that Sowell himself would draw that conclusion.

In general, immigration historians avoid making sweeping claims for the causal importance of ethnicity. This is partly because their interest has focused on specific ethnic groups, whom they perceive as unique creations—the flowers of history and often its victims. Another reason for the relative particularity of the ethnic approach is the paucity of grand social theory assigning a central role to ethnicity. Unlike class, theorists have rarely taken ethnicity seriously as a universal and necessary property of social systems. Accordingly, it has lacked the broad, explanatory significance that is often imputed to class.[26] Only within special topics in which economic interpretations have come under attack has the predominance of ethnicity over class in American history been asserted explicitly. The study of election returns, for example, produced an "ethnocultural school" of historians who have devoted many pages to showing how and when ethnic identifications have outweighed economic interests in determining voting behavior.[27]

In summary, it seems fair to say that the culturalist position in the study of immigration history has remained fragmented while the materialist position has undergone a steady dilution. This theoretical disarray is producing a third approach in which neither ethnicity nor class is understandable without reference to the other—yet neither can be reduced to the other. Bodnar's *The Transplanted* took an important step in that direction, but an incomplete one. His strategy, although far from materialist, was nevertheless reductive. It enclosed ethnic experience within a class structure presented as fractured but inflexible. We see the immigrants deploying their many cultural resources (family, religion, folklore) to cope with the constraints of class. Class remains unaffected and inert, however, and ethnicity seems incapable of reaching much beyond it. The extent to which a predetermined working class frames the author's perspective becomes clear in the one chapter devoted to an immigrant middle class. Here Bodnar treats as a self-interested minority the "self-employed shopkeepers, fraternal officials, and other businessmen who fostered fragmentation by separating themselves from their humble moorings."[28]

An unwillingness to step outside of a fixed class framework appears also in Bodnar's treatment of the second generation. We see the children of immigrants only insofar as they stayed within their parents' world. Conflicts between generations are screened out, along with changes in self-definition that accompanied those conflicts. By treating particular ethnic groups as if they have little meaning apart from the classes in which they function, Bodnar emptied them of the color and flavor that make their identities meaningful. Ethnic identity as a contested choice never enters the picture at all.

A workable synthesis will have to emerge from a perspective in which ethnicity and class are recognized as distinct but overlapping dimensions of society. Each extends beyond the other, but where they intersect, each forms a medium in which the other is experienced. Our question now is whether, among the Europeans who emigrated to the industrial heartland of the United States in the nineteenth and early twentieth century, the interaction of class and ethnicity reveals any consistent relationship.

A starting point may be found in a striking feature of American labor history. Many labor historians have shown that the industrial era produced intense and frequently violent class conflicts. Yet these bitter struggles, we are told, rarely created in working people any settled consciousness of belonging to a class that was permanently or essentially opposed to the classes above it.[29] What Marxists call "class consciousness"—the articulated resistance of one class to the perceived power of an adversarial class—has boiled up episodically in American history and then (so the argument goes) simply subsided.

Preoccupation with the problem of an unstable, repeatedly deflated class consciousness has diverted American labor history from another kind of class sentiment that is harder to observe but more tenacious. It exists whenever people are aware of sharing similar attitudes, a common life-style, and a common position in society without feeling antagonistic to other classes and without adopting any self-conscious group strategy. Class awareness, as I shall call this relatively passive form of self-identification, is simply the subjective correlate of class structure. American historians have only begun to study it.[30]

The distinction between awareness and militant consciousness is useful because the latter is so visible, so overt, in widely available historical records. The distinction invites quick access to what is most energetic in group behavior without forcing that militant consciousness to represent the entire class for which it claims to speak. Moreover, the distinction is just as applicable and even essential in studying ethnicity as it is in understanding class. As Katherine Verdery has shown in the case of Transylvania, awareness of having a particular ethnic heritage need not entail a corresponding program of collective action. In other words, at the most active level, both class and ethnicity are "strategic options" rather than inescapable fates.[31] They are identities that can be mobilized, and when that happens they acquire a special power.

To realize that both class and ethnicity become empowered through mobilization is not to deny structural differences between the two categories. It is simply to make them comparable, and thus to explore connections between them empirically without presupposing that one is subordinate or reducible to the other. Have classes and ethnic groups mobilized concurrently in American history? Or has each marched to a different drummer? Answers to that question should shed some light on the pattern and direction of American immigration history.

On first inspection, the behavior of the immigrants whom Bodnar studied reveals no consistent relation between ethnic and class consciousness. Instead, one finds a perplexing oscillation between outbursts of class conflict, episodes of interethnic conflict, and longer periods of withdrawal into the private world of a familiar ethnic enclave. When these scattered data are examined within the larger contours of American history, however, the suggestion of a pattern emerges. During the early decades of industrialization, ethnic attachment thwarted and disrupted class consciousness. As the Industrial Revolution matured, however, ethnic and class assertiveness became entwined and mutually supportive for almost half a century.

Before the 1850s, industrialization proceeded relatively slowly and undramatically. Manufacturing establishments remained scattered and generally small; capital and manpower were overwhelmingly engaged in the conquest of a vast interior. Drawn by the general expansion of the economy, mass immigration became visible in the 1830s, well before there was much awareness of factory operatives as a class distinct from their employers. Instead of massing in factories, immigrants toiled in a great variety of occupations and situations—commonly in the poorest jobs but often in skilled and specialized work for which prior knowledge had qualified them. A study of 2,664 adult male Scottish immigrants who came to the United States before 1855 showed, for example, that before emigration about a third had earned their living from a remarkable variety of crafts. A smaller proportion of these Scottish males had been farmers (28 percent), a still smaller one servants and laborers (16.4 percent).[32] This diversified work experience must have forestalled any immediate inclination to identify, consistently or predominantly, with one class or another. The newcomers' primary allegiance (beyond relatives and neighbors) would have to be to their fellow countrymen, especially to those already established in America.

And, indeed, each of the ethnic groups who were drawn into the early American factories and mines found in their new homeland compatriots comfortably settled in business and the professions. The mass immigration of the 1830s merely resumed the migration from northwestern Europe that had begun in the eighteenth century. Accordingly, the Germans, English, Scots, Irish, Welsh, and Jews had already made their presence and institutions felt in preindustrial settings. All of them had developed a middle class able to exert influence and leadership across class lines. In Philadelphia, for example, a largely assimilated Irish-American middle class controlled both the religious and the secular institutions that molded the group consciousness of the peasants who came in such torrential numbers after the Famine.[33] The mid-century immigrants would never become so completely associated with an industrial working class as would the newer groups who arrived in the late nineteenth century.

Along with objective circumstances that separated ethnic consciousness from class consciousness in the early industrial era, immigrants to the United States encountered a culture that made ethnic identities more meaningful than class identities. Native-born Americans relished national and racial stereotypes. The American habit of thinking about others in terms of ethnocultural inequalities and differences undoubtedly reinforced the stereotyping propensities immigrants had brought with them. On the subject of class, however, American predelictions were much less supportive of attitudes formed in Europe. American culture discouraged overt display of rank and privilege. Immigrants marveled that "no kind of work is looked down upon here," that the poor man does not have to doff his cap to his betters, that farmers and artisans "have practically the same manners" and "enjoy the same degree of respect as the merchant and the official," that capitalists and workers march together in parades. "It is an American political creed to be one people," a happy Norwegian immigrant wrote home in 1848. "This elevates the lowly and brings down the great."[34]

There was, to be sure, a widening gap between wealth and poverty in Jacksonian America and along with it an amorphous class consciousness. But prevailing American ideologies softened and blurred the conflict. The Whig party preached a true harmony of interests between labor and capital; it attracted many working-class votes in doing so. The Jacksonians espoused class struggle. They interpreted it, however, as a battle between a privileged set of idlers and the broad mass of hard-working "producers," which included honest employers as well as employees. Both parties converted the incipient class consciousness of antebellum America into a definition of the nation's moral center.[35] What immigrant workers heard as well as what they saw created a presumption that the burden of class would not weigh heavily on them.

Still, workers' resentments sputtered in urban settings and might have built up strongly if ethnic divisions had not supervened. When a workers' movement showed a certain promise in the mid-1830s, immigrants in some numbers joined the upthrust of trade unionism and strikes in several major cities. Some unions in New York City welcomed German and Irish craftsmen. Unrest even spread to unorganized Irish dock workers and building laborers. The movement soon collapsed, however. Heightened animosities between native and foreign workers followed in the 1840s.

One might have expected a reversal in the fifties, a revival of class consciousness. By then industrialization was transforming key cities and towns, turning artisans into wage workers and removing them almost completely from the "genteel" society of business and professional people. Yet brave attempts early in the decade to organize city-wide federations of unions in New York, Cincinnati, and elsewhere, bringing native Americans and Irish together with German workers, came to nought.[36] Instead, an unprecedented mobilization of ethnic consciousness throughout American society either dwarfed or absorbed class antagonisms. In place of the economic issues that had aroused the "producing classes" in the Jacksonian era, problems of national identity and of defending a cultural heritage from foreign and domestic enemies dominated political and social life.

The great crisis over slavery that convulsed the Union in the 1850s may not at first glance look like an ethnic mobilization. But it is well to bear in mind that the most intense sectional feeling emanated from the most homogeneous regional cultures—from New England and its western extensions on one side and the deep South on the other. Compromise failed when both Yankees and white Southerners perceived the other as plotting to overthrow a long-established way of life, which each believed was at the core of its identity. Spokesmen for the two groups had come to see one another as separate peoples with incompatible social systems.[37]

Many Americans, especially in the mid-Atlantic and border states, shrank from both sides. But they too rallied in great numbers around issues of ethnic identity, as if the heterogeneous, centrifugal, uncontrolled expansion of the country had become suddenly intolerable. To whites who regarded themselves as old-fashioned Protestant Americans rather than guardians of a sectional heritage, Catholic and foreign influence presented the great threat to national (i.e., ethnic) unity. That influence could seem more alien than the sectional enemy and was also closer at hand. For several years a fledgling American (or Know-Nothing) party and the equally untried Republican party competed to become the chief defender of American institutions, one from the Slave Power, the other from a despotic church. Although principled Republicans despised the illiberal side of the Know-Nothings, the general compatibility of their appeals as the protectors of a free country was widely recognized.[38]

An unprecedented influx of European and Chinese immigration, pouring into the growing cities and the new minefields of the North and West, gave native-born wage-earners special reasons for feeling endangered. They confronted the proximity of more numerous alien rivals just when the mechanization of production was undercutting their own economic independence. It is little wonder that working-class whites provided the shock troops of the Know-Nothing movement, or that Catholic immigrants clung desperately to their own ethnic institutions: their parishes, saloons, gangs, and Democratic political clubs. The mobs that invaded German and Irish neighborhoods in Baltimore, Louisville, and other cities in 1855, the pitched battles that ensued, and the spectacular electoral victories of Know-Nothing candidates in half a dozen states made dramatically clear the intensity of a second ethnic mobilization cross-cutting that of Yankees and Southerners.[39]

The antebellum era reveals, therefore, an alteration between class and ethnic militancy in the course of which ethnicity became the ever more active and manipulable force. Class awareness survived, of course, but trapped and partly hidden within a maze of ethnic assertiveness. In the Civil War era, the mobilization of competing sectional and religious identities—all in the name of race and nationality—brought ethnic consciousness so strongly to the fore that class consciousness could not coalesce effectively. Its reemergence as a significant force in public life was discouraged and deferred.

After the Civil War, the institutions through which immigrants and other Americans worked out their ethnic and national affiliations underwent a vast elaboration. Churches, political machines, fraternal orders, and other voluntary societies stabilized communities while linking the classes within them.[40] Yet the inflamed ethnic consciousness of the 1850s and 1860s subsided in the postwar years while class consciousness revived, notably among skilled workers. Surges of discontent, feeding on the impersonality of big corporations and the insecurities of unregulated labor markets, swept across the industrial areas of America. As strikes multiplied, large numbers of working people and others caught a vision of a cooperative economy. Among the upper classes, fears of social revolution provoked a reciprocal solidarity. It is difficult, however, to discern during those post-Civil War decades a clear pattern in the interplay of class and ethnicity. Sometimes, as in the Chinese Exclusion Act of 1882, the ethnocultural structure resonated to class grievances and reinforced them; sometimes it deflected or muffled them.

As class antagonisms peaked in the mid-1880s, we find again the alternation between class and ethnic mobilizations that marked the antebellum era. Among workers, the increasingly radical class consciousness of the late nineteenth century crested in an extraordinary wave of strikes in the spring of 1886. Skilled and unskilled, immigrants and natives, joined hands in a passionate hope of changing the industrial system. This special, millennial moment passed in 1887–88. Under a barrage of legal and ideological attacks from business interests, the Knights of Labor and the independent labor parties allied with the Knights collapsed in bitter factional wrangles.[41] Only then, after class mobilization had failed, did a comparable surge of militant ethnic consciousness boil up in its wake.

The ethnic struggles of the late 1880s turned on traditional cultural issues. They turned not on economic exploitation—not on wages, the eight-hour day, or collective bargaining—but on the control of education (i.e., the heritage that would be passed on to the young) and the regulation of private life, especially the consumption of alcohol. As in the 1850s, Protestant moralists spearheaded an assault on the drinking habits that Irish and German immigrants took for granted. Simultaneously, the old-stock reformers made a national issue of the marital customs of Mormons, while also launching a drive to Anglicize Catholic and Lutheran parochial schools. Immigrant voters, furious at these invasions of their "personal liberty" and their rights as parents, inflicted stunning defeats on the dominant Republican party in many states from 1889 to 1892.[42] In some places the collapse of class mobilization was the immediate cause of the ensuing ethnic militancy. Within a week after a local election in 1887 in Clinton, Iowa, an industrial town on the Mississippi River, the defeated labor candidate for mayor and his friends founded the American Protective Association, which became the chief anti-Catholic organization of the late nineteenth century. The embittered mayoral candidate blamed his defeat on the failure of the Irish mill workers to support him.[43]

Without further research and deeper analysis it is hard to say whether the experience of the 1880s resembles that of the 1850s sufficiently to suggest a pattern rather than an episodic fluctuation. What can be argued with some confidence is that an erratic or inverse fluctuation of class and ethnic mobilizations is far less apparent in the first half of the twentieth century. Instead, the two forms of assertive solidarity became more closely entwined, rising and falling together and eventually—in the 1930s—merging. An amalgam of class and ethnic consciousness in the early twentieth century completed the making of an immigrant working class.

To understand this remarkable new phase in American social history we will have to return to my preliminary distinction between awareness and consciousness, that is, between relatively persistent structures of society and more volatile movements of ideological assertiveness. Throughout the ups and downs of militant group consciousness in the nineteenth century, the underlying structure of classes that crystallized early in the century apparently remained firmly in place. It was, in brief, a localized structure. Most of the time it offered a modicum of personal contact between classes, a cross-class ethic of fairness, and a credible hope of escaping oppressive conditions by moving away.[44] For the most part, the social structure of nineteenth-century America seemed to contemporaries relatively porous and uncoercive. Class awareness was generally soft and blurred.

Around the end of the nineteenth century, however, prevailing perceptions of inequality between classes hardened drastically. By the 1890s, according to a study by James Livingston, an assumption that industrialization "was producing a permanent working class and a class society according to the European model informed almost every contemporary analysis of economic development, regardless of the analyst's political sympathies."[45]

The accuracy of these perceptions, and especially the degree of social change that they reflect, remains uncertain, but there is little doubt that a quantum increase in the spatial segregation of social classes occurred as local communities lost cohesiveness and autonomy. Retreating into exclusive neighborhoods or fleeing entirely from the cities, the middle and upper classes created suburban enclaves that firmly resisted metropolitan annexation. Simultaneously, huge factories gathered their work force into nearby, class-segregated districts.[46] Further reinforcing the experiential boundary between middle and working classes was the development of country clubs, "service" clubs, vacation resorts, automobiles, private schools, and public high schools permeated by genteel values. A banker in William Dean Howells's novel, *A Traveler from Altruria*, summed up the resulting class awareness: "There is as absolute a division between the orders of men, and as little love, in this country as in any country on the globe. The severance of the man who works for his living with his hands from the man who does not work for his living with his hands is so complete, and apparently so final, that nobody even imagines else."[47]

Yet millions did imagine else, including Howells himself, and much of the history of the early twentieth century is about efforts to deal with these gaping rents in the social order. On one side of the division that Howells described, a native-born middle class, feeling squeezed between an oligarchy above and a restive lower class beneath, rallied to the broad political movement that called itself "progressive." More directly relevant to the story of the immigrants was a simultaneous although largely separate mobilization of working people—a class-conscious movement to cope with a new class structure. A weak, tenuous federation of unions blossomed in the early twentieth century into a durable mass movement, particularly in certain basic industries. For almost the entire period 1901–19, the number of strikes (relative to the number of nonagricultural employees) soared above anything recorded in the previous century.[48]

The institutionalization of class consciousness within an expanding labor movement provided a context in which ethnic fragmentation of the industrial work force was reduced. Just as the new class structure fostered a multiethnic working-class culture, so the unionizing struggles of the early twentieth century forged in some industries a multiethnic solidarity. In a study of the anthracite coal industry, Peter Roberts marvelled in 1901 that the "the foreigners" have formed unions "which are more compact and united than any which ever existed among the various English-speaking nationalities who first constituted these communities. It is conceded by men intimate with the situation throughout the coal fields during the last strike, that its universality was more due to the Sclav than to any other nationality."[49]

Admittedly, "class" was in the air in the early twentieth century, challenging as never before the old American confidence in individual opportunity. But that alone cannot account for the solidarity, to say nothing of the communal passion, that immigrant communities now displayed during strikes in the coal fields and elsewhere. These uprisings expressed not only class assertiveness, but also and simultaneously a new-born ethnic consciousness, especially among recent immigrants from southern and eastern Europe. Those newcomers became self-consciously ethnic in the very throes of discovering a wider class identity.

Peasants drawn to the United States after 1880 from Italy, Hungary, and Slavic lands came with scant awareness of a world outside their own village. Identity for them was very parochial. The nation was an idea in the minds of educated elites, far beyond their ken. In America these immigrants formed little communities restricted to an immediate neighborhood or even to people from a single village. Then, around the turn of the century, leaders of the little communities began to build wider networks of communication among them, invoking the ties of a common language, culture, and often religion. Some, who were labor activists or radical intellectuals fleeing from repression in the old country, stressed the solidarity of class. Necessarily, however, they organized along national lines and thus promoted awareness of a national as well as a class identity. Others, with middle-class goals, appealed directly to the idea of the nation as a great community struggling for realization. National fraternal societies and ethnonationalist newspapers sprang up alongside the burgeoning labor organizations. While ethnic consciousness was gaining as a vehicle for class consciousness, it was also fueled by rivalry between the two.[50] Both impulses widened horizons, and many former peasants must have felt the enlargement of their identity as a single consciousness-raising experience.

If the new immigrants from southern and eastern Europe had found among their fellow countrymen in America an entrenched middle class capable of guiding their acculturation, the ethnic bond would surely have impeded class consciousness. But no such elite was on hand.[51] Few southern and eastern Europeans had settled in the United States before the 1870s. Still less than 5 percent of the total foreign-born population in 1880, they came in the next two decades almost without precursors.[52] In the nineteenth-century immigrant communities of Germans, Irish, and others, the influence of a successful, Americanized middle and upper class had strongly counteracted class grievances. Within the new immigrant communities, class and ethnic feelings could more easily spring up together as complementary focuses of social consciousness.

To organize their local communities, the newcomers had either to create their own leaders, or fall under the control of bosses, politicians, and priests who neither spoke their language nor shared their heritage. At the end of the nineteenth century, therefore, the New Immigration produced its own thin middle class of shop owners, saloon keepers, newspaper editors, priests, and officers of fraternal societies. A large proportion of such local leaders came from peasant stock. Sharing the sympathies and experiences of their neighbors and customers, they were close to the laboring masses. The dependence of this petite bourgeoisie on a vastly larger body of factory hands meant that the new ethnic communities in the early twentieth century belonged to a relatively undifferentiated working class.[53]

By the outbreak of World War I, the rising ethnic consciousness in the new immigrant communities was finding expression in nationalist as well as class programs. In the nineteenth century, only the Irish had supported a broad movement for liberation of their homeland. Beginning in 1914, movements to free one's own people from oppression overseas spread through a dozen ethnic groups ranging from Jewish Zionists to pan-African black nationalists, each group resonating to the excitement that gripped the others.[54]

In principle, the ethnic nationalisms of the war years clashed with a radical class consciousness because the socialists and anarchists who opposed the war appealed for proletarian solidarity among all the wretched of the earth. At an emotional rather than ideological level, however, the aroused class consciousness and the militant national consciousness of the war years were symbiotic. They flowed together. As a working class, the immigrants in 1917 threw themselves into the largest strike wave the United States had seen up to that time. As ethnics who identified with the United States, with the old country, and with one another, they caught a patriotic fever in which victory for America, liberation of the homeland, and justice for the working class intermingled. The fusion of a hyphenated national consciousness and a multiethnic class consciousness was grounded in a tremendous, expectant yearning for a better life, here in America and through America's leadership in the Old World as well. "For why this war?" asked a Polish steelworker at a union meeting in Pennsylvania. "For why we buy Liberty bonds? For the mills? No, for freedom and America—for everybody. . . . For eight-hour day."[55]

This was a new stage in the making of an immigrant working class, not only because of the alignment of class and ethnic sentiment, but also because of the direction in which the alignment pointed. The distinctively ethnic mobilizations of the nineteenth century, among immigrants and natives alike, were basically defensive. People rallied to save their own traditions from the intrusions of outsiders—to protect especially their religion, language, and mores from proselytizers, public officials, and unwelcome neighbors. The early class mobilizations were also largely defensive in looking back to the imagined harmony of a producers' Eden before the coming of the factories and foreigners. For all such movements—ethnic and class alike—the point of reference was anterior to the polyglot reality of contemporary America. In the twentieth century, however, a basic urge to change the world infused both class and ethnic consciousness, connecting them through a common web of protest and a common reference to a future that all could hope to share. In spite of clashing ideologies and divergent cultures, the immigrant working class was becoming aware of itself as a segment of America, marked partly by its disadvantage relative to the older strata but drawn together also by intuitions of a single destiny.

After World War I, the dreams of a brave new world of class solidarity and national liberation shattered. Both working-class and ethnic consciousness thereupon underwent a precipitous decline, and in doing so demonstrated again how interdependent they had become. Labor union membership and the number of strikes dwindled year by year; ethnic nationalism virtually collapsed. Even the Zionist movement survived only by shelving its political agenda and concentrating on philanthropic projects. The immigrants, demobilized and demoralized, put up only feeble resistance to the victorious immigration restriction movement.[56]

But the twenties turned out to be hardly more than an interlude in the making of the immigrant working class. Under the hammering of the Great Depression, the ethnic and class militancy that had begun to coalesce before and during World War I returned. Now led by a second generation, born in America, a resurgent ethnic working class built on the experience of the Progressive era. The linkage created then between the labor unions and the Democratic party gave the next generation a potentially powerful organizational basis. As voters, the immigrants and their children became the central component in the

New Deal coalition. As workers, they brought the American labor movement the greatest gains in its history.[57]

In the perspective of our own time, the victories of the 1930s and 1940s loom as a culminating moment in the history of the immigrant working class. After a century of intermittent struggle and adaptation, its triumphs in the mid-twentieth century surely owed much to the accumulated experience of earlier mobilizations. Perhaps even more vital, however, was the complementary and reinforcing alignment between class and ethnic identities. In establishing a civic and not just an economic presence in America, the urban ethnics benefited from having a middle class that still inhabited the "moral universe" of the masses.[58] Both joined in a political uprising that drew as much on ethnic as on class consciousness.

On the ethnic side, however, the consciousness that informed the organizing drives and political campaigns of the 1930s and 1940s had changed significantly since World War I. After an intervening period of intense Americanization, many of the immigrants—and especially the second generation—no longer identified with a homeland beyond the sea. The hyphenated loyalties of 1917, which had associated the American cause with irredentist and national liberation movements, now energized an inclusive American nationalism—a nationalism celebrating the heterogeneous origins and the allegedly egalitarian spirit of the American people. This inclusive nationalism, affirming as it did the Statue of Liberty as the supreme American symbol, harmonized with the class consciousness of the period because it located the true and essential America in the "common man."[59] For all who chafed over some kind of exclusion, for all who felt they had been left out of the American Dream, the ethnic and class consciousness of the 1930s expressed an overwhelming demand for incorporation. In the great strike at Bethlehem Steel in 1937, second-generation immigrant workers vowed, "You are not going to call us 'Hunky' no more."[60]

The substantial success and eventual irony of this last mobilization of the immigrant working class can be read in the statistics of its *embourgeoisement* during the 1940s and after. In employment rates and income levels the major white ethnic groups made such spectacular gains that by the 1970s they outranked white Protestants in annual income.[61] Understandably, both class and ethnic consciousness sharply declined after World War II. This in turn reduced class polarization in voting and the vigor of the labor unions. What is more, nearly all of the local institutions that sustained traditional identities—such as lodges, taverns, national parishes, and political machines—were gravely weakened.[62] The causes of this massive demobilization lie beyond the scope of the present essay. But the fact should not be missed that the immigrant working class lost its raison d'être in the course of attaining the incorporation it had sought for so long.

Presented in the form I have given it here, the history of the multiethnic working class that forged America's industrial revolution suggests a developing, rather than a constant or merely erratic, relationship between class and ethnicity in American history. In questioning the image of an obdurately cautious immigrant culture preoccupied with survival, we have glimpsed the outline of a dramatic narrative. We have discovered a protagonist whose shape and purpose change as the larger social order evolves and whose story has a beginning, a climax, and an end. It is surely not the story that Marcus Lee Hansen would have told had he lived to complete his work. But it may suggest the continuing relevance of the panoramic, narrative history that he wrote.

NOTES

An earlier version of this chapter was presented at the annual conference of the Atlantic Association of Historians, October 25, 1986, in Annapolis Royal, Nova Scotia, where I benefited from the comments and criticism of Stephen E. Patterson, Gilbert Allardyce, and Sam Nesdoly. This version is a product of a Mellon Senior Fellowship at the National Humanities Center. I am also greatly indebted to the critical perspicacity of William Freehling and Olivier Zunz.

1. Moses Rischin, "Marcus Lee Hansen: America's First Transethnic Historian," in *Uprooted Americans: Essays to Honor Oscar Handlin*, ed. Richard Bushman, Neil Harris, David Rothman, Barbara Miller Solomon, and Stephan Thernstrom (Boston: Little, Brown, 1979), pp. 319–47. Less sympathetic, but also useful, are: Allan H. Spear, "Marcus Lee Hansen and the Historiography of Immigration," *Wisconsin Magazine of History* 44 (Summer 1961):258–68; and Carlton C. Qualey, "Marcus Lee Hansen," *Midcontinent American Studies Journal* 8 (Fall 1967):18–25. A document of special personal interest is a brief memoir by C. Frederick Hansen, "Marcus Lee Hansen—Historian of Immigration," *Common Ground* 2 (Summer, 1942):87–94.

2. *The Atlantic Migration, 1607–1860: A History of the Continuing Settlement of the United States*, ed. Arthur M. Schlesinger (Cambridge: Harvard University Press, 1940), p. 11. *The Immigrant in American History*, ed. Arthur M. Schlesinger (Cambridge: Harvard University Press, 1940) was basically the Commonwealth Fund Lectures on American history, which Hansen delivered at the University of London in 1935.

3. John J. Appel, *Immigrant Historical Societies in the United States 1880–1950* (New York: Arno Press, 1980).

4. Oscar Handlin, *The Uprooted: The Epic Story of the Great Migrations That Made the American People* (Boston: Little, Brown, 1951). See also Maldwyn A. Jones, "Oscar Handlin," in *Pastmasters: Some Essays on American*

Historians, ed. Marcus Cunliffe and Robin W. Winks (New York: Harper and Row, 1969), pp. 245–61.

5. John Higham, *History: Professional Scholarship in America*, rev. ed. (Baltimore: Johns Hopkins University Press, 1983), pp. 239–61.

6. Fred Matthews, "Louis Wirth and American Ethnic Studies: The Worldview of Enlightened Assimilationism, 1925–1950," in *The Jews of North America*, ed. Moses Rischin (Detroit: Wayne State University Press, 1987), p. 141, n19; Morton G. White, *Social Thought in America: The Revolt Against Formalism* (New York: Viking Press, 1949). *The Atlantic Migration* was only the first of a projected three-volume work, so it is difficult to say what form Hansen would have given to the American side of the immigrant experience had he lived to write the later volumes. But there is no evidence in his collected essays that he would have departed from the pattern of prototypical, individual progress.

7. White, *Social Thought in America*, pp. 110–14, 183–95.

8. Marcus Lee Hansen, "The Problem of the Third Generation Immigrant," republication of the 1937 address with introductions by Peter Kivisto and Oscar Handlin (Rock Island: Swenson Swedish Immigration Research Center and Augustana College Library, 1987).

9. Emmanuel LeRoy Ladurie, "History That Stands Still," in *The Mind and Method of the Historian* (Chicago: University of Chicago Press, 1981), pp. 1–27. See also Fred Matthews, " 'Hobbesian Populism': Interpretive Paradigms and Moral Vision in Recent American Historiography," *Journal of American History* 72 (June 1985):92–115.

10. John Bodnar, *The Transplanted: A History of Immigrants in Urban America* (Bloomington: Indiana University Press, 1985).

11. Bodnar, *The Transplanted*, pp. 210–12.

12. Quoted from Robert F. Berkhofer, Jr., "Comments," *American Historical Review* 84 (December 1979):1328.

13. Hansen, *The Atlantic Migration*, p. 306. Another indication of the temporal and conceptual distance between the two books is the contrast between Bodnar's opening invocation of "the overall social system" and Hansen's closing salutation to "one people." Present-day readers may not agree that there is an "overall social system," but the phrase will arouse nothing more critical than a yawn. Any allusion to "one people," however, immediately puts us on guard.

14. Bodnar, *The Transplanted*, pp. xv, xx–xxi.

15. Herbert Gans, "Symbolic Ethnicity: The Future of Ethnic Groups and Cultures in America," *Ethnic and Racial Studies* 2 (January 1979):1–20.

16. Jon Elster, *Making Sense of Marx* (New York: Cambridge University Press, 1985), pp. 318–97; Max Weber, *From Max Weber: Essays in Sociology*, ed. H. H. Gerth and C. Wright Mills (New York: Oxford University Press, 1946), pp. 181–94.

17. Donald L. Horowitz, *Ethnic Groups in Conflict* (Berkeley: University of California Press, 1985); Werner Sollors, *Beyond Ethnicity: Consent and Descent in American Culture* (New York: Oxford University Press, 1986); Robert Norton, "Ethnicity and Class: A Conceptual Note with Reference to

the Politics of Post-Colonial Societies," *Ethnic and Racial Studies* 7 (July 1984):426–32; John L. P. Thompson, "The Plural Society Approach to Class and Ethnic Political Mobilization," *Ethnic and Racial Studies* 6 (April 1983):127–53. Michael Banton, *Racial Theories* (Cambridge: Cambridge University Press, 1987) places contemporary theories about race and ethnic relations in a context of earlier theories and persistent conceptual problems. A valuable symposium is *Theories of Race and Ethnic Relations*, ed. John Rex and David Mason (Cambridge: Cambridge University Press, 1986).

For an illuminating analysis of the tangled meanings of "community" I am indebted to Thomas Bender, *Community and Social Change in America* (New Brunswick: Rutgers University Press, 1978), pp. 5–11.

18. Horace B. Davis, *Toward a Marxist Theory of Nationalism* (New York: Monthly Review Press, 1978); Walker Connor, *The National Question in Marxist-Leninist Theory and Strategy* (Princeton: Princeton University Press, 1984).

19. Pierre van den Berghe, "Class, Race and Ethnicity in Africa," *Ethnic and Racial Studies* 6 (April 1983):221–22. See also the more elaborate definitions proposed in articles by Walker Connor, van den Berghe, and James McKay and Frank Lewins in *Ethnic and Racial Studies* 1 (October 1978):377–427.

20. M. G. Smith, "Ethnicity and Ethnic Groups in America: The View from Harvard," *Ethnic and Racial Studies* 5 (January 1982):1–22.

21. Barbara J. Fields, "Ideology and Race in American History," in *Region, Race, and Reconstruction: Essays in Honor of C. Vann Woodward*, ed. J. Morgan Kousser and James M. McPherson (New York: Oxford University Press, 1982), pp. 143–77; Stephen Steinberg, *The Ethnic Myth: Race, Class, and Ethnicity in America* (New York: Atheneum, 1981). For an application of this approach see Joe William Trotter, Jr., *Black Milwaukee: The Making of an Industrial Proletariat, 1915–1945* (Urbana: University of Illinois Press, 1985).

22. Michael Omi and Howard Winant, *Racial Formation in the United States from the 1960s to the 1980s* (New York: Routledge and Kegan Paul, 1986), pp. 30–37, 47–50; J. Stone, ed., *Internal Colonialism*, special issue of *Ethnic and Racial Studies* 2(July 1979); David M. Gordon, Richard Edwards, and Michael Reich, *Segmented Work, Divided Workers: The Historical Transformation of Labor in the United States* (Cambridge: Cambridge University Press, 1982); Edna Bonacich, "Advanced Capitalism and Black/White Relations in the United States: A Split Labor Market Interpretation," *American Sociological Review* 41 (February 1976):34–51.

23. Herbert Gutman, *Work, Culture, and Society in Industrializing America: Essays in American Working-Class and Social History* (New York: Alfred A. Knopf, 1976). See also John Higham, "Current Trends in the Study of Ethnicity in the United States," *Journal of American Ethnic History* 2 (Fall 1982):5–15.

24. T. Jackson Lears, "The Concept of Cultural Hegemony: Problems and Possibilities," *American Historical Review* 90 (June 1985): 567–93.

25. Thomas Sowell, *Ethnic America: A History* (New York: Basic Books, 1981), and *Marxism: Philosophy and Economics* (New York: Morrow, 1985), p. 208.

26. Frank Parkin, *Marxism and Class Theory* (New York: Columbia University Press, 1979), pp. 31–43.

27. Paul Kleppner, "Piety, Federalism, and the Shaping of U.S. Politics," *Mid-Stream* 22 (July–October 1983):401–18, is an especially pointed summary of the literature.

28. Bodnar, *The Transplanted*, p. 117.

29. Nick Salvatore, "Response to Sean Wilentz, 'Against Exceptionalism: Class Consciousness and the American Labor Movement, 1790–1920,'" *International Labor and Working-Class History* no. 26 (Fall 1984):29. I am also indebted to, although unpersuaded by, Wilentz's argument, pp. 1–24, for the continuity of class consciousness in American labor history.

30. Stuart Blumin's pioneering essay, "The Hypothesis of Middle-Class Formation in Nineteenth-Century America: A Critique and Some Proposals," *American Historical Review* 90 (April 1985):299–338, is an important exception. For more elaborate theoretical statements of the levels of class formation see Jurgen Kocka, "The Study of Social Mobility and the Formation of the Working Class in the 19th century," *Le Mouvement Social* no. 111 (June–August 1980): 104–7, and Ira Katznelson, "Working-Class Formation: Constructing Cases and Comparisons," in *Working-Class Formation: Nineteenth-Century Patterns in Western Europe and the United States*, ed. Ira Katznelson and Aristide R. Zolberg (Princeton: Princeton University Press, 1986), pp. 13–22.

31. Katherine Verdery, "The Unmaking of an Ethnic Collectivity: Transylvania's Germans," *American Ethnologist* 12 (February 1985):62–83; Peter Eisinger, "Ethnicity as a Strategic Option: An Emerging View," *Public Administration Review* 38 (January–February 1978):89–93.

32. Gordon Donaldson, "Scots," in the *Harvard Encyclopedia of American Ethnic Groups*, ed. Stephan Thernstrom (Cambridge: Harvard University Press, 1980), pp. 912–13. Because these figures very likely underrepresent unskilled rural labor, the variety of skilled trades may be more telling than the percentages.

33. Dale Light, "The Reformation of Philadelphia Catholicism," *Pennsylvania Magazine of History and Biography* 112 (July 1988):375–405, and "The Role of Irish-American Organizations in Assimilation and Community Formation," in *The Irish in America: Emigration, Assimilation and Impact*, ed. P. J. Drudy (Cambridge: Cambridge University Press, 1985), pp. 113–41, amplify aspects of an important argument summarized in Light's "Irish-American Organizations in Philadelphia," *American Catholic Studies Newsletter* 15 (Spring 1988):12–6.

34. Frederick Hale, ed., *Danes in North America* (Seattle: University of Washington Press, 1984), pp. 106, 116; H. Arnold Barton, ed., *Letters from the Promised Land: Swedes in America, 1840–1914* (Minneapolis: University of Minnesota Press, 1975), p. 247; Theodore C. Blegen, ed., *Land of Their*

Choice: The Immigrants Write Home (St. Paul: University of Minnesota Press, 1955), pp. 86, 199, 203, 433–34.

35. Marvin Meyers, *The Jacksonian Persuasion: Politics and Belief* (New York: Vintage Books, 1960), pp. 10–15, 18–32; Daniel Walker Howe, *The Political Culture of the American Whigs* (Chicago: University of Chicago Press, 1979), pp. 21, 29–37, 138–39; Sean Wilentz, *Chants Democratic: New York City and the Rise of the American Working Class, 1788–1850* (New York: Oxford University Press, 1984), pp. 157–68, 212–16, 237–48; Friedrich Lenger, "Class, Culture and Class Consciousness in Ante-Bellum Lynn: A Critique of Alan Dawley and Paul Faler," *Social History* 6 (October 1981): 317–32. On a widening gap between rich and poor, see William Chambers, *Things as They Are in America* (London, 1854), p. 199; Massachusetts Board of Education, *Twelfth Annual Report* (Boston, 1849), pp. 57–59; Jeffrey G. Williamson and Peter H. Lindert, *American Inequality: A Macroeconomic History* (New York: Academic Press, 1980), pp. 44–46; Edward Pessen, *Riches, Class, and Power Before the Civil War* (Lexington: D. C. Heath, 1973).

36. Wilentz, *Chants Democratic*, pp. 220–23, 250–251, 364–86; Steven J. Ross, *Workers on the Edge: Work, Leisure and Politics in Industrializing Cincinnati, 1788–1890* (New York: Columbia University Press, 1985), pp. 142–57, 172–91; Susan E. Hirsch, *Roots of the American Working Class: The Industrialization of Crafts in Newark, 1800–1860* (Philadelphia: University of Pennsylvania Press, 1978); Bruce Laurie, *Working People of Philadelphia, 1800–1850* (Philadelphia: Temple University Press, 1980); Amy Bridges, "Becoming American: The Working Classes in the United States Before the Civil War," in *Working-Class Formation*, ed. Katznelson and Zolberg, pp. 171–89.

37. Michael F. Holt, *The Political Crisis of the 1850s* (New York: John Wiley and Sons, 1978), pp. 184–99, 242–56; William E. Gienapp, *The Origins of the Republican Party 1852–1856* (New York: Oxford University Press, 1987), pp. 415–35; William Dusinberre, *Civil War Issues in Philadelphia, 1856–1865* (Philadelphia: University of Pennsylvania Press, 1965); Eric Foner, *Free Soil, Free Labor, Free Men: The Ideology of the Republican Party before the Civil War* (New York: Oxford University Press, 1970), p. 310.

38. Foner, *Free Soil*, pp. 226–60; Joel Silbey, *The Partisan Imperative: The Dynamics of American Politics Before the Civil War* (New York: Oxford University Press, 1985), pp. 112, 137.

39. Michael F. Holt, "The Politics of Impatience: The Origins of Know-Nothingism," *Journal of American History* 60 (September 1973):309–31. See also Peter H. Henderson, "Rowdyism and Reform: Political Participation and Institutionalization in Baltimore's Election Violence, 1854–1860," unpublished seminar paper, Johns Hopkins University, 1987.

40. Mary Ann Clawson, "Fraternal Orders and Class Formation in the Nineteenth-Century United States," *Comparative Studies in Society and History* 27 (October 1985):672–95; Roy Rosenzweig, *Eight Hours for What We Will: Workers and Leisure in an Industrial City, 1870–1920* (New York: Cambridge University Press, 1983); Martin Shefter, "Trade Unions and Political Machines: The Organization and Disorganization of the American Working

Class in the Late Nineteenth Century," in *Working-Class Formation*, ed. Katznelson and Zolberg, pp. 235–46.

41. Richard Jules Oestreicher, *Solidarity and Fragmentation: Working People and Class Consciousness in Detroit, 1875–1900* (Urbana: University of Illinois Press, 1986), pp. 103–221. More broadly, see also Oestreicher's discriminating article, "Urban Working-Class Political Behavior and Theories of American Electoral Politics, 1870–1940," *Journal of American History* 74 (March 1988): 1257–896.

42. Richard Jensen, *The Winning of the Midwest: Social and Political Conflict, 1886–1896* (Chicago: University of Chicago Press, 1971); Paul Kleppner, *The Third Electoral System, 1853–1892: Parties, Voters and Political Cultures* (Chapel Hill: University of North Carolina Press, 1979), pp. 303–36. Here and henceforth I have drawn on an earlier and somewhat more detailed outline of the course of ethnic mobilization: John Higham, "The Mobilization of Immigrants in Urban America," *Norwegian-American Studies* 31 (1986):3–33.

43. John Higham, *Strangers in the Land: Patterns of American Nativism, 1860–1925* (New Brunswick: Rutgers University Press, 1955), pp. 59–62.

44. David Grimsted, "Ante-Bellum Labor: Violence, Strike, and Communal Arbitration," *Journal of Social History* 19 (September 1985): 5–28; John S. Gilkeson, Jr., *Middle-Class Providence, 1820–1940* (Princeton: Princeton University Press, 1986); Robert H. Wiebe, *The Segmented Society: An Introduction to the Meaning of America* (New York: Oxford University Press, 1975).

45. James Livingston, "The Social Analysis of Economic History and Theory: Conjectures on Late Nineteenth-Century American Development," *American Historical Review* 92 (February 1987):83

46. Olivier Zunz, *The Changing Face of Inequality: Urbanization, Industrial Development, and Immigrants in Detroit, 1880–1920* (Chicago: University of Chicago Press, 1982), is the most important study of this transition. But see also: Jon C. Teaford, *City and Suburb: The Political Fragmentation of Metropolitan America, 1850–1970* (Baltimore: Johns Hopkins University Press, 1979); Robert O. Schulze, "The Role of Economic Dominants in Community Power Stucture," *American Sociological Review* 23 (February 1958):3–14; Helen Campbell, Thomas Knox, and Thomas Byrnes, *Darkness and Daylight; Or, Lights and Shadows of New York Life* (Hartford: A. D. Worthington, 1892), p. 477.

47. William Dean Howells, *A Traveler from Altruria* (New York: Harper and Brothers, 1908), pp. 44–45. Explicit class awareness, centered especially in the middle class, pervaded the short stories in the *Saturday Evening Post*, for example, Emery Pottle, "The Weekend: A Story for Those Who Earn and Spend a Modest Competence," July 30, 1904, pp. 6–9. See also: Price Collier, *America and the Americans from a French Point of View* (New York: Charles Scribner's Sons, 1987), pp. 4–7, 50–51; Reed Ueda, *Avenues to Adulthood: The Origins of the High School and Social Mobility in an American Suburb* (New York: Cambridge University Press, 1987); and the classic study by Robert

S. Lynd and Helen M. Lynd, *Middletown: A Study in Contemporary American Culture* (New York: Harcourt, Brace, 1929).

48. P. K. Edwards, *Strikes in the United States, 1881–1974* (New York: St. Martin's Press, 1981), pp. 15–16. See also David Montgomery, "The 'New Unionism' and the Transformation of Workers' Consciousness in America, 1909–1922," *Journal of Social History* 7 (Summer 1974):509–29.

49. Peter Roberts, *The Anthracite Coal Industry* (New York: Macmillan, 1901), p. 172. See also: Paul Krause, "Labor Republicanism and 'Za Chlebom': Anglo-American and Slavic Solidarity in Homestead," and James R. Barrett, "Unity and Fragmentation: Class, Race, and Ethnicity on Chicago's South Side, 1900–1922," in *"Struggle a Hard Battle": Essays on Working-Class Immigrants*, ed. Dirk Hoerder (DeKalb: Northern Illinois University Press, 1986), pp. 144–69, 229–53; Victor R. Greene, *The Slavic Community on Strike: Immigrant Labor in Pennsylvania Anthracite* (Notre Dame: University of Notre Dame Press, 1968); Michael Novak, *The Guns of Lattimer: The True Story of a Massacre and a Trial August 1897–March 1898* (New York: Basic Books, 1978). Leon Fink's probing study, *Workingmen's Democracy: The Knights of Labor and American Politics* (Urbana: University of Illinois Press, 1983), pp. 219–23, suggests that some of the seeds of a forward-looking, multiethnic class consciousness may be found in the labor uprising of the 1880s.

50. Robert A. Slayton, *Back of the Yards: The Making of a Local Democracy* (Chicago: University of Chicago Press, 1986), pp. 110–48; John J. Bukowczyk, "The Transformation of Working-Class Ethnicity: Corporate Control, Americanization, and the Polish Immigrant Middle Class in Bayonne, New Jersey, 1915–1925," *Labor History* 25 (Winter 1984):61–65, 70–71.

51. The eastern European Jews did find an entrenched middle class waiting for them in America, but so different was it from themselves in religion and culture as well as class that the newcomers would not submit to its guidance or control.

52. *Statistical Abstract of the United States* (Washington: Government Printing Office, 1925), p. 31

53. Bukowczyk, "The Transformation of Working-Class Ethnicity," pp. 58–59; Ewa Morawska, *For Bread with Butter: The Life-Worlds of East Central Europeans in Johnstown, Pennsylvania, 1890–1940* (New York: Cambridge University Press, 1985), pp. 224–43; Josef Barton, "Eastern and Southern Europeans," in *Ethnic Leadership in America*, ed. John Higham (Baltimore: Johns Hopkins University Press, 1978), pp. 159–68. The multiethnic and interracial company towns of West Virginia offer an extreme example of the working-class solidarity that could develop in the absence of a countervailing ethnic middle class. See David Corbin, *Life, Work, and Rebellion in the Coal Fields: The Southern West Virginia Mines, 1880–1922* (Urbana: University of Illinois Press, 1981), pp. 61–86.

54. Higham, "Mobilization," pp. 20–23. See also Judith Stein, *The World of Marcus Garvey* (Baton Rouge: Louisiana State University Press, 1986).

55. David Montgomery, *The Fall of the House of Labor: The Workplace, the State, and American Labor Activism, 1865–1925* (Cambridge: Cambridge University Press, 1987), pp. 384–85.

56. Naomi W. Cohen, *American Jews and the Zionist Idea* (Hoboken: KTAV Publishing House, 1975), pp. 25–32; Higham, *Strangers*, p. 311. A vivid impression of the passivity of immigrant communities in the late 1920s and early 1930s is conveyed in Louis Adamic, "Thirty Million New Americans," *Harper's* 169 (November 1934):684–94.

57. On the significance of the "New Americans" in the electoral victories of the New Deal see especially: Kristi Andersen, *The Creation of a Democratic Majority, 1928–1936* (Chicago: University of Chicago Press 1979), pp. 30–38, 105–14; John H. Shover, "The Emergence of a Two-Party System in Republican Philadelphia, 1924–1936," *Journal of American History* 60 (March 1974):996–98; Richard Jensen, "The Cities Reelect Roosevelt: Ethnicity, Religion, and Class in 1940," *Ethnicity* 8 (June 1981):189–92. On their role in a revitalized labor movement, see Peter Friedlander, *The Emergence of a UAW Local, 1936–1939: A Study in Class and Culture* (Pittsburgh: University of Pittsburgh Press, 1975), and Thomas Göbel, "Becoming American: Ethnic Workers and the Rise of the CIO," *Labor History* 29 (Spring 1988):173–98.

58. David Montgomery, "Nationalism, American Patriotism, and Class Consciousness among Immigrant Workers in the United States in the Epoch of World War I," in *"Struggle a Hard Battle,"* ed. Hoerder, pp. 330–33.

59. Roy Rosenzweig, " 'United Action Means Victory': Militant Americanism on Film," *Labor History* 24 (Spring 1983):274–88.

60. Morawska, *For Bread with Butter*, p. 273.

61. Stanley Lieberson, *A Piece of the Pie: Blacks and White Immigrants since 1880* (Berkeley: University of California Press, 1980), pp. 242–70; Andrew M. Greeley, *The American Catholic: A Social Portrait* (New York: Basic Books, 1977), p. 62.

62. Paul R. Abramson, *Generational Change in American Politics* (Lexington: D. C. Heath, 1975), pp. 12–45; Granville Hicks, *Where We Came Out* (New York: Viking Press, 1954), pp. 227–29; Ronald W. Edsforth, *Class Conflict and Cultural Consensus: The Making of a Mass Consumer Society in Flint, Michigan* (New Brunswick: Rutgers University Press, 1986), pp. 212–16; Philip Gleason, "Americans All: World War II and the Shaping of American Identity," *Review of Politics* 43 (October 1981):483–518; Edward R. Kantowicz, *Polish-American Politics in Chicago, 1888–1940* (Chicago: University of Chicago Press, 1975), p. 223; Peter Kivisto, *Immigrant Socialists in the United States: The Case of Finns and the Left* (Rutherford: Fairleigh Dickinson University Press, 1984), pp. 192–95.

Hansen's Hypothesis as a Model of Immigrant Assimilation

Scholarly papers tend to be ephemeral. Of all those written, few are presented publicly, and fewer still are published. Among that modest number, a mere handful gain even a transient position in bibliographies and on reading lists. Rare indeed is the academic essay that redirects the focus of its specialty and extends its influence across decades—a category in which Marcus Lee Hansen's "The Problem of the Third Generation Immigrant" clearly belongs.

Success, however, has its price in scholarship as well as in other endeavors. As time passes, a work that has joined its discipline's bibliographic Hall of Fame becomes as much a part of folklore as a piece of literature. Our understanding of it sometimes deteriorates into a caricature of the author's original message. That outcome may be especially likely if the core, or at least if a critical part, of the author's thesis can be captured in aphorisms such as "what the son wishes to forget the grandson wishes to remember."[1]

The Swenson Swedish Immigration Research Center and the Augustana College Library have produced a welcome edition of Hansen's "Third Generation" essay. In his introduction to this republication, Peter Kivisto points out that scholars have taken four different approaches to explicating Hansen's message. One group has tested his comparisons of the second and third generations and has declared them empirically unverifiable. A second has read those comparisons as metaphors rather than as hypotheses and has found them full of insight. A third group has extended Hansen's message to make religious identity as well as ethnic that to which the third generation "returned." The fourth has made Hansen a forecaster of the "new ethnicity" that has played such an important role in scholarly discourse since the late 1960s.[2]

In the context of that set of approaches, and in response to them, I will address four issues in this discussion. First, because of the confusion that has surrounded Hansen's message, I will briefly restate the points he made fifty years ago. Next, I will call attention to some elements of Hansen's argument that students of ethnicity have neglected—in particular, Hansen's warnings about the pitfalls of immigrant history and the distinction between the phenomena of "interest" and "return." Third, paying heed to those slighted aspects of the essay, I will analyze the model of American immigrant history that Hansen implicitly proposed and discuss the conditions under which it would support his conclusions. Finally, I will examine the adequacy of Hansen's model for describing the history of immigrant groups in eras and places other than those familiar to him.

The "Problem" of the Third Generation According to Hansen

Hansen selected, as the organizing theme of his paper, the problems faced during the successive generations of a people's history in America. During an immigrant group's first sixty years in the United States, he argued, each generation—the pioneers themselves, their children, and their grandchildren—faces a special problem rooted in and characteristic of its social position within the overall population. The problem of the first generation is to make the adjustments necessary to survive economically, to function within an alien culture, and to learn about democracy. That of the second generation is "to inhabit two worlds at the same time." The problem of the third generation, briefly expressed, is properly interpreting the history of the first two.[3]

Hansen saw the third generation as a secure group endowed with the education to appreciate the culture that the first generation had, in its faltering way, carried with it from Europe. The third generation has affluence and, accompanying that, the social acceptance to which the second generation could only aspire. At the same time, however, Hansen saw that the third generation's fresh sense of pride entails its own dangers, that can be subsumed under the rubric of an impulse to filiopietism.[4]

Hansen's message to the third generation emerging among the Swedes, and indirectly to those that would eventually come of age among other groups, was a call to broad vision. As each group comes to recognize its common "heritage of blood," he advised, it must ask "how can this impulse be organized and directed so that the results growing therefrom will be worthy of the high instincts from which it has sprung." It must seek also to determine how their efforts can become "a dignified tribute to the pioneers and at the same time be a contribution to the history of the United States which has received all Europeans on a basis of equality and which should record their achievements in the same spirit of impartiality."[5]

The "Problem" of the Third Generation after Hansen

The precis that I have just presented bears only a loose resemblance to readings of Hansen's essay offered by some other commentators. There is an interesting irony in the situation. The problem of the third generation, according to Hansen, was understanding the history of the preceding two. We, however, have made Hansen's problem—and ours—understanding the history of that third generation.

Analyzing the interpretative complexities that subsequent readings of Hansen, as well as his own vagueness, have engendered requires the pursuit of three issues. The first concerns the accuracy of Hansen's contrast between second generation flight and third generation interest. The second involves an evaluation of his recommendations and warnings to third generation historians. The last demands scrutiny of the concept of third generation return.

Flight versus Interest

Critics have given considerable attention to Hansen's distinction between the second and third generations. As Peter Kivisto notes in the Introduction, John Appel, in an article published in 1961, made the most explicit test of the contrast. Appel argued that the founders of the American Jewish Historical Society and those who set up similar organizations for a diverse set of nationalities including Germans, Irish, Italians, Scots, and Swiss, "were a mixed lot of first-, second- and subsequent-generation Americans."[6] Appel did concede, however, that the American Jewish Historical Society—and presumably other such organizations—became less defensive in their orientation and less inclined to heroic accounts of early settlers when third generation men and women became heavily involved.[7]

In an article, "Problems and Possibilities in the Study of American Immigration and Ethnic History" (1985), I also touched, albeit indirectly, on the issue of generational flight and interest. The article argued that the study of immigration and ethnicity remained outside the mainstream of American history, and it attempted to trace the impact of that marginality on the kind of work done in the field. It proposed that efforts to use immigration and ethnicity as a base from which to analyze American history encounter strong resistance rooted in the common assumption that the topics were transient phenomena and in an intellectual milieu that stresses the paradigms of class and race for explaining society's vertical and horizontal divisions. As a result of this marginality, the writing of an immigrant people's history had, by default, become primarily an endeavor undertaken by men and women belonging to—and especially involved with—that ethnic group.[8]

In my opinion, "Problems and Possibilities" proved the point that "most histories about an ethnic group are written by people of that nationality." It also supported a corollary that "scholars in ethnic history tend not to study groups other than their own."[9] In addition, its data concerning the timing of the publication of scholarship on various nationalities were consistent with the expectation that half a century or more must expire after the major influx of a group to the United States before such works begin to appear in large numbers.[10]

Because testing Hansen's third generation assumption was not my purpose, I did not systematically investigate the generational backgrounds of individual historians of ethnicity. However, I feel that too many exceptions exist in the form of ethnic historians who are second generation Americans for Hansen's generalization to go unchallenged. Indeed, Hansen himself was second generation, the son of a Danish immigrant father and of a Norwegian immigrant mother.[11] Therefore, we are left with the plausible hypothesis that the third generation in America marks the beginning of ethnic historical work about an ethnic group and a less convincing assumption that it is the third generation Americans who do that research.

Some of the confusion over Hansen's principle of third generation interest may involve a variation of a problem familiar to quantitatively oriented historians—the ecological fallacy in which a researcher attempts to make judgments about individual members of a population on the basis of data gathered about the whole. If that is so, one appropriate response is not to discard the principle but to apply it at the proper level of aggregation. Perhaps Hansen's concept of generation should be interpreted as a measure of collective rather than individual status.

Hansen's illustrations of his principle indicate that he understood the first two decades after a group's arrival in America to constitute its first generation, the next two its second, and so forth. The standard assumption, and the one that Hansen made loosely, has been that most members of an ethnic group have been in the United States the same number of generations as the nationality itself. That generalization, however, overlooks an important dimension in the distribution of the group's population. If a reasonably large volume of immigration from the homeland persists, an immigrant people established in America for three generations will still have a large contingent of first and second generation members, including young people as well as older ones.

Perhaps the offspring of immigrants who come to America late in the history of their nationality's movement to this country experience a telescoped process of assimilation. Although biologically and genealogically members of the second generation, they may be, in other respects, part of the third. Because their parents joined an existing subculture rather than faced the need to create one, the members of this later second generation may be able to move ahead more quickly socially and economically. Moreover, because of the presence of a large, acculturated third generation that can provide role models, and because prejudice against the group is likely to be waning, this cohort may not be as vulnerable as its predecessor to the classic symptoms of second generation marginality.

Hansen's own life offers an interesting variation on this theme. His father, Markus, had come to the United States from Langeland in 1871 at the age of twenty. He was clearly part of the first wave of the Scandinavian influx that began in the years immediately following the Civil War. Marcus Lee Hansen, however, was the sixth of the pioneer's seven children and was not born until 1892.[12] Thus, although he grew up during the second twenty years of Scandinavian experience in post-Civil War America, he must have been among the last-born of the second generation cohort. As a result, his years as a productive scholar coincided with the third twenty-year block of Scandinavian-American history. In a sense, therefore, he was a second generation scholar working in a third generation milieu.

If the preceding hypotheses are correct, Hansen's principle should be reformulated. At the risk of creating my own ecological fallacy, I would like to suggest that it can also be equipped with a new dynamic. In its fresh form, the "principle of third generation interest" would state that by the time a European ethnic group has had a major presence in the United States for three generations, prejudice against it will have waned and many of its members will have achieved middle-class standards of income and education. The successful will include not only many in the third generation, but also numbers of people who have been in the country for just two generations and who, because of the opportunities afforded them, have been able to reconcile the duality in their cultural background. Under those circumstances, the group can expect to experience a burst of interest in its history and culture, with the successful second generation playing a surprisingly important role in those scholarly endeavors.

The Historiography of the Third Generation

For Marcus Hansen—as for Oscar Handlin, who helped bring his "Third Generation" essay to a larger audience in the 1950s[13]—immigrants were at the core of the American experience. They were neither an alternative to it, nor a testament to its diversity. Although he did not define explicitly what the content of immigrant history should be, Hansen did state that the measure of the success of immigrant history societies would lie in the answer to two questions: "Did they, when the time was appropriate, write the history of the special group with whom they were concerned on broad impartial lines, and did they make a contribution to the meaning of American history at large?"[14]

Hansen's example of successful third generation history was quite revealing. He pointed to the experience of the Scotch-Irish and to the themes of life in the colonial backcountry emphasized by their historians in the late nineteenth century. It was in those accounts that Hansen saw the seeds of the frontier thesis that his Harvard mentor, Frederick Jackson Turner, had given formal expression. From Hansen's perspective, however, Turner's contribution had been to organize and name a theme that was in the intellectual air thanks to the effects of third generation Scotch-Irish interest.[15]

Was Hansen's exhortation to broad historical vision, which would make the ethnic group being studied a means better to appreciate the whole American experience, only a warning against a potential problem? Alternatively, did Hansen believe that the third generations of his era were actually succumbing to the temptations of filiopietism? The issue is problematic. Hansen, who claimed that the principle of third generation interest "is applicable in all fields of historical study," used as his principal nonethnic example the revival of Southern patriotism embodied in Margaret Mitchell's *Gone With the Wind*. His description of the new Southern patriotism, however, was without obvious approval or disapproval; it in no way indicated that he was persuaded by the movement's reinterpretation of the Civil War.[16]

Two pieces of evidence suggest, however, that Hansen had real misgivings about the immigrant history of his era. In an enigmatic statement in the essay on the role of immigrants in American society Hansen remarked, "How much of a problem the forty million actually were will not be known until their history is written *with realism as well as sympathy*" (my emphasis).[17] Unless he chose his words carelessly, Hansen's phrasing indicates that he thought the former to be in shorter supply than the latter.

Hansen's condemnation of some elements of third generation historiography was more direct in an address entitled "Who Shall Inherit America?" that he delivered before the National Conference of Social Work in Indianapolis, just ten days after the presentation of his more famous paper. "Amateur historians and racketeering publishers," he stated in describing the first fruits of third generation interest, "combine to draw up a volume of biographies of insignificant people and pawn it off upon the eager purchaser as a history of that group in

American life." Even more carefully researched efforts, he added, were likely to lose their credibility by making excessive claims.[18]

In "Problems and Possibilities," I discussed problems in third generation historiography of the post-Hansen era that, although not as blatant as those he condemned, were consistent with the kind of distortion he had feared. For example, third generation histories have emphasized the role of discrimination in the group's American experience and, in their focus on individual nationalities, have slighted comparative studies. I also claimed that the coincidence after World War II between the societal coming of age of the "new immigrant" groups and the general expansion of the discipline of history had led to imbalances of coverage and interpretation. New immigrant nationalities have been receiving much more attention than old immigrant peoples in America longer than three generations. Likewise, as the nation's tolerance for diversity increased, interpretations in those later histories have become more receptive to the idea that immigrants held tenaciously, and with some success, to their European cultures.[19]

Hansen would not have been surprised when the new immigrant nationalities began eventually to experience third generation interest of the kind he anticipated in the 1930s for the Scandinavians. In "Who Shall Inherit America?" he simply said that it was "a little too early" to trace the evolution of those "who are generally classified as the 'new immigrants.' "[20] More important to his overall view of immigrant history, however, he would not have been surprised either by apparent diminution of interest in the old immigrant groups that occurred with the passage of time. The constituency interested in immigrant history and societies for its promotion, Hansen argued, inevitably "becomes gradually thinned out as the third generation merges into the fourth and the fourth shades off into the fifth."[21]

Of course, Hansen could not have foreseen the expansion in historical writing that would create an imbalance in the overall amount of scholarly attention devoted to each set of groups. Had he enjoyed a fair share of years, Marcus Lee Hansen probably would have modified his ideas about the focus and content of his field of history. He would have absorbed the findings of other scholars and would undoubtedly have continued to contribute his own insights. Unfortunately, Hansen died prematurely, and our assessment must be of his ideas as they were frozen at the stage of the late 1930s. In terms of those, Hansen would not have expected, and might not have welcomed being identified as a precursor of, the intellectual evolution of immigrant history into ethnic history that occurred after World War II.

Third Generation "Return"

If my exegesis of "The Problem of the Third Generation Immigrant" has merit, then it is necessary to examine critically the prevailing interpretation offered by numerous scholars who, whether in agreement or disagreement with Hansen, have credited him with positing a hypothesis of third generation return. Vladimir C. Nahirny and Joshua Fishman associated the word *return* with Hansen in their 1965 article on "American Ethnic Groups: Ethnic Identification and the Problem of Generations."[22]

Eugene Bender and George Kagiwada placed the phrase "third-generation return" in quotation marks when they made it part of the title of their 1968 article, "Hansen's Law of 'Third- Generation Return' and the Study of American Religio-Ethnic Groups."[23] Likewise, in his 1971 article, "The Emergence of Ethnic Interests: A Case of Serendipity," John M. Goering put his discussion of Hansen under the heading "Ethnic Scales and Third-Generation Return."[24]

Contrary to this popular assumption, Hansen, at least in the article now under scrutiny, did not use the word *return* in connection with the third generation. He spoke and wrote instead of "the principle of third generation interest," which he succinctly expressed in the previously cited comment "what the son wishes to forget the grandson wishes to remember." The distinction between *return* and *interest* is not merely semantic; the two words underlie entirely different models of ethnic history.

Hansen proposed his "principle of third generation interest" as a theory that "anyone who has the courage to codify the laws of history must include." He defined it as a principle that "makes it possible for the present to know something about the future."[25]

How serious he intended those remarks to be is problematic; my feeling is that his purpose was rhetorical and that he may even have been speaking with tongue in cheek. Nevertheless, Hansen must have considered his principle to be at least a good generalization, if not a law. Therefore, to speculate on the dynamic behind the phenomenon is not unreasonable.

Those who speak and write of the "return" of the third generation use what Hansen termed "interest" as a surrogate variable for measuring the intensity of a generation's ethnicity. There are as many different definitions of ethnicity as there are scholars in the field, and in the context of this discussion, the word is meant to cover a potpourri of attitudes and behaviors. Among the most important of those are a sense of identity based in membership in a non-American people, a willingness consciously to form primary relationships at least partly on the basis of that affiliation, and an attachment to the culture and perhaps to the language of the group.

"Return," therefore, can have two different implications. On the one hand, it may refer to an actual restoration of ethnicity from the depths experienced during the second generation to a level closer to the heights felt by the pioneers. On the other, "return" may simply refer to an emergence from a closet. In that context, ethnicity does not decline and revive; what changes with the passing decades is the willingness to acknowledge it. The third generation, either because society is more tolerant or because the grandchildren of the immigrants come to recognize the high price paid in surrendering one's culture, embraces what the second thought it had to scorn.

The model of return, therefore, breaks the paradigm of the melting pot. It suggests the permanence, or at least the "revivability," of ethnicity. In doing so, it calls into question the assumption of inevitable assimilation that is best symbolized in the Census Bureau's longtime practice of classifying the grandchildren of immigrants as the native-born offspring of native-born parents. Perhaps more important, it leaves open the possibility that ethnicity may remain a vital force past even the third generation.

At various points in "The Problem of the Third Generation Immigrant," Hansen equated interest with mundane phenomena such as "curiosity," an "attitude of inquiry," and a "feeling of pride" in ancestors.[26] Ultimately, however, he endowed it with the mystical qualities of a "spontaneous and almost irresistible impulse"[27] to learn about one's heritage. The indefinite and overlapping quality of those descriptions complicate efforts to understand "Hansen's law." Nothing in the article, however, necessarily leads to the conclusion that he equated third generation interest with return as that phenomenon has been described in the preceding paragraphs.

Little in the family or personal history of Marcus Lee Hansen would have made him a likely spokesperson for a movement of "ethnic return." His father, the immigrant, was something of an Americanizer, who became a Baptist after arriving in the United States, trained for the ministry in that denomination, and spent forty years establishing Baptist churches for Danish and Norwegian newcomers to the prairie. The household in which Hansen grew up was trilingual, with English receiving attention equal to that given Danish and Norwegian. As a graduate student working under Frederick Jackson Turner at Harvard, Hansen described himself as of Danish stock, but he listed "Scandinavian" rather than a specific tongue as a non-English language that he read and spoke.

When he visited Scandinavia in the 1930s, Hansen found himself uncomfortable both in Danish and in Norwegian. Finally, as Moses Rischin has noted in his important essay on the man he identifies as "America's first transethnic historian," Hansen deliberately avoided publishing a single article focused on Scandinavian America.[28]

Rather than anticipate an ethnic revival, Hansen's article seems instead to presume a more or less continuous diminishing of the force that today's scholars call ethnicity. According to the author, the third generation consists of people of "different professions, different positions in life and different points of view," who have in common only "the heritage of the blood."[29] A generation or two later even that shared sense would also be gone, Hansen predicted, and with its demise membership in ethnic societies would wither in keeping with "the life-course of every organization of this nature."[30]

If Hansen did not anticipate a resuscitation of what commentators in our era attribute to ethnicity, what did he foresee as the consequence of the revival of third generation interest? Although the personal satisfaction of those who gained knowledge of their heritage might be its own reward, surely that outcome alone would not have rationalized his judgment that writing the history of the great migration was "the most challenging duty now facing American historians."[31] For Hansen, a historical appreciation of the immigrants would offer the benefit of a second opportunity to create for the United States a culture that truly represented the breadth of the American experience.

Hansen recognized that the common people who made up the bulk of the immigrant influx were not especially able transmitters of culture. At the same time, he believed that European civilization so pervaded the societies from which they came that they inevitably brought with them an appreciation of music and art and, if not real culture, at least the seeds of it. Although the European pioneers had not been able to bring those seeds to fruition in an American soil made infertile by Yankee glorification of the practical,[32] Hansen hoped that the many contacts to be established by members of the prosperous and educated third generation with popular culture abroad would "constitute a new opportunity that is to knock" for adding selected features of continental culture to "the heritage of America."[33]

On one level, therefore, Hansen was quite different from modern proponents of third generation return. The possibilities that the descendants of the immigrants were not fully integrated into the economic structure of the United States and that they operated, voluntarily or involuntarily, in semisegregated networks of primary and secondary relationships do not seem to have shaped his thought. Indeed, his own experience would have led him toward opposite assumptions. Instead of pointing to the tenacity of what today is called ethnicity, Hansen was, in effect, calling for a reimportation of some of what had been lost.

Hansen's emphasis on culture, and, within that ill-defined concept, on music and art, calls to mind too quickly the pathetic remnants of the immigrant heritage that survive in contemporary ethnic song and dance festivals. Making that equation, however, deflects attention from his true objective. The core of Hansen's message addressed the need to end the hegemony of British culture in American life. In that regard, he seems to have shared the resentments expressed by spokespersons for the "new ethnicity." Perhaps, on that deeper level, Hansen was a forerunner of the advocates of ethnic return.

"They made a bad blunder," Hansen said of earlier Americans, "when consciously or unconsciously they decreed that one literature, one attitude towards the arts, one set of standards should be the basis of culture." He asked, "Was it not a short-sighted view that decreed that the people who came first should have a continent reserved for the particular strain of culture that they represented?" American culture will be predominantly British, he admitted, "but why shouldn't there have been added to its wearing qualities some of the lighter and brighter features offered by immigrants from the Mediterranean and some of the deeper feelings brought in by immigrants from Eastern Europe."[34]

Hansen's Model

Reconciling the seeming contradiction between Hansen's principle of third generation interest and his assumption that substantive ethnicity was waning requires a systematic decomposition of his argument. Assume that interest is a variable which, at least indirectly, is measurable. Likewise, its value can change with shifting situations. In that case, "third generation interest" is just a particular case of that general variable.

In the language of quantitative analysis, interest seems to be a dependent variable. Its value for a particular case—or, in this context, for a particular generation—can be estimated as a function of the values of a set of independent variables. Each independent variable, however, will not necessarily make an equal contribution to the sum. Each of those values, therefore, will have associated with it a weight reflecting the relative importance of that variable it measures. In the terms of one standard analytical procedure, the preceding paragraph describes a regression equation of the simplified form:

$$Y = b_1X_1 + b_2X_2 + \ldots + b_nX_n$$

Under certain constraints, the weight (b_i) assigned to an independent variable (X_i) measures the proportional contribution made by that variable to the final value (Y). Although purists might be uncomfortable with the terminology, interest can be interpreted as an effect produced by a combination of causes, each of which has an impact, proportional to its importance, on the outcome.

The problem is to envision a model that allows a continuing decline in ethnicity to combine with other variables to make the value of interest peak in the third generation. Before such a model could be accepted as plausible, it would have to be subjected to statistical test. Collecting the data that would be used in those tests would require a major research project, an important part of which would involve devising reliable scales for measuring the phenomena being observed. Although I am not ready to offer those data, I would like, at a theoretical level, to discuss what variables might be in the model and how they might fit together.

A consideration of the elements that comprise the phenomenon termed *interest* can give some insight into the combination of independent and dependent variables that make up the model. Interest is distinct from ethnicity but obviously bears some relationship to the intensity of ethnic feelings. Likewise, Hansen's "law" tied interest to attitudes and values that ebb and flow with passing generations. Finally, Hansen also suggested that, in the third generation, interest manifests itself partly through scholarship and the writing of history.

At the moment, the last element described in the preceding paragraph—the volume of secondary literature produced concerning an ethnic group—seems to offer the most direct measure of Hansen's concept of interest. Of course, even that simple measure could require special handling to compensate for special circumstances. For example, it might be appropriate to count scholarly works more heavily than popular ones. Likewise, measuring an ethnic group's share of a period's historical literature, rather than the raw number of studies concerning it, might lessen distortions introduced by changes over time in the overall amount of scholarship produced.

For the sake of convenience, all the independent variables to be included in the model can share a common scale. Consider them to range from a low value of 0 to a high value of 100. If each of those variables was to be displayed on a graph, that range of values would form the vertical, or y, axis.

Inasmuch as the intention is to measure the change in interest across generations, the appropriate horizontal, or x axis, should indicate the passage of time. Its values could range from 0 years to 100, with each succeeding set of twenty years constituting a generation. Such a finely detailed range increases computational accuracy and—assuming that such a scale could be devised—simplifies the discussion. In reality, however, the data available may not be adequately precise or voluminous to permit its use. Provided the researcher were willing to adapt the specific statistical techniques employed, alternatives could be sought. The range selected, for example, might become 1 to 20, with each number from 1 to 20 representing a five-year period, and with each set of four years comprising a generation. In an even more compressed arrangement, the range might become 1 to 5, with each number from 1 to 5 representing a generation.

The first—in the sense of most obvious—independent variable to be included in the model would be ethnicity. This discussion has argued that Hansen, at least implicitly, described ethnicity as being continually in decline. Rather than portray it as withering at a constant rate, as the dotted line in Figure 1 would represent, I would prefer to postulate a very sharp drop between the first and second generation, followed by an increasingly slow decline thereafter (Fig. 1, solid line). That would allow a low "ethnic hum" to exist almost indefinitely as a motif in the society.

The next component of the model addresses the ability to do scholarship. An underlying assumption related to this component is that a rise in social status is a prerequisite for the expansion of scholarship on the ethnic group by group members. More than one variable may be necessary to measure social status, for example, an education variable, or one that addressed the issue of timing of entry into the profes-

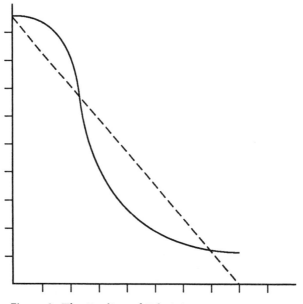

Figure 1. The Decline of Ethnicity

sions. Likewise, a variable concerning income could have an impact because it tells something about a group's ability to provide education or to have the time for scholarship. Given the extent of overlap between those candidates, a single variable combining the three as a factor may prove the ultimate solution. In any case, all three variables would probably follow the same graphic form—a slow increase between the first and second generation, a much more rapid rise between the second and third, and a gradual leveling off thereafter (Fig. 2).

The third variable to be included in this effort to create a model for Hansen's article has to be a measure of the reaction among the native core of America's population to the immigrants and their descendants. That variable may be envisioned either as a decline in prejudice or as an increase in tolerance. A particular researcher may imbue the choice with some political or social message; mathematically, however, it is inconsequential. As a contrast to the declining value of ethnicity, let us here consider it an increase in toleration. Once again, the graphic representation of the variable would show a slow increase between the first and second generations, a marked improvement between the second and third, and a gradual leveling after that. The overall pattern is similar to that in Figure 2, but, in regard to the time

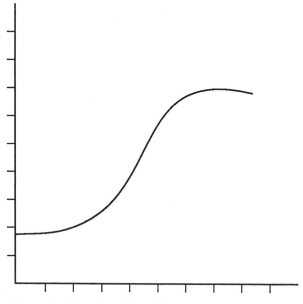

Figure 2. The Rise of Social Status

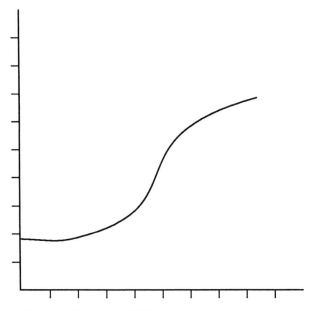

Figure 3. The Rise of Tolerance

scale, the increases in toleration would trail the improvements in income and education, as can be seen in Figure 3.

Generation is the final and most difficult variable to incorporate in the model. Hansen's insight was that generation encompasses more than the passage of time. It involves as well the continuity and the tension that exist between grandparents, parents, and children. The tension component is naturally based in normal parental efforts to nurture their offspring and in the necessity for the latter eventually to establish their independence. To have a public as well as a private impact, however, the tension may have to interact with a historical event of general importance. In regard to ethnicity, therefore, the generation variable reflects especially the impact that being from immigrant stock has on the pioneers, their descendants, and the relationships between them. It measures, in effect, the rapport between later generations and the first.

Built into the definition of generation is an assumption that the values of the variable are autocorrelated; in other words, each value depends in part on the one preceding it. Moreover, the form of the correlation between generations is negative in that a low value follows a high and vice-versa. Finally, insofar as immigration constitutes a shock that aggravates normal levels of generational conflict, the range of values for this variable will be temporarily wider than normal before returning to its standard limits.

Relationships like that just attributed to generation frequently appear in time-series analyses. Indeed, if the focus is kept on the impact of the immigrant experience on the public manifestation of intergenerational tension, the variable would seem to take a form similar to a standard one described in econometric literature as a complementary sine and cosine function, with a damped fluctuation leading eventually to equilibrium (Fig. 4).

The model proposed here expresses accurately the argument presented by Marcus Lee Hansen in "The Problem of the Third Generation Immigrant." Moreover, the description it offers of the processes of acculturation and assimilation seems consistent with the findings of the scholarly literature in the field and with commonsensical extensions of those works. A key remaining issue in regard to Hansen's essay concerns whether or not the model supports the idea of third generation interest without third generation return. I think it does.

According to the model, the variables representing education or an income-occupation-education factor, tolerance, and generational rapport all register relatively high values in the third generation. Only the variable representing ethnic identity is in decline at that time. Such

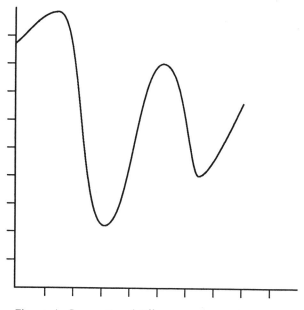

Figure 4. Generational Effects

a combination is consistent with a judgment that the third generation would form a "window of ethnic interest." In the second generation, the higher value of ethnicity would not be enough to offset the lower values on the other variables. In generations subsequent to the third, high values on tolerance and the factors associated with education or social status would not be enough to offset the continuing decline in ethnicity and the movement of generational rapport toward equilibrium.

Conclusion

The model analyzed in the preceding section attempted to represent in an abstract form the historical processes that Marcus Lee Hansen implicitly described as underlying the first three generations in an immigrant group's experience in the United States. The discussion showed that if a particular set of conditions holds, the model supports Hansen's judgment that an "interest" in a people's immigrant heritage would emerge during that third generation. The model, however, does not necessarily tie the dynamic bearers of that interest to any specific generations. Moreover, the logic of the model is such that a phenomenon of third generation interest could arise at the same time that substantive indicators of ethnic behavior, which would indicate incomplete assimilation of the group into the American mainstream, continues to decline. Finally, the model's logic also supports the conclusion that the phenomenon of ethnic interest should decline subsequent to the third generation

It is tempting to close this discussion on such indicators of success. Unfortunately, such a step would continue the neglect of dimensions of the issue that Hansen omitted from his discussion. Hansen based his essay and the model underlying it on a narrow band of historical experience. They focus on the United States in its great age of immigration, an era that Hansen assumed was finished. The restrictive legislation of the 1920s had "cut down the normal inflow to a tenth of its one-time volume," he noted, and the depression of the 1930s had made emigration from the United States exceed immigration to it. Moreover, Hansen did not believe that a restoration of economic health would reverse the situation. "The quotas will be filled," he predicted, "but even then the number of the arrivals will be so small in comparison with the nation's population that we can say that immigration has come to an end."[35]

Within the limited framework in which he was operating, Hansen treated generational flight and interest as a patterned phenomenon repeated in the history of each immigrant group. The Scotch-Irish of the 1890s could serve as an example for the Scandinavians of the 1930s, who, at some later date, might fulfill the same function for one of the new immigrant groups. Hansen, however, did not incorporate the possibility that the experiences of one nationality affected those of others. In particular, he did not consider that either the successful integration of one group into the mainstream or the revival of its heritage might alter the overall societal attitude toward diversity in the population.

Hansen's hypothesis implied that American views on heterogeneity—whatever they were—had been constant for each generation and immigrant group relevant to his research. Of course, attributing a constant effect to a factor is not the same as stating that it has no impact. Nevertheless, the presumption of constancy meant the model of his argument did not have to include a variable representing the society's attitude toward ethnic differences in general, as opposed to its tolerance for individual alien groups.

The limits of Hansen's focus and his assumption that the phenomenon under investigation was constant raise a number of issues about his argument. Would Hansen's model be adequate for comparing societies that differed from each other in the value they placed on homogeneity or heterogeneity? Even within the restricted context of American history, would the model correctly describe the ebb and flow of generational interest in ethnicity if it were applied to groups arriving in the United States in an era with attitudes different from those that prevailed when the bulk of Hansen's European subjects came? Indeed, was Hansen even correct in his analysis of the period he examined?

Perhaps thinking in terms of graphs can once again assist in the search for answers to the questions posed in the preceding paragraph. A constant societal attitude toward heterogeneity would appear on a graph of the kind used above as a horizontal line spanning the generations. The height of that line on the y axis might indicate a lower value, if the society espoused a melting pot ideology, or a higher one, if it accepted cultural pluralism. Depending on the location of the line, Hansen's model might operate in a fashion remarkably different from that seen in the American history. Most notably, a society with a toleration score higher than that implicitly assigned the United States in Hansen's original model might experience less of an initial loss of ethnicity and no pattern of alternating generational flight and interest.

Illustrating, accounting for, and assessing the impact of a change in outlook within a single nation, however, is more difficult. Is an increasing level of overall tolerance itself a predictable part of the process of immigration history; that is, is it simply a parallel to the growing acceptance granted specific immigrant groups with the passage of time? Or, is it more likely that an increase—or decrease—in general

tolerance is a reaction to a specific historical development or event?
The definition chosen has important implications for the working of
the expanded model.

If a change in society's attitude toward heterogeneity is part of a
learning experience associated with the gradual, successful absorption
of immigrants, then an increase in general tolerance across three waves
of immigration might follow a curve similar to that in Figure 5. The
pattern in that graph suggests that as the third generation in each wave
achieves success and is able to present its culture positively, the level
of societal acceptance of ethnic diversity improves. Accordingly, the
variable would have a dual impact. It would encourage a revival of
ethnic interest among groups in the country for three generations, as
predicted by Hansen. In addition, it would lead to a permanent read-
justment of societal attitudes that could affect the immigration histories of groups coming to the nation later. In particular, it would
make it less likely that such a group would experience a severe second
generation flight from ethnicity. That, in turn, would minimize the
need, in the next generation, for a renewal of interest. Within the
context of American history, it would explain whatever greater tendency to ethnic retentiveness that might be found among new immigrant groups in comparison with old immigrant ones. I would also

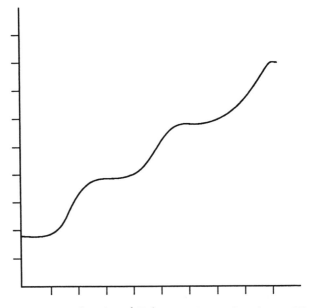

Figure 5. The Rise of Tolerance Across Immigrant Waves

suggest that the newest immigrant groups now arriving on American shores may prove even more inclined toward maintaining their ethnic identities and heritages.

If, however, changes in societal attitudes are the effects of specific historical events, then there may be no underlying predictability to that variable. Its values would reflect, in part, the impact of what statisticians describe as "random shocks." At a logical extreme, such a possibility could vitiate Hansen's hypothesis. The phenomenon of third generation interest might not develop from any underlying dynamic in the immigrant experience; the supposed pattern might simply be an accident. The interest expressed by the old immigrant groups on which Hansen focused might have been a by-product of improvements in their image made possible by the coming of the seemingly less assimilable new immigrants. Likewise, the revival perceived among the latter nationalities in recent decades might be tied to the lessons of World War II, and especially to rejection of the ethnic hatred embodied in the Holocaust, or perhaps to the legitimation of the social strategy seeking recognition of permanent ethnic interests as encountered in the Black Power movement of the 1960s.[36]

Of course, the response of societal attitudes to random shocks might have only modest implications for Hansen's hypothesis. It might simply reduce that variable to a wild card, capable, in some cases, of accentuating the phenomenon of third generation interest, and, in others, of dampening it. If the effects were truly random, the most likely outcome would be that late-arriving groups would have essentially the same set of experiences as those coming during an earlier era. The reinforcement that a positive societal attitude to diversity might provide for third generation interest among one set of immigrant groups would not necessarily carry over to their successors. Interim developments restoring the society's emphasis on the need for homogeneity—such as a renewal of the nativist feelings spurred by a fresh set of socioeconomic and cultural threats seemingly posed by a fresh wave of immigrants—could cause later groups to face the same challenges as their predecessors and to pass through the same three-generation process of adaptation that Hansen described. Thus, although the model he implied would blur important details in the story, it would still lead to basically correct generalizations.

This discussion ends, therefore, by leaving the door open. It seems that even fifty years after its appearance, Hansen's third generation hypothesis, when properly understood, offers many insights into an important block of American immigrant history. Whether or not it is the key to understanding the process of immigrant adaptation, and whether or not it qualifies as anything approaching a law of history, remain problematic. We shall never know, however, unless first we ask the right questions.

NOTES

1. Marcus Lee Hansen, "The Problem of the Third Generation Immigrant," republication of the 1937 address with introductions by Peter Kivisto and Oscar Handlin (Rock Island: Swenson Swedish Immigration Research Center and the Augustana College Library, 1987), p. 15.

2. Kivisto, "Hansen's Classic Essay After a Half-Century," in Hansen, "The Problem of the Third Generation," pp. 6–7.

3. Ibid., pp. 11–19.

4. Ibid., pp. 17–20.

5. Ibid., p. 19.

6. John J. Appel, "Hansen's Third Generation 'Law' and the Origins of the American Jewish Historical Society," *Jewish Social Studies* 23 (January 1961):3–20.

7. Appel, "Hansen's Third Generation 'Law,' " p. 18.

8. Thomas J. Archdeacon, "Problems and Possibilities in the Study of American Immigration and Ethnic History," *International Migration Review* 19 (Spring 1985):112–34.

9. Archdeacon, "Problems and Possibilities," p. 117.

10. Ibid., p. 120.

11. Ibid.; Moses Rischin, "Marcus Lee Hansen: America's First Transethnic Historian," in *Uprooted Americans: Essays to Honor Oscar Handlin*, ed. Richard Bushman, Neil Harris David Rothman, Barbara Miller Solomon, and Stephan Thernstrom (Boston: Little, Brown, 1979), pp. 329–30.

12. Ibid., p. 329.

13. Oscar Handlin, "A Classic Essay in Immigrant History," *Commentary* 14 (November 1952); reprinted in Hansen, "The Problem of the Third Generation," pp. 8–10.

14. Hansen, "The Problem of the Third Generation," p. 21.

15. Ibid., pp. 24–25.

16. Ibid., pp. 15–16.

17. Ibid., p. 12.

18. Marcus Lee Hansen, "Who Shall Inherit America?," *Interpreter Releases* 14 (July 6, 1937):231.

19. Archdeacon, "Problems and Possibilities," pp. 188–223.

20. Hansen, "Who Shall Inherit America?," p. 229.

21. Hansen, "The Problem of the Third Generation," p. 21.

22. Vladimir C. Nahirny and Joshua Fishman, "American Ethnic Groups: Ethnic Identification and the Problem of Generations," *Sociological Review* 13 (November 1965):311–26.

23. Eugene Bender and George Kagiwada, "Hansen's Law of 'Third-generation Return' and the Study of America's Religio-Ethnic Groups," *Phylon* 24 (Fall 1968):360–70.

24. John M. Goering, "The Emergence of Ethnic Interests: A Case of Serendipity," *Social Forces* 49 (March 1971):379–84.

25. Hansen, "The Problem of the Third Generation," p. 15.

26. Ibid., p. 17.

27. Ibid., p. 19.

28. Rischin, "Marcus Lee Hansen," pp. 329–30, 336, 341.

29. Hansen, "The Problem of the Third Generation," p. 19.

30. Ibid., pp. 20–21.

31. Hansen, "Who Shall Inherit America?," pp. 226–27.

32. Hansen, "The Problem of the Third Generation," p. 14.

33. Hansen, "Who Shall Inherit America?," p. 231.

34. Ibid., pp. 229–30.

35. Ibid., p. 229.

36. Nathan Glazer's contribution to this volume was influential in helping to develop the ideas in this paragraph.

Just Call Me John:
Ethnicity as *Mentalité*

This essay is intended as a meditation upon a theme that historians of past generations have addressed in many ways and pursued along many lines with a depth, sophistication, and empathy without parallel in the history of our nation. It is the theme of America's historic ethnicity, a theme that Marcus Hansen was the first to approach with high historical imagination, to adumbrate in international and transethnic terms for the totality of our history, and to project, at least posthumously, to the forefront of the American historical consciousness. So enduring has been Hansen's influence that his planned epic of the making of a multiethnic people still awaits a synthesis that will penetrate to the core historical needs of all Americans by telling not only of the great saga of immigration and its proximate effects, but also of the full meaning of the American story in rich and intimate human detail that goes beyond ethnicity and is consonant with it, as Hansen surely intended.

Heretofore, in a nation segmented along so many diverse lines and legally segregated down a number of deep faults and heir to so many ethnic and other often pejoratively accented status discriminations and habits of thought, no democratic frame of ethnic discourse sufficient to encompass all Americans had a chance of acceptance. Indeed, for much of the twentieth century, polemically keyed metaphors and catchphrases persisted in diverting attention away from the historical study of everyday ethnicity, blunting our perceptions both of the continuities and discontinuities shaping our distinctively individual and group selves, and dimming our capacity to derive meaning from our diverse lives and acknowledging them to be what they have been and even might become. Ever since Michael-Guillaume Jean de Crèvecoeur, the first voice of our "national consciousness" as he has been called, chose to pass as Hector St. John and to proclaim America the country of new men and new women, Americans in season and out have been prone either to flaunt or to camouflage the telltale marks of their palpably different ancestries. Not unlike Crèvecoeur, although seeking to affirm their Americanness, they have been wary that in some way they might be compromised by the acknowledgment of their complexity. In a nation so diverse, with its people ever in flux, the potential stresses to which the integrity of any identity may be subject remains a perpetual source of discomfiture, ever lurking just below the surface. It would almost seem as if at the very founding of the nation, a John the Brokenhearted (the literal translation for *Crèvecoeur*) had been invented both to proclaim the creation of a new people and to forewarn Americans, as he did in sundry ingenious ways in his *Letters from an American Farmer* and other writings, of the ironies and paradoxes inherent in their quest for an original national identity.[1]

In these reflections upon our historic ethnicity, I shall single out a number of intellectual events of the past decade or so that enlivened my understanding of a theme first illuminated by the pioneering efforts of Marcus Hansen. I will allude to a conference on ethnicity that quickened my capacity for perceiving America's historic ethnicity as a living force; to the role of ethnicity as *mentalité* in furthering our ability to link the American past with the American present; to the relationship of the only two ethnic ancestry enumerations in our history to the prevailing ethos; to the implications of our ethnically sensitive scholarship for a full-scale reconceptualization of the American past; and to the shade of Marcus Hansen, who was the first to ask so many of the important questions.

Inadvertently, in 1974 a conference on ethnicity at the Center for the Study of Democratic Institutions, which—as an officer of the Immigration History Society—I helped organize, extended a plumb line into America's historic ethnicity by reaching back to our nation's earliest beginnings. Following upon the most revolutionary decade in the history of American ethnic and race relations, culminating in major civil rights legislation, an amended immigration law, and the ethnic heritage act, as well as much else, simultaneously and singularly capped by racial upheaval and ethnic revival, it seemed essential to ground our understanding of the contemporary intergroup climate in a larger historical matrix. Most important, it appeared crucial that the two leading senior savants of American ethnic and race relations, Gunnar Myrdal and Donald R. Young, take part so that their differing views, which long had conditioned our apprehension of race and ethnic relations, serve as departure points for subsequent discussion. Myrdal, author of the social science classic, *An American Dilemma*, the single most influential work on American race relations in the generation after World War II, and Young, the first sociologist to attempt "an integrated study of the minority peoples in the United States" on the assumption that "the problem of race relations are remarkably similar regardless of what groups are involved," graciously accepted our invitation to participate.[2]

Like Robert E. Park, the pioneer student of race relations, Young did not see blacks as an exceptional group victimized by a unique form of racial prejudice due to the failure of whites to live up to American ideals as did Myrdal, but as the most severely penalized of all minority groups, whose condition, if thoroughly investigated, would shed light on all of American society and on all its minority groups. A resumption then of the colloquy between the monistic-minded Swede and the pluralistic-minded American who had served as chief consultant and critic to Myrdal during the preparation of his study in the late thirties of "The Negro Problem and Modern Democracy" would launch the conference on both a fittingly historical and contemporaneous note.[3] Regrettably, this was not to be. Young's growing deafness forced him to withdraw, and the conference was deprived of a live-witness retrospective of his views on ethnicity that was sorely missed.

Subsequent correspondence with Young, however, made vivid the resilience of his personal ethnicity, and gave depth and meaning to biographical clues that had led to the initial surmise that he was an old American ethnic, at least nominally. Young proved to be far more, for the thumbnail ethnolinguistic self-portrait that he sent me extended back two centuries. And amplified by Ada Young, his widow, it revealed him to be singularly attuned to the vagaries of American ethnicity. With the intimacy and intensity of a self-conscious ethnic Young had a profoundly individualized sense of self that Park could not have been expected to share. "Your guess is correct," wrote Young,

> I am a Pennsylvania German. Although I count myself bilingual, as were my parents and all my grandparents, I spoke only English with my parents, only Pennsylvania "Dutch" with my grandmother and either the dialect or English with my grandfather. (These were my maternal grandparents. My paternal grandparents died before I was born.) I was born in the house in which I now live, but lived in it very little in my youth because my father's work as a civil engineer specializing in railroad location and construction moved us about quite a bit.
>
> We are, of course, of very mixed national origin. My own ancestry, which probably is typical since I am related to a goodly proportion of the community of my generation, includes French, English, an early settler named Vasqueau who probably was a Basque, as well as several German lines. One ancestor changed his name from Jung to Young when he moved from Lancaster, Pa. to Niagara Falls with a Mennonite group in about 1810 [and] another changed his name from Ramsey to Rems to make it sound more German when he moved to this part of the country. [Young in turn apparently changed his

middle name back to Ramsey.] Perhaps this mixture accounts in part for the lack of identification with Germany as a homeland.[4]

Shortly after his death in 1977, Ada Young, in a brief communication, completed her late husband's ethnobiographic sketch.

> He spoke Pa. German every time the plumber came here. Our son took some lessons but never used it. Several years ago a course was given at the local vocational school; several of my friends enjoyed it. You can still hear it at the local grocery store. I don't know when the first Young or Ramsey came to [the] U.S.A. but one my husband came to talk about came as a redemptioner so I suppose that would be late 1700s. His mother belonged to the D.A.R. so I assume some of the ancestors fought in the revolution.[5]

Better than any single document that I have ever encountered in the literature of immigration and ethnic history, this capsule-size family biography of a latter-day American farmer from Macungie, Pennsylvania, telescopes the little-told tale not simply of long-term generational ethnic continuities, but, by implication at least, dramatizes the dynamics of the less visible family histories of a considerable proportion of the American people. Summarily dispatched into ethnic anonymity in our time with the ugly epithet *WASP*, old American ethnics have been denied an appreciation of their own distinctive and complex pasts with an indifference once reserved by historians for peoples on the fringes of public consciousness at one time, along with all of America's ethnics, they had found a spokesman in none other than the dean of the New History.

> "In a way, all of us except the red Indian, are foreigners, with reminiscences of a mother-country other than that in which it is our good fortune to live" [insisted James Harvey Robinson during World War One]. "If we are of English or Dutch extraction, we may be separated by nine or ten generations from our ancestors who lived in Europe; but this does not necessarily break the tie with peoples beyond the Atlantic whose blood flows in our veins. I certainly feel myself an Englishman by eight or nine removes. . . . We are all hyphenated, excepted the poor black man, who is scarcely ever suspected of a double allegiance. . . ."[6]

Understandably, Robinson's spirited appreciation of hyphenated America in the midst of World War I was not likely to spur American historians, Hansen and a few others excepted, to grapple with problems that could only seem intractably divisive in a nation sundered down the middle along major ethnic lines as it has been in no other war in American history. The unself-conscious Young story, by contrast, evokes an entirely different dimension of ethnicity. In a world that has lived in peace for two successive generations, it is suggestive of the intricately wrought family histories of older and newer American ethnics alike, of their cognizance of their ethnic selves, and of the formation and even reformation of ethnic identities over the centuries. Linked to the development as well of local and regional intra-, inter-, and polyethnic configurations, the resultant galactic flux, surprisingly, has barely been remarked as social process, its ethnic divagations and disjunctive informality remaining largely uncharted and unrelated to our understanding of historic ethnicity and the functioning of our society.

Yet at no other time has the study of America's historic ethnicity in a bewildering variety of abiding guises and forms been welcomed so universally. Generously affirmed for all and granted official American sanction, it has been endowed with a name. "The advent of the name is always a great event even though the thing named has preceded it; for it signifies the decisive moment of conscious awareness," noted Marc Bloch, a historian like Hansen, of "the hidden forces which determine behavior and the structure of society."[7]

In our era, ethnicity has become a *mentalité*, to appropriate a succinct French term that has not quite been domesticated to the American or any other language, yet that seems peculiarly suited to our needs. Fresh, devoid of false precision, and applicable to all, ethnicity as *mentalité* is expressive of the self-evident, no less than the latent, vestigial, adoptive, self-generating, and symbolic ethnic modes that have come to be recognized as inseparable from our common humanity and integral to our ethic of democracy and civilization. As Americans have become impregnated with a new cosmopolitan outlook, such once-favored designations as nationality, people, minority, and race have fallen into abeyance, if not into disuse. By contrast, ethnicity, reechoing with the long-term, if not quite with eternity, and overarching the planet, carries with it none of the patronizing overtones that charged the everyday language of ethnic discourse until quite recently and that may have prompted Marcus Hansen, with uncharacteristic sociological bravura, to mint the term "the third generation immigrant" (or as he spoke of it originally, in January 1935 before a public audience at the University of London, as "the third generation theory") to address the problem of ethnicity in indubitably American accents before the Augustana Historical Society in 1937.[8]

Clearly, we live in an age of ethnicity, an age whose culturally democratic and pluralistic impulses Hansen had championed and was committed to understanding. Emerging out of the second Thirty Years' War that began in 1914, a war far more apodictic in its devastation even than its namesake, there followed in its wake, as in the wake of its predecessor three centuries before, an era of mounting cosmopolitanism, internationalism, and a sense of mission. If in the eighteenth century an incipient toleration for religious differences in western Europe came to moderate historic hostilities and eventually opened the way to a new consensus respecting the rights of the individual and the individual's relationship to the state, by the latter half of the twentieth century, a second Thirty Years' War, fueled in its final phase by a demonic racism and totalitarianism, has been followed by a second age of enlightenment wedded to a vision of one world where the representatives of all humanity were to be recognized as equal and where the ideals of individual rights and of ethnic individuality were to become the twin towers of a new transethnic civilization incorporating yet transcending its diverse elements. In this new age, the United States of America again was destined to emerge as the exemplar of an ethnically open society.

By contrast, Hansen's foreshortened life was inseparable from an era of extreme nativism, isolationism, and racism, one that appeared singularly conclusive for the story of American ethnic and immigration history. The congealing of American public opinion on the immigration question, the withering obsession and fear of the genetic and cultural impact of "inferior" races upon American life and institutions, and the triumphal drive to define and virtually foreclose the composition of the American people for all time culminated in the year that Hansen completed his doctoral dissertation. Bringing down the curtain on an epic drama that, like the epic of the frontier, had placed its stamp upon American life at every level, the immigration law of 1924 appeared final. As visas and 3 percents turned a promised land into an "almost . . . forbidden land," as Hansen put it in an obiter dictum interjected into his doctoral dissertation, he more than ever felt driven to elucidate the larger meaning of the immigration story as a means for nurturing an ethnically diverse and authentic American culture. Anticipating "a budding movement for cultural democracy," as Rudolph Vecoli has phrased it, Hansen envisioned the historian as the prime catalyst for the regeneration and legitimation of a diverse and cosmopolitan America. In the last year of his life, most notably in his Augustana and Indianapolis jeremiads, Hansen virtually appeared to be keynoting a public campaign, which he had quietly heralded in 1929, in his study, "The Second Colonization of New England," to disseminate a program for the re-Americanization of America that would join newer and older Americans in a commonly shared history.[9]

This was the burden of Hansen's classic "Third Generation" address and of his little-known last public statement, "Who Shall Inherit America?" that followed. In both he unmercifully indicted second generation immigrants out of hand for being "traitors," the culpable addicts of a "queer hunger" for a "true Americanism," as Saul Bellow subsequently labeled the second generation's longing for acceptance that drove many of them to tailor their "appearance and style to what were . . . journalistic publicity creations and products of caricature."[10] Yet, as Hansen saw it, cultural redemption was destined to come in the lives of the successors to this lost generation. In remarks that seem clairvoyant and bear a familiar ring a half-century later, but which proved premature then, Hansen in his last address optimistically projected an American ethnic renaissance based on a renewal of generational, geographic, familial, and personal ties and affections:

> To be proud of blood and descent is one of the most common of human desires. Pride is easily extended from a person to a country and a wanderer in the field of genealogy often strays into the field of history. He is proud of his grandfather but just as proud of the civilization that he represented and whereas his grandfather cannot be recalled to life while the civilization can the former is often forgotten in the awakened interest in the latter. A trip back to the ancestral village often reveals that the home has disappeared and with it all objects of personal interest. But new scenes and strange customs are viewed sympathetically and vivid impressions are left upon the mind of one who is American in birth, reactions and influence.
>
> Such developments multiplied several million times are now transpiring or about to take place. A large proportion of the American people is just entering the third generation stage and many contacts that they will establish with popular culture abroad will constitute the new opportunity that is to knock. In a recognition of this fact and by a skillful handling of the situation there may be selected from the revived interest those features of cultural life that should be added to the heritage of America.

To facilitate the selection process, Hansen proposed a "museum of American culture. . . . rich in funds and staffed by men of learning and ingenuity who consider it the greatest of all callings to let the American people know something about the thirty or forty nationalities that contributed blood, ideas and labor to the founding of the nation during the first three hundred years of its existence."

Even better, more direct, and more likely to take hold quickly, insisted the historian, would be "a thousand enterprises springing up from the people," with each community library

> the collector of an historical exhibit that will reflect the cultural background of the people that first settled the surrounding countryside. Should some forward-looking librarian undertake to fill the hall cases with pioneer articles, prayer books and guide books printed in some

foreign tongue, needle work and utensils unknown to the native homestead, some worthy citizen might object especially if it involved the removal of relics of the Revolution or Civil War. But the incident in itself could be the occasion for a lesson on national culture and might spur the representatives of other groups into an effort to secure their proper share of recognition. If, on every hand, the impression-able mind of the youth of the country were reminded of the multiple origin of the American people, all presented in a truthful, dignified and tolerant way, little by little, daily life would select what it found useful or pleasant from the gifts that were still available and that a previous generation had blindly refused.

In closing, Hansen bade his last audience to remember that the his-torian understood the ultimate irony, that the immigrants' "real in-fluence in cultural development begins only when most observers say that it has come to an end."[11]

Hansen's prognostications, of course, have been realized at many levels, if not quite in the modes that he envisaged. Hansen might have experienced a sense of déjà vu when in 1980, for the first time in the nation's annals, the Bureau of the Census conducted a comprehensive enumeration of all Americans by ethnic ancestry. At only two junc-tures in American history, in 1927 and in 1980, have ethnic, as dis-tinguished from immigration, statistics either been compiled or in part extrapolated from the census records. Conducted a half-century apart, America's ancestral stock-taking could not have been more differently inspired. In the first, in which Hansen had a hand, only people of European origin were enumerated; in the second, everyone was in-cluded. In 1927, the objective of the Quota Board empowered with working out the details of the Johnson-Reed law that reduced immi-gration into the United States to 150,000 annually was to exclude as many "inferior" immigrants as the formulaic ingenuity of the times permitted. To do so, quotas were to be keyed not simply to the two-generational "foreign-stock" segment of the white population of the United States in 1920, but to be determined as well by a study of the ethnic origins of the American people in 1790, which then was to be statistically factored into the final quota calculations.

Undertaken in an entirely different spirit and with radically dif-ferent assumptions was the landmark 1980 ethnic ancestry enumer-ation, for it was to be as dramatically inclusionist as its forerunner had been blatantly exclusionist. In June 1976, at a White House con-ference on ethnicity spearheaded by Michael Novak, some sixty rep-resentatives of diverse ethnic groups recommended that the United States Bureau of the Census frame questions for the 1980 census that would record the ethnic origins of all Americans. Heretofore, for more than a century, the Bureau of the Census had collected data for first and second generation Americans of European origin, but all earlier generations had been lumped together indiscriminately under the rubric "native of native parentage." This was no longer to be. "This report," noted the Census Bureau, "presents 1980 census information on the population size and geographic distribution of more than 100 ancestry groups in the United States. The general ancestry question was based on self-identification, provided no prelisted categories, and allowed for one or more ancestry responses. This was the first census to collect ethnic data on persons regardless of the number of generations removed from their country of origin."[12]

The objective of the 1980 ethnic census was primarily to secure a reasonably accurate statistical profile of the American people for cultural purposes, with, as Novak put it, its many "implications for education, for humanistic studies, for social studies, for television and the popular arts, for public communication, and for political and social analysis." The availability of such census data was seen to be especially valuable as well in projecting the nation's unique multiethnic makeup and demonstrating the unsurpassably diverse ethnic linkages of the American people to peoples throughout the world.[13]

Some fifty years earlier, Hansen had been commissioned by the American Council of Learned Societies to ascertain the ethnic proportion of three of America's minor stocks, the Dutch, the French, and the Swedes, in the thirteen original states in 1790, as well as the ethnic composition of the population in the outlying regions. Apparently, he also proved to be the sole critic of the prescribed "nomenclature" methodology that was employed and to which the researcher for the major stocks, the genealogist Howard Barker, was fervently committed.

No more devastating indictment of historical or social science methodology is ever likely to be composed than the thirteen-page memorandum that Hansen prepared arraigning the "distinctive names" or "nomenclature" system for ascertaining the national origins of the population of the United States in 1790. Hansen directed his criticism primarily at the "distinctive names" method applied by his colleague to the study of the Irish, whose history and records the young historian had been studying with fresh eyes in Ireland in preparation for his projected immigration epic. Barker's assumptions that names distinctive for a province remain fixed in the course of a century and more, that names distinctively associated with a province also were distinctive for emigrants from that province, that ten readings of one name had the same significance as single readings of ten names, and that names that looked Irish were in fact Irish, all were simply not so, wrote

Hansen. Finally, the comptometer, he lamented, went against everything his historian's instincts and long immersion in immigrant life and the original sources had taught him. "The impossibility of acquiring direct genealogical information" for 450,000 families and "the risk involved in classifying those names by their national appearance, due to the changes which took place in their forms, especially in regions where several nationalities were present or where a minor stock was completely overshadowed by a predominant stock" led to "fantasies," he insisted. "Millions for research but not one cent for nonsense,"[14] exclaimed Hansen on a final note of exasperation after completing his assignment.

More than six decades later, leading social scientists bringing differing perspectives to bear on their evaluation of the 1980 ethnic ancestry census appeared uniformly accepting of its basic premise. Like Hansen earlier, however, they raised questions regarding its reliability, its methodology, and its practical value. Minimal comment was accorded the gross statistics of ethnic ancestry, namely that of 83 percent of Americans who responded to the question directly, 52 percent registered a single specific ancestry, whereas 31 percent reported a multiple ancestry, including seventeen "unique" triple-origin ancestries. Apparently, had sufficient funding allowed, double-origin ancestries also would have been tabulated.[15]

Significantly, the first and most comprehensive critique of the 1980 census was a detailed preliminary appraisal of ethnic ancestry census procedures by the demographer Ira Lowry. While severely criticizing the Bureau of the Census for not knowing how to conduct an ethnic census, Lowry conceded that no better alternative had been proposed. After commending the Bureau for resisting the most outrageous proposals, he attributed its failure to conduct a methodologically scientific ethnic census primarily to politics; to pressure from the science lobby determined to perpetuate accepted census concepts and methods for the sake of long-term consistency; and to the failure of social science "to offer valid methodological instruction." From the outset, the "low order of response consistency in ethnic self-identification," to which the census advisory panel appointed by the National Research Council had pointed to earlier, underlined the census's methodological insufficiencies. In order that ethnic data acquire "functional significance," Lowry recommended 1) that a reliable method of ethnic identification be established; 2) that "the degree of ethnic enclosures" of "the numerically important ethnic groups" that "would reveal the implicit ethnic structure of American society be measured"; and 3) that "a scale of intensity for ethnic self-identification" be established so that distinctions may be made between those for whom ethnic ancestry is significant and those for whom it is trivial and negligible.[16]

Taking an entirely different tack, Stanley Lieberson, a leading sociologist, was impressed with the conspicuous presence in the ethnic ancestry census of a new ethnic group that he denominated "unhyphenated whites." He observed that these self-identifying or unidentifying nonethnics, comprising the 6 percent of the respondents who recorded themselves as "American" or "United States" and the remaining 10 percent who recorded no ancestry at all, were significantly different from other white Americans on a number of counts. Relying on National Opinion Research Center (NORC) surveys, Lieberson noted first that the consistency in the responses to the question of ethnic identity were far lower for whites from northwestern Europe, descended primarily from ancestors who came to the United States earlier, than for whites whose ancestors came later. Second, this pattern, he reported, was especially marked in the more isolated regions of the South, where both the highest proportion of "unhyphenated whites" and of Americans of four or more generations were to be found. Predominanty rural and Protestant, they also were of a lower educational level and of lower social and economic status than were ethnic whites. Significantly, in earlier NORC social surveys, blacks too were disproportionately represented among those who identified themselves simply as American or of no ancestry.[17] By ethnic criteria, unclassified whites, an expanding group, Lieberson ventures to predict, clearly would appear to be as marginal to mainline ethnic America as were ethnically unidentifying blacks.

Finally, Paul Magosci, a leading historian of nationalism and of ethnicity in the United States, called for greater sensitivity and precision in ethnic ancestry tabulations. After commending the open-ended self-identification method as being "in the best tradition reflecting freedom of choice," Magosci offered suggestions for improving the upcoming 1990 ethnic ancestry census, particularly the ancestry classification system, which he called "a useful first draft" in need of emendation and refinement. As Magosci saw it, the major problem, was that the commendably wide variety of responses encouraged by the ethnic self-identification method complicated ethnic and ancestry classifications and often led in the tabulation process to the nullification of the respondent's free choice. After noting that apparently a minimum number of five thousand, as in the case of Dominica Islanders and Saudi Arabians, warranted a distinct ancestry group classification, Magosci recommended an increase in the number of European group classifications. To the fifty European-derived groups of a total of 128 ancestry group classifications listed not in the published reports, but in the unpublished "Code List for Ancestry Entries," Magosci urged that sixteen more be added, for example, Acadians, Bretons, Catalans, Corsicans, Jews, Pennsylvania-Germans, and Scotch-Irish. Like all the other ancestry group classifications, these proposed ancestry entries were to be "based on the situation in the United States."[18] Thus far, apparently no criticisms of methodology have been voiced from the perspective of peoples of non-European origin nor has it been suggested that the 1,500 ethnic designations compiled by the Bureau of the Census had a validity for which no provision was made in the ethnic ancestry census.

Clearly, the American consensus has moved a long way since Benjamin Franklin, in his classic essay, *Observations Concerning the Increase of Mankind*, expressed his preference for "purely white people," excluding "Spaniards, Italians, French, Russians, and Swedes [who] are generally of what we call a swarthy Complexion" from the white category as well as "Germans, the Saxons, only excepted, who with the English, make the principal body of White People on the Face of the Earth." Although no longer referring to his natural partiality for "the Complexion of my Country," nearly three decades later, Franklin reiterated his fond wish that America be peopled by Englishmen. "You do wrong to discourage the emigration of Englishmen to America," wrote Franklin to an English friend. "Why should you be against acquiring by this fair means a repossession of it [America], and leave it to be taken by foreigners of all nations and languages, who by their numbers may drown and stifle the English. . . ."[19]

Franklin's attachment to "purely white peoples" like himself, as he so well knew, was unlikely to shape immigration patterns. Yet, in the face of seemingly intractable social problems in the mid-nineteenth century, a passion for Anglo-American ethnic homogeneity would become compulsive at times and culminate in repeated appeals to racial Anglo-Saxonism. In a series of articles in the Boston *Daily Advertiser*, no less a public figure than the subsequent grand old man of Boston Unitarianism, Edward Everett Hale, broached a scheme for the dispersal of the Irish that would be revived invariably for a dozen other groups into our own day. In his proposal for the distribution of the Irish among the natives across the nation in a ratio of eight to a hundred, Hale argued that it would "stimulate the absorbents" and lead, as it had in colonial New England, to their being Protestantized. Furthermore, insisting that Irish Catholicism was "a matter of national pride rather than . . . a matter of faith," Hale breathlessly concluded: "The Irishman must be surrounded by Americans. His children must be Americans. He must not be left in clans in large cities."[20]

The ready acknowledgment by most Americans in 1980 of a distinctive ethnic consciousness extending across the whole ethnic spectrum ranging from an ingenuous, if often vague and ambiguous, identification with a single ethnic ancestry for the majority to a considered, residual, token, or simply romantic association with two or more ethnic groups for others, is reflective of our age of ethnicity, of ethnicity as *mentalité*. If the many elusive aspects of our ethnic matter-of-factness often tinged with ambivalence have yet to be effectively integrated with insight and authority into a more profound understanding of the entire American experience, it has not been for lack of a growing recognition by historians of the critical challenge to American self-knowledge that such an enterprise entails and of its potential importance for providing our history with a unifying perspective.

It was, of course, Marcus Hansen in his foray into historical counterpoint who first proffered the idea of immigration as a key to an understanding of the total American experience. Fully convinced that the immigrants of the nineteenth and twentieth centuries were the true-blue latter-day American counterparts of the seventeenth- and eighteenth-century pioneers and colonists, Hansen opened the way to a total reconceptualization of American immigration and ethnic history. "The Puritan who landed in Massachusetts Bay with his blunderbuss and Bible was an immigrant," wrote Hansen. "The peasant from Eastern Europe who . . . passed through Ellis Island with a pack upon his back was a colonist. They were all colonists, all immigrants. And all were engaged in providing America with ancestors."[21] Reversing Hansen's focus, a new generation of American colonial historians has responded energetically to his vision of America as a nation linked by the common thread of the immigration experience. By depicting seventeenth- and eighteenth-century colonists as true-blue immigrants, historians of colonial America have been completing the Hansen circle, endowing Americans of all origins, colonial no less than twentieth century, with real rather than with largely mythical ancestors. To fully understand this transformation, every phase of the colonial immigrant experience is being examined: the European context, the pre-American experience, the interplay of cultural and religious ties and affinities, the continuing relations of immigrants with their places of origin, and the varied accommodations that they made. Even the poorly defined ethnically opaque years that Hansen called the era of "The First Americanization"—extending from the end of the American Revolution to the end of the War of 1812 and perhaps somewhat beyond—when immigration presumably fell to a low ebb, have elicited a new scholarship. Despite formidable obstacles, it is intended to bridge the substantial gap in our knowledge of the makeup and making of the initial second and third generations of the American people.[22]

What can it all mean in the light of Hansen's passion for "Americanization," for "that spiritual unity which makes up a nation" to which he was so ardently committed even as he was to American diversity? If, as he put it, it was "the ultimate fate of any national group to be amalgamated into the composite American race," clearly it was to be a differential long-term process for which Hansen, who everywhere about him avidly sought out the tracings of ethnicity, proffered no formula. Hansen's final charge to his students in his one-year sequence in American immigration history at the University of Illinois may come closest at least to conveying his anthropological ardor for ethnic individuality and diversity. "All the people we see are somehow related to the history of immigration; every name and every blending of features and almost every personal reaction mean something. You may be bored by scenery and by books, but you should never be bored by people." Surely, John Higham's penetrating delineation of what he has called "pluralistic integration" makes full provision for the variety and ambiguity historically inseparable from the American ethnic way to which Hansen implicitly pointed. If Hansen would have admonished the 1980 ethnic census for punching out its share of quantifiable nonsense by grace of the computer as he had the comptometer guesstimates a half-century earlier, he hardly would have questioned the need for ethnic stock-taking in a nation pledged to upholding diversity.[23]

Hansen might also have recognized the conundrum of American identity so poignantly symbolized in the life of America's first man of humane letters, whose very name has long continued to baffle the most fervent admirers of his writings. In 1781, that most emblematic and cosmopolitan of all proto-Americans, Michael-Guillaume Jean de Crèvecoeur, variously known over the preceding two decades as St. John, J. Hector St. John, John St. John, Crèvecoeur, and J. Hector St. John de Crèvecoeur, artfully summed up his personal drama of identity on the eve of the publication of his soon-to-be-famous *Letters from an American Farmer*.

In reply to Benjamin Franklin, who was confused as to his correspondent's identity and the spelling of his name, the doubly hyphenated Anglo-French-American assured his fellow countryman that he indeed was he.

> The reason of this mistake proceeds from the Singularity of ye french Customs, which renders their Names, allmost arbitrary, & often leads them to forget their family ones; it is in Consequence of *this*, that there are more alias dictos in this than in any other Country in

Europe. The name of our Family is St. Jean, in English St. John, a name as Antient as the Conquest of England by Wm. the Bastard. [Crèvecoeur then continued] I am so great a Stranger to the manners of this, tho' my native Country (having quitted it very young) that I Never dreamt I had any other, than the old family name—I was greatly astonished when at my late return, I saw myself under the Necessity of being Called by that of Crèvecoeur. . . .[24]

Ever since, ambivalence about ethnic identity has been a running commonplace of the American experience, of which there are no end of illustrations. Most recently, a prominent candidate for high political office was taunted repeatedly for misrepresenting the year of his birth, cropping his surname, and pursuing life, liberty, and happiness in a style that offended many Americans because, it has been suggested, they saw in him many troubling aspects of themselves. Predictably, the most thorough student of the 1980 ethnic ancestry census, looking as American as apple pie, could not recall how he had identified himself in the ethnic census. The son of an Anglo whose grandmother was Hispanic, as a child in Texas, he had learned Spanish before he had learned English.[25]

This discussion is intended as a commentary on the ethnic dimension of the American experience, on the perennial and profound human need to simultaneously sustain larger and smaller identities, equivocal as they often may be, in the American spirit of the 1980 ethnic self-identifying census. Surely that complex phenomenon is the central theme in the study of America's historic ethnicity, of the creation and recreation of the American people over the course of three centuries, of a people whose varied ethnocultural pasts have lived on in themselves in some form. Remittently divided and united in the course of our history, the periodic genesis, regenesis, and sorting out of diverse American ethnic and other identities—no less than the recasting of a larger American national identity—ever constitutes a challenge to our understanding of the drama of a multiethnic people.

For Hansen's successors, the extension backward and forward and the deepening of his nineteenth-century saga of the great North Atlantic migration to encompass the South Atlantic and the Pacific migrations from Africa, Asia, and Latin America, continues to exert a categorical claim on their talents. At hand for the first time in our history, we have an unparalleled array of original sources, an extraordinary profusion of splendid historical monographs, and an unprecedented number of monumental works of collaborative scholarship. Most important, perhaps, the prevailing *mentalité* of ethnicity makes a finely textured, no less than a deeply imagined, epic of ethnic America feasible at last, one that will do justice to our felt sense of American and world realities.

NOTES

1. See John Higham, *Send These to Me: Immigrants in Urban America* (Baltimore: Johns Hopkins University Press, 1984), pp. x–xiii, 3–4; Rudolph J. Vecoli, "Return to the Melting Pot: Ethnicity in the United States in the Eighties," *Journal of American Ethnic History* 5 (Fall 1985): 17; Moses Rischin, "Creating Crèvecoeur's 'New Man': He Had a Dream," *Journal of American Ethnic History* 1 (Fall 1981):33–36.

2. Gunnar Myrdal, *An American Dilemma* (New York: Harper and Brothers, 1944), pp. x, 52, 1185–86; G. Myrdal to Donald R. Young, May 15, 1974 (copy in author's possession). See *The Center Magazine* 7 (July–August 1974):17–73; Donald R. Young, *American Minority Peoples* (New York: Harper and Brothers, 1932), p. xiii.

3. Young, *American Minority Peoples*, p. 574; Higham, *Send These to Me*, pp. 27–220; Fred. H. Matthews, *Quest for an American Sociology: Robert E. Park and the Chicago School* (Montreal: McGill-Queen's University Press, 1977), pp. 184–85; David W. Southern, *Gunnar Myrdal and Black-White Relations* (Baton Rouge: Louisiana State University Press, 1987), pp. 10–11, 86; Walter A. Jackson, "The Making of a Social Science Classic: Gunnar Myrdal's *American Dilemma*," *Perspectives in American History*, New Series 2 (1985):232–33, 250.

4. *Who's Who in America 1942–1943* (Chicago: A. H. Marquis, 1942), p. 2420; Donald R. Young to Moses Rischin, June 26, 1974. Young's understanding of the role of language in the making of Americans is particularly revealing (*American Minority Peoples*, pp. 465–66):

> It is usually stated that a knowledge of English is the first prerequisite to proper assimilation. To an extent this is true: but it must not be forgotten that the Pennsylvania Germans and other rural groups as well, have been "Americanized" for generations in spite of a limited knowledge of the English language. Language is only a tool, and while it is essential that the communication tool of the community be learned quickly and thoroughly there may be advantages in not discarding the old too soon. Identical thoughts can be expressed in English, German, Italian, or Chinese, and it is much easier to grasp ideas expressed in the speech of childhood than in one learned in later life. . . . Any program of assimilation which considers its first duty to be the wiping out of all alien tongues without delay, and fails to make use of the best tool for conveying ideas to the immigrant, that is, his primary language, is paying more attention to surface polishing than to true assimilation. It is not the means of expression, but the attitudes and actions which count, for they require no greater substitute of English in the foreign-born generations than is dictated by the English-speaking contacts of the individual.

5. Ada Young to Moses Rischin, undated [ca. February 1979]. Also see Don Yoder, "The Pennsylvania Germans: Three Centuries of Identity Crisis," in *America and the Germans*, ed. Frank Trommler and Joseph McVeigh (Philadelphia: University of Pennsylvania Press, 1985), vol. 1, pp. 41–65.

6. James Harvey Robinson, Introduction to Marcus L. Ravage, "The Loyalty of the Foreign-Born," *Century* 74 (June 1917):201–2. See Oscar Handlin, "Ethnicity and the New History," in *Truth in History* (Cambridge: Belknap Press, 1979), pp. 392–94, 400–2; Higham, *Send These to Me*, 175ff.; Moses Rischin, ed., *Immigration and the American Tradition* (Indianapolis: Bobbs-Merrill, 1976), pp. xxxi–xxxvi, 191–208.

7. Marc Bloch, *The Historian's Craft* (New York: Random House, 1964), pp. 168, x. See also Nathan Glazer and Daniel P. Moynihan, eds., *Ethnicity: Theory and Experience* (Cambridge: Harvard University Press, 1975), pp. 1–3, and Rowland Berthoff, "Writing a History of Things Left Out," *Reviews in American History* 14 (March 1986):4–6.

8. Michael Vovelle, "Ideology and *Mentalités*," in *Culture, Ideology and Politics: Essays for Eric Hobsbawm*, ed. Raphael Samuel and Gareth Stedman Jones (London: Routledge and Kegan Paul, 1982), pp. 2–11; Francois Furet, *In the Workshop of History* (Chicago: University of Chicago Press, 1984), pp. 8, 15–16; J. Revel, "*Mentalités*," in *Dictionnaire des Sciences Historiques*, ed. Andre Burguiere (Paris: Presses Universitaires de France, 1986), pp. 450–56; Olivier Zunz, "Genèse du pluralisme americain," *Annales* no. 2 (March–April 1987):429ff. See Herbert J. Gans, "Symbolic Ethnicity: The Future of Ethnic Groups and Cultures in America," in *On the Making of Americans: Essays in Honor of David Riesman*, ed. Herbert J. Gans, Nathan Glazer, Joseph R. Gusfield, and Christopher Jencks (Philadelphia: University of Pennsylvania Press, 1979), pp. 193–230.

9. See Moses Rischin, "Marcus Lee Hansen: America's First Transethnic Historian," in *Uprooted Americans: Essays to Honor Oscar Handlin*, ed. Richard Bushman, Neil Harris, David Rothman, Barbara Miller Solomon, and Stephan Thernstrom (Boston: Little, Brown, 1979), pp. 324 ff.; Hansen, "The Second Colonization of New England," *The Immigrant in American History*, ed. Arthur M. Schlesinger (Cambridge: Harvard University Press, 1940), pp. 154–74, was originally published in 1929 in the *New England Quarterly*. Also see Vecoli, "Return to the Melting Pot," p. 10; Richard Weiss, "Ethnicity and Reform: Minorities and the Ambience of the Depression Years," *Journal of American History* 66 (December 1979):581.

10. Saul Bellow, "Writers and Literature in American Society," in *Culture and Its Creators: Essays in Honor of Edward Shils*, ed. Joseph Ben-David and Terry Nichols Clark (Chicago: University of Chicago Press, 1977), p. 177; Oscar Handlin, ed., *Children of the Uprooted* (New York: G. Braziller, 1966), pp. xiii–xxii; Victor Greene, *American Immigrant Leaders 1800–1910* (Baltimore: Johns Hopkins University Press, 1987), pp. 9–10.

11. Marcus Lee Hansen, "Who Shall Inherit America?," *Interpreter Releases* 14 (July 6, 1937):231–33. See Odd S. Lovoll, *The Promise of America: A History of the Norwegian-American People* (Minneapolis: University of Minnesota Press, 1984), pp. 216–21.

12. Nancy Sweet, U.S. Bureau of the Census, Washington, D.C., February 17 and 24, 1987, to Moses Rischin (telephone conversation); United States Department of Commerce, Bureau of the Census, *1980 Census Population: Supplementary Report, Ancestry of the Population by State: 1980* (Washing-

ton: Government Printing Office, 1983), pp. 1, 8; also see Charles A. Price, "Methods of Estimating the Size of Groups," in the *Harvard Encyclopedia of American Ethnic Groups*, ed. Stephan Thernstrom (Cambridge: Harvard University Press, 1980), pp. 1033ff; James P. Allen and Eugene J. Turner, *We the People: An Atlas of American Ethnic Diversity* (New York: Macmillan, 1988).

13. *Empac* no. 10 (October 1976):3–5.

14. M. L. Hansen to A. M. Schlesinger, January 2, March 8, 1928; M. L. Hansen to W. F. Willcox, January 2, 1928; "A Consideration of the System of 'Distinctive Names' as a Method for Determining the National Origins of the American Population" (memorandum, January 1928), pp. 1–13; M. L. Hansen to W. F. Willcox, January 2, 1928; A. M. Schlesinger to M. L. Hansen, March 2, 1928 (all in Schlesinger Papers, Columbia University). See American Council of Learned Societies, *Report of the Committee on Linguistic and National Stocks in the Population of the United States* (Washington: Government Printing Office, 1932), pp. 360ff. Also see Thomas L. Purvis, "The National Origins of New Yorkers in 1790," *New York History* 67 (April 1986):134–37, for a recent assessment of the surname methodology for New York.

15. Sweet to Rischin, February 24, 1987.

16. Ira S. Lowry, "The Science and Politics of Ethnic Enumeration," *Rand Corporation Papers* 6435 (January 1980): 1, 3, 5, 20–21.

17. Stanley Lieberson, "Unhyphenated Whites in the United States," *Ethnic and Racial Studies* 8 (January, 1985):159, 173ff; also see Thomas J. Archdeacon, *Becoming American: An Ethnic History* (New York: Free Press, 1983), pp. 230–31.

18. Paul Magosci, "Are The Armenians Really Russians?—Or How the U.S. Census Bureau Classifies America's Ethnic Groups," *Government Publications Review* 14, no. 2 (1987):135, 137–38, 147–48.

19. Ralph Ketcham, ed., *The Political Thought of Benjamin Franklin* (Indianapolis: Bobbs-Merrill, 1965), p. 71.

20. See Reginald Horsman, *Race and Manifest Destiny: The Origins of American Racial Anglo-Saxonism* (Cambridge: Harvard University Press, 1981), passim; Edward Everett Hale, *Letters on Irish Emigration* (Boston: Phillips, Sampson, 1852), pp. 34–36.

21. Hansen, *The Immigrant*, pp. 9–10.

22. See Jon Butler, *The Huguenots in America* (Cambridge: Harvard University Press, 1983), pp. 1–9; Ned C. Landsman, *Scotland and Its First American Colony, 1683–1765* (Princeton: Princeton University Press, 1985), pp. 256ff; Stephanie Grauman Wolf, "Hyphenated America: The Creation of an Eighteenth-Century American Culture," in *America and the Germans*, vol. 1, ed. Frank Trommler and Joseph McVeigh (Philadelphia: University of Pennsylvannia Press, 1985), pp. 66ff; Bernard Bailyn, *The Peopling of British North America* (New York: Alfred A. Knopf 1986), pp. 7–9 and *Voyagers to the West* (New York: Alfred A. Knopf 1986), p. xix; Carl A. Brasseaux, *The Founding of New Acadia* (Baton Rouge: Louisiana State University Press, 1987); Henry A. Gemery, "European Emigration to North America, 1700-1820: Numbers and Quasi-Numbers," *Perspectives in American History*, new series

1 (1984):283–89; Rischin, "Creating Crèvecoeur's 'New Man,' " pp. 31–33; Marcus Hansen, *The Atlantic Migration, 1607–1860: A History of the Continuing Settlement of the United States*, ed. Arthur M. Schlesinger (Cambridge: Harvard University Press, 1940), p. 53ff.

23. Hansen, *The Immigrant*, p. 167; C. Frederick Hansen, "Marcus Lee Hansen—Historian of Immigration," *Common Ground* 2 (Summer 1942):5; Higham, *Send These to Me*, p. xiii; Hansen, "The Problem of the Third Generation Immigrant," republication of the 1937 address with introductions by Peter Kivisto and Oscar Handlin (Rock Island: Swenson Swedish Immigration Research Center and Augustana College Library, 1987), p. 24.

24. Crèvecoeur, *Letters from an American Farmer* (New York: Everyman, 1912), p. 245; also see, Rischin, "Creating Crèvecoeur's 'New Man,' " p. 38.

25. See Richard Rodriquez, *Hunger of Memory* (Boston: D. R. Godine, 1982) for an eloquent contemporary portrayal of the dilemmas of ethnicity and Werner Sallors, *Beyond Ethnicity: Consent and Descent in American Culture* (New York: Oxford University Press, 1986), p. 208ff for a discussion of generation as metaphor.

PART TWO

Hansen and Various Groups

Hansen, Herberg, and American Religion

Now universally regarded by scholars in the field as a classic, Hansen's celebrated essay, "The Problem of the Third Generation Immigrant," attracted no notice whatsoever until fourteen years after its original publication. It was brought to the attention of *Commentary*'s readers in November 1952, as being especially pertinent to the contemporary situation of American Jews. Three years later, Will Herberg popularized "Hansen's law"—a term he introduced—by arguing in his widely read *Protestant-Catholic-Jew* that the statement "what the son wishes to forget the grandson wishes to remember" was one of the main conceptual keys to understanding the postwar "revival of religion." Thus the applicability of Hansen's third generation thesis to religious phenomena was what put his 1938 essay into general circulation. It was, indeed, in precisely this context that the essay first came to be regarded as a classic, despite the oblivion into which it had fallen after its original publication. These facts seem to me sufficiently intriguing to justify a closer look at the relationship between Hansen's essay and religion. My aim is simply to open the subject; if my observations seem at times speculative, I would claim as warrant the venturesome example Hansen set in his original discussion.

The original lecture being the obvious place to begin, we note first that it was delivered under the auspices of a church-related organization—the Augustana Historical Society—to an audience whose historical identity was inseparable from the religion around which their life as a social collectivity was structured. Hansen was quite conscious of the aegis under which he spoke. Indeed, he felt some concern that the religious context might lead his audience to put an unduly narrow construction on the message he wanted to get across. This uneasiness played no small part in shaping his treatment of "the problem of the third generation immigrant," as a brief review of his lecture will show.[1]

Those whose expectations were formed by Herberg and other recent commentators may feel surprise, if not bewilderment, on looking into the original lecture; the "problem," as Hansen himself explains it, is not what they have been led to expect. The problem is not to determine whether such a thing as "the principle of third generation interest" actually exists, or to account for its origins, or to establish how extensively its influence is felt. All these matters are, for Hansen, quite unproblematic. He simply *asserts* the principle as one of "the laws of history ... applicable in all fields of historical study," and asserts further that it derives from an "almost universal phenomenon" of human psychology ("what the son wishes to forget the grandson wishes to remember"). Although he calls the third generation principle a "theory," he makes no effort to verify it in a rigorous way. Rather he "illustrates" its operation by more or less offhand references to the contemporary interest in the history of the South—not disdaining to instance the case of *Gone With the Wind*, "written by a granddaughter of the Confederacy"—and to the emergence of immigrant historical societies.[2] Only after having dealt with what posterity regards as the heart of the matter in a series of generalizations so impressionistic that they might be said to fall into the "armchair" category does Hansen get around to the "problem."

What then *was* the problem? Simply this: How was the third generation's interest in its group heritage—assumed as a given—to be "organized and directed" in such a way as to produce the most fruitful historiographical results? Because the Augustana Historical Society was one of the organizations exemplifying third generation historical interest, the "problem" had immediate application to Hansen's audience.[3] And it was in suggesting how they ought to deal with it that he betrayed the uneasiness alluded to above.

Two general principles, according to Hansen, ought to guide the third generation's historical work: it should avoid "self-laudation" and hew to "broad impartial lines," and it should aim to "make a permanent contribution to the meaning of American history at large." To elucidate the former, Hansen admonished his audience on five points that related directly to the religious matrix from which the Augustana Historical Society sprang. They must look beyond the church in telling the story of their past; they should study first the context in which the church was planted and grew; they ought to give particular attention to groups "that broke with the faith of the old country"; they were not to overlook the political influence of the Augustana Synod; finally, they must also pay attention to groups that were the church's "competitors in the matter of interest, affection and usefulness."[4]

Hansen's remarks on the second general principle, although of considerable intrinsic interest, do not bear directly on the religious dimension. His guidelines on avoiding group "self-laudation" reveal very clearly, however, that he was sensitive to the religious aspect of the immigrant's historical heritage and group consciousness. They indicate with equal clarity that he regarded it as something that could easily distort a group's historical self-understanding. It would be rash to conclude, on this evidence alone, that Hansen had little historical interest in matters religious. What the lecture does establish beyond peradventure is that he did not find in the third generation principle the special significance for religious development that later commentators emphasized.

Although it is proverbially difficult to prove a negative, a strong case can be made to show that "The Problem of the Third Generation Immigrant" was unknown to the intellectual world in general until 1952. First, the form in which it was published—as a pamphlet by a local historical society—gave it far less visibility than it would have had as a journal article. Hansen quite possibly never saw it in print himself, for he died in May of the year it was published (1938). Thus he never had a chance to call it to the attention of colleagues, or to develop more systematically the principle of third generation interest. He did refer to the principle in speaking to an audience of social workers a few weeks after the Augustana lecture, but that talk attracted little attention at the time and was not made known to scholars until 1979.[5] It seems reasonable to conclude that Arthur M. Schlesinger, Sr., did not know about the Augustana lecture, for he did not include it, or make any reference to it, in the volume of Hansen's essays that he edited as *The Immigrant in American History*. Neither did C. Frederick Hansen say anything about "The Problem of the Third Generation Immigrant" in a biographical memoir of his brother, entitled "Marcus Lee Hansen—Historian of Immigration," which was published in 1942.[6]

It is true that Margaret Mead's *And Keep Your Powder Dry* (1942), a widely read analysis of the American character, makes interpretive use of a third generation concept. But despite the fact that the two are sometimes mentioned together, there is no reason to believe that Mead was acquainted with Hansen's essay. She does not refer to Hansen—or any other historian, for that matter—in text or notes; where he perceived a third generation interest in ethnic roots, Mead stresses the third generation's being completely cut off from their immigrant heritage and wishing to identify, not with their grandfathers, but with the "founding fathers."[7] In contrast to the second generation problem, which was a sociological commonplace, not much had yet been written about the situation of the third generation when *Keep Your Powder*

Dry appeared. But Mead's interpretation was consistent with the prevailing assumption that the third generation was the most "fully assimilated," and we can safely assume that Hansen had nothing to do with forming her ideas on the subject.[8]

It would be tedious to list all the relevant works of the period that do not mention Hansen's third generation essay. But because something more ought to be said to establish the presumption that it was unknown, let us look at two particularly revealing cases. The first of these works in which we could surely expect to find a reference to the Augustana lecture, if it were known, is the compendium of articles on immigration and ethnicity edited by Brown and Roucek. The first edition, *Our Racial and National Minorities*, appeared in 1937, the year before Hansen's lecture was published; hence its non-appearance there signifies nothing. There were, however, two later editions of the book, in 1946 and 1952, both of which had the main title, *One America*. Each of the later editions included a contribution by Samuel Koenig on "Second- and Third-Generation Americans." Although he cited a wide range of literature—more than fifty footnotes in a fifteen-page article—Koenig made no reference to Hansen's essay either in 1946 or 1952. Nor was that essay included in the lengthy bibliographies that accompanied each edition, although an obscure Hansen monograph of 1931 turned up in all three (among the readings listed for Portuguese Americans), and the latter two also included *The Atlantic Migration* and *The Immigrant in American History*.[9]

The second particularly revealing bit of negative evidence involves the writings of Edward N. Saveth. We know that he was much impressed by "The Problem of the Third Generation Immigrant" because he included it in his book of readings, *Understanding the American Past*.[10] That volume, however, appeared two years after Hansen's essay was republished in *Commentary*. Although Saveth cited the 1938 Augustana Historical Society publication as his source, it seems clear that his attention was called to the essay by seeing it in *Commentary*. We might draw that inference simply because he was at the time an employee of the American Jewish Committee, and could therefore be expected to be familiar with the contents of the magazine it published. There is, however, more conclusive evidence, namely, Saveth's failure to allude to the third generation essay in his earlier discussions of Hansen as an immigration historian. Although he praised Hansen's work in a 1946 *Commentary* article and in his standard monograph, *American Historians and European Immigrants, 1875–1925*, in neither case did he give evidence of acquaintance with the essay he later reprinted.[11]

If we can take it as at least provisionally established that Hansen's essay was unknown to the world at large until 1952, what were the circumstances of its immediate acceptance then as a classic? Nathan Glazer, a young scholar already deeply interested in ethnicity, came across Hansen's essay among the materials he was researching at the New York Public Library. Much struck by it, Glazer, an associate editor of *Commentary*, called the essay to the attention of his colleagues, who agreed that it would be of interest to readers of the magazine. It appeared in the November 1952, issue with a slightly altered title ("The Third Generation in America"), and with the subtitle or caption: "A Classic Essay in Immigrant History." Oscar Handlin, a frequent contributor whose recently published *The Uprooted* made him the preeminent academic authority on immigration, added an introductory note.[12]

Although his remarks dealt mainly with Hansen's career, what Handlin had to say about the essay itself is of particular interest. After noting Hansen's message about how an immigrant group should write its own history, Handlin called attention to "the applicability to Jewish immigrants of Hansen's striking theses." Among these he mentioned the latter's "views on the second and third generation," but the point he stressed "above all perhaps" was Hansen's "prediction as to the limited survival span in America . . . of the effective *distinctive* life of the group itself." Jewish readers, Handlin thought, would be surprised to discover the parallels between their own group experience and that of others, seemingly unlike them. They might also reflect, he concluded somberly, on the distinctiveness of Jewish group life and on "whether, to what degree, and how American Jews . . . can hope to escape the complete amalgamation which Hansen seems to predict."[13] From the viewpoint of group survival, this was a distinctly pessimistic reading that stands in sharp contrast to the emphasis Will Herberg was soon to lay on the law of third generation return.

After its republication, Saveth and Glazer were the first to take note of Hansen's essay. Saveth, as we saw, reprinted it in 1954, but his introductory comments were brief and noncommittal. Although he observed that it dealt with "the relationship of groupings in the American population to ancestral cultures," he did not draw attention to the principle of third generation interest or speculate on its implications.[14] Glazer, who rediscovered Hansen, was also the first to stress this aspect of the essay. His treatment, unlike Saveth's, was strongly theoretical. In "Ethnic Groups in America: From National Culture to Ideology" (1954), he hailed Hansen for perceiving that the third generation tends, in some sense, "to return to the first," and he linked that perception to his own bold interpretation of the overall pattern of American ethnic development as moving from identification with relatively concrete cultural attributes (e.g., language) to a more abstract "ideological" phase. An earlier version of Glazer's discussion included a paragraph arguing that religion functioned for some immigrant groups as a transmuted form of spiritual commitment to the old country.[15] In thus including religion among the aspects of Old World culture transformed in the New World, and "returned to" by third generation immigrants, Glazer anticipated certain aspects of the interpretation Will Herberg was soon to advance in *Protestant-Catholic-Jew.*

Herberg's book was published in the fall of 1955, but *Commentary* readers had been given a preview of two chapters in the August and September issues.[16] The book, a paperback edition of which appeared in 1960, attracted much attention because of the brilliant way it explained how a "revival of religion" could be taking place in a society that seemed simultaneously to be growing more and more secularized. The explanation, Herberg suggested, was to be found in the social psychology of an immigrant-derived people. The Augustana lecture provided one of the principle keys to understanding the situation, for it was in accordance with Hansen's law that members of the third generation were "returning" to the churches and synagogues as a means of reestablishing contact with their ancestral heritages. The religious dimension of an ethnic heritage was, in Herberg's view, best suited for third generation "remembering" for several reasons. In the first place, it had persisted more successfully than language and customs, which had been eroded by assimilation. At the same time, immigrant religious traditions had been sufficiently Americanized to suit the mentality of the third generation. Moreover, religion helped the members of the third generation to locate themselves in the "lonely crowd" by providing an answer to the "aching question" of social identity, Who am I? Finally, religion was much-prized in American society, whereas foreign "nationality" was regarded as narrow, ethnocentric, even divisive.

Herberg thus portrayed the religious revival as deriving in large part from the fact that religion served as a kind of residuary legatee of ethnic feeling. But why was religion itself so widely regarded as a good thing? Why did public figures like President Eisenhower insist so strongly that religion was indispensable to national well being? The reason, Herberg said in an answer that anticipated the civil religion discussion of the late 1960s and early 1970s, was that the American ideology was a profoundly spiritual construct embodying such values as freedom and individual dignity, as well as more mundane elements associated with material prosperity. As such, it had always been closely linked to religion. In the early days, the linkage was to Protestantism exclusively; with the coming of the immigrants and the adjustment of their religious traditions to the new environment, Catholicism and Judaism took their places alongside Protestantism as "the three great faiths of democracy." Hence, Protestantism, Catholicism, and Judaism were socially praiseworthy because they constituted three equally acceptable ways for the individual to manifest his or her commitment to the "spiritual values" underlying the American Way of Life—which was, in Herberg's view, the real religion of Americans.

Hansen's law and the process of spiritual amalgamation just described presumably accounted for the modulation of ethnic identity into religious identity that Herberg dealt with under the rubric of "the triple melting pot." Although this expression seemed to imply greater diversity (three melting pots instead of one), the phenomenon to which it referred was the gradual assimilation of a large number of different nationality groups into three major religious denominations: Protestantism, Catholicism, and Judaism. The evidence for the sociological reality of the triple melting pot was thin—Herberg relied principally on an early 1940s' study of intermarriage trends in New Haven—but a number of other observers agreed that, as immigrant "nationalities" faded away, the "residual group differences . . . [were] racial and religious."[17]

In fact, the assumption that Protestants, Catholics, Jews, and Negroes (not yet called blacks) constituted the principal social groupings in the American population is still to be found in Glazer and Moynihan's *Beyond the Melting Pot* (1963) and in Milton M. Gordon's *Assimilation in American Life* (1964).[18] Although largely forgotten in the racial turmoil and reassertion of ethnicity that ensued shortly after the publication of these works, the belief was widely held in the 1950s that religion was becoming a more important sociological category for understanding contemporary American society. Herberg's book, which was the most influential single work in establishing this view, thus simultaneously popularized Hansen's law and linked it firmly to an interpretation of the relationship of ethnicity, religion, and American culture very broadly considered.

Although Herberg treated Hansen's law as applicable to the American religious scene generally, he was, of course, best acquainted with the Jewish situation, and the evidence clearly indicates that Jews were particularly sensitive to the role of generational transition in the contemporary revival of Judaism as a religion. The very prominence of Jewish scholars in the recovery and elaboration of Hansen's essay constitutes one bit of evidence because it testifies to a special alertness to the issue on their part. The essay was reprinted in a Jewish publication, and every one of the commentators mentioned so far—Handlin, Saveth, Glazer, and Herberg—was also Jewish.

The appearance of Herberg's book brought Hansen to the attention of a wider audience. But even then, Jewish writers seemed more preoccupied by the Hansen thesis than Protestant or Catholic commentators. Thus Glazer featured it in his review of Herberg, and in an independent analysis of "The Jewish Revival in America." While reviewing Herberg favorably, Marshall Sklare cautioned against making too much of Hansen and the triple melting pot idea and in developing the generational component of his analysis of "symbolic Jewishness" (which anticipated "symbolic ethnicity" by twenty years); Herbert Gans explained how his interpretation differed from "the well-known thesis of Marcus Hansen." C. B. Sherman maintained, a few years later, that Jews were the only group whose experience "suppl[ied] proof of Hansen's thesis."[19]

Protestant and Catholic reviewers of course took note of the generational angle, but they tended to lay greater stress on the more distinctively religious aspects of Herberg's discussion. The *Christian Century*, for example, featured the work of David Riesman and Will Herberg in an editorial entitled, "The Lonely Crowd at Prayer." Although it summarized the generational interpretation (without mentioning Hansen), its main purpose was to criticize the "pallid . . . religion" that threatened to "let us all disappear into the gray-flannel uniformity of the conforming culture."[20] Herberg's earlier work had attracted favorable attention from Catholics, and they greeted *Protestant-Catholic-Jew* with enthusiasm. Immediately upon its publication, the influential Jesuit weekly, *America*, devoted a feature article to the book. Here Gustave Weigel, S. J., who was the leading American Catholic theologian involved in ecumenical activities, pronounced the sociological interpretation (including Hansen's law) "facinating and enlightening." But he added immediately: "Dr. Herberg draws something profound, however, from the facts he reports and organizes." That more profound point had to do with Herberg's assertion that religion was considered "a good thing" because it buttressed the American Way of Life.[21]

Weigel's reaction was typical in the sense that Catholics tended to value Herberg's work primarily for the critique it offered of the nature of American religiosity. They were impressed, to be sure, by the sociological analysis—including what one reviewer called "the interesting law of the assimilation of immigrants"[22]—but no Catholic observer seriously suggested that anything like a "third generation return" played a significant role in making American Catholicism what it was in the 1950s. Although Catholic faith and piety were flourishing, there was no "revival" in the sense of a recovery from an earlier slump. On the contrary, the Catholic community had been growing vigorously over the past generation in numbers, institutional strength, and spiritual vitality. The Catholic dimension of the post-World War II "revival of religion" was, in other words, a straight-line continuation and intensification of developments that had been evident for a long time. Catholics of Italian background were thought to be becoming more regular in their church-going, but that, too, was a straight-line progression rather than a reversion to an earlier pattern.

Catholic reformers of the 1950s did, to be sure, talk a great deal about the immigrant heritage of the American church. But the talk was overwhelmingly negative in its assessment of that heritage insofar as it still made itself felt in the mid-twentieth century. What else but their memories of nativist hostility made Catholics so suspicious and standoffish? Why were they burdened with a siege mentality? Whence came their anti-intellectualism? Why had they exerted so slight an influence on the cultural life of the nation? It was clearly time, according to Catholic reformers, for the church in America to come out of its "immigrant ghetto" and plunge into "the mainstream of American life." The hope, in other words, was not that the grandchildren of the immigrants would return to the ancestral religion, which they had never left in massive numbers; it was, rather, that they would more effectively leave behind them the psychological and cultural encumbrances that were their inheritance from immigrant days.[23]

If the Hansen thesis didn't really apply to the religious situation of American Catholics, it seemed even less appropriate as a general explanation of the religious upswing among Protestants. Their situation was illuminated by other features of Herberg's analysis—for example, the melding of religion and Americanism—but the "new immigrants" included too few Protestants for the Hansen effect to be regarded as a major factor in their situation in the 1950s. Hansen himself, as we have seen, gave no indication of thinking that the third generation would be more fervent church-goers. What his discussion revealed was an anxiety that the continuing religious attachments of his audience might unduly restrict their study of the immigrant past. And it seems unlikely that any considerable number of later Protestant observers were persuaded that a third generation return had much to do with the postwar revival of religion so far as it affected their own denominations.

The situation among Jews was strikingly different. Although the most widely heralded, Will Herberg was only one among a cluster of Jewish observers to point out that the generational issue was crucial to an understanding of the religious situation of American Jews, and to make the further point that the heightened participation of the third generation in religious activities was to be understood in functional terms—that is, as a means of giving young Jews a sense of who they were and thereby maintaining group identity and boundaries. In addition to earlier works cited by Herberg as consistent with his interpretation (for instance, Sklare's *Conservative Judaism*), two studies (by Glazer and Gans) arriving at very similar conclusions were published so soon after he wrote that we can safely assume the authors were thinking along the same lines before they read Herberg. A few years later, Erich Rosenthal gave the impression he was merely summing up what knowledgeable observers already knew. He wrote: "It appears, then, that the basic function of Jewish education is to implant Jewish self-consciousness rather than Judaism, to 'inoculate' the next generation with that minimum of religious practice and belief that is considered necessary to keep alive a level of Jewish self-consciousness that will hold the line against assimilation."[24]

The preceding establishes that Hansen's thesis really applied much more to Jews than to Protestants or Catholics, and that Herberg's exaggeration in this matter by no means vitiates his whole interpretation; nor does it dim the brilliance of his contribution to our understanding of the religious situation at midcentury. If our concern was primarily with Herberg's analysis, we should have to look further into how his exaggeration affected the overall argument of his book. But because our interest here is in Hansen's thesis as it relates to religious developments, the more pertinent line of inquiry is *why* the law of third generation interest fits the case of Jews more closely than that of Protestants or Catholics. Because of the nature of the inquiry, the discussion that follows has a more speculative quality than that preceding it.

First, Jews might be expected to find almost any third generation thesis particularly relevant to their situation because the American Jewish population was entering a third generation phase in the 1950s. As many as four out of five American Jews derived from the great East European migration that entered the United States in the last quarter of the nineteenth century and the first fifteen years of the twentieth.[25] This was a much higher proportion than "new immigrant" stock comprised among Catholics, to say nothing of Protestants. This meant that the fortunes of the Jewish group as a whole were linked to what happened to the grandchildren of the immigrants in a way that was not true for either of the other two major religious bodies. Little had been written about the third generation by midcentury; hence it is understandable that Hansen's essay—easily the boldest and most original discussion of the subject in existence—seemed particularly apt to Jews when it was rediscovered by a Jewish researcher, republished in a Jewish magazine, and elaborated upon by other Jewish commentators.

But there was more to it than where Jews as a group stood in terms of generational stages. Hansen's discussion of immigrant psychology involved religion more directly in the case of Jews because religion and ethnicity stood in a different relationship for them than for Catholics or Protestants. This is not the place for an elaborate discussion of the nature of Judaism, or of the relation of Judaism as a religion to Jewishness as a nationality or a species of ethnicity.[26] It is, nevertheless, clear that Judaism is an "ethnic religion" in a way quite different from the manner in which Catholicism was an ethnic religion for Irish, or Polish, or Italian immigrants (to confine the discussion to Catholic groups whose religion is considered to be closely related to their ethnicity, and whose situation I know better than that of American Protestants).

From the viewpoint of Judaism as a religion, God's covenant with Abraham made His earthly descendants a chosen race, a royal priesthood, a people set apart. God took them for His own in a special way: setting forth the law they were to follow, chastising their lapses, guiding them through the desert, overcoming their foes, and bringing them at length to the land He had promised would be theirs. In this sense, Judaism is a highly particularistic religion—one that involves a quite definite historical people, in real and identifiable times and places, under the care of a God who, although He is the creator and ruler of all, revealed Himself only to them, and promised to be with them until the end of days. Judaism, on this account, is not a missionary religion; it is something that belongs uniquely to Jews and can hardly, without changing its nature, be spread abroad to others who do not share the original inheritance. Jewishness and Judaism are thus interlinked theoretically as well as practically in a way that, for example, Irishness and Catholicism could never be, for however close the historic connection between religion and nationality, the theoretical distinction between being Catholic and being Irish—or Polish, or Italian, or whatever—could always be clearly drawn.

The intimate linkage between religion and group identity meant that when Jewish immigrants, and their children of the second generation, fell away from adherence to, and the practice of, Judaism as a religion—which they did in massive numbers—it left a kind of vacuum at the center of their group identity. As with all immigrants, the problematic nature of group identity was very much heightened when

Jews reached the third generation stage because, unlike their parents
and grandparents, these young people did not have living memories
of the beliefs and customs that had been abandoned. Moreover, upward
mobility had dispersed the packed ghettos, resulting in more frequent
contacts with gentiles and magnifying the danger of assimilation for
a generation of Jewish youngsters who had difficulty explaining to
themselves why they were different from anyone else. In these circumstances, second generation parents, who were conscious of being
Jews even though they might not be believers, turned to the practice
of Judaism as a religion, and insisted on a modicum of Jewish religious
education for their children, in order, as a Rosenthal puts it, to "inoculate" the next generation against assimilation. The religious dimension, historically at the core of being Jewish, was thus optionally
cultivated, not from strictly religious motives, but as a means of giving
concrete content to a group identity that could not be so easily specified
in any other way.[27]

Herberg took note of the uniqueness of the Jewish situation with
respect to Hansen's law, but he interpreted it differently from the
interpretation offered here. In the case of Italian or Polish immigrants,
he said, there was nothing left for the third generation to "remember"
but the religion, so that Hansen's law resulted in "the disappearance
of the 'Italianness' or the 'Polishness' of the group, or rather its dissolution into the religious community." Catholicism, for these third
generations, thus replaced ethnicity. In the case of the Jews, however,
third generation remembering of religion resulted in a reinforcement
of ethnicity because, among the Jews alone, the "religious community
bore the same name as the old ethnic group and was virtually coter-
minous with it."[28]

It is, perhaps, a fine point, but this seems to me almost to suggest
that the difference arose from a peculiarity of labeling—"Jewishness"
signifying both religion and ethnicity—rather being rooted in a more
intimate substantive linkage between Judaism and Jewishness than existed between Catholicity and Italianness or Polishness. In addition,
Herberg speaks as though Hansen's law operated in conventional fashion with these Catholic groups, but in an anomalous way with Jews.
I would maintain, rather, that Herberg offered no real evidence for its
operation in any way among Catholic immigrants, and that the Jews
were actually the paradigmatic case of its operation, which led him to
assume its application to other groups as well. The more basic difference this implies might be summarized as follows: Herberg seems to
take for granted that the religion of Catholic immigrant nationalities
was abandoned in the second generation and returned to by the third,
in accordance with Hansen's law. I would argue, however, that the

religion of these ethnic groups did not have to be "returned to" because it had persisted through all three generations—although not, to be sure, without differences in understanding and practice in which generational shifts were involved as well as other factors.

Herberg was certainly correct, however, in suggesting that American circumstances encouraged the tendency to stress the religious aspect of Jewishness at midcentury. Freedom of religion is one of the cornerstones of the American system; the courts have often defended minority religious positions even when they affect public policy areas such as education and conscientious objection to military service, and the need to cultivate feelings of tolerance, brotherhood, and interfaith understanding was preached with increasing insistence in the era of World War II. American Jews strongly supported the interfaith work of the National Conference of Christians and Jews; indeed, Nicholas Montalto has shown that this organization, formed in 1926, received most of its funding from Jewish sources during the first fifteen years of its existence.[29]

Montalto links this support to the policy pursued by the American Jewish Committee of stressing the religious rather than the ethnic dimension of Jewishness. Writing as a convinced proponent of the new ethnicity, Montalto laments what we might call the AJC's "religious strategy," and even implies that it, rather than Hansen's law, accounted for the existence of Herberg's triple melting pot.[30] The latter point strikes me as overdrawn, but Montalto has undoubtedly called attention to matters Herberg overlooked that are highly relevant to the emergence of Judaism as one of the "three great faiths of democracy." His discussion, however, is not without significant omissions of its own.

According to Montalto, the AJC adopted the religious strategy primarily because its leadership was dominated by third and fourth generation German Jews, strongly assimilationist in orientation, who shared the prevailing American antipathy for "organizations smacking of ethnic separatism." On this account, he argues, they promoted a "sectarian view of Judaism" that was misguided in the long run because it involved Judaism's "denying part of itself—the ethnic part."[31] Although one can understand how an ethnic enthusiast of the 1970s might reach such a conclusion, it leaves out far too much of the background of the 1930s to be a satisfactory explanation for the heavy stress placed on the religious character of Jewishness. More specifically, it fails to give anything like adequate weight to the influence of Nazi anti-Semitism and to the overall effect of the wartime crisis in enhancing the intellectual respectability and public importance of religion. Matters, incidentally, which Herberg likewise failed to underline.

Nazi anti-Semitism must surely be regarded as the greatest single force affecting American Jewish life in the 1930s. It not only stimulated anti-Semitism in this country, but it also shaped the thinking and reactions of Jews and other persons concerned about intergroup relations.[32] And what was the nature of Nazi anti-Semitism? It was racial—Jewish blood, even in the smallest proportion, made anyone in whom it coursed an abomination, a defiler of the Aryan purity of the Germanic *Volk*. But Nazi anti-Semitism was not only the paradigmatic exemplar of racism, it was part and parcel of an insanely elaborated form of nationalistic ethnocentrism, the dangers of which had been a staple of liberal commentary since the 1920s.

In view of the frightening growth of racial anti-Semitism, it was virtually unthinkable that American Jews would want to insist on the ethnic quality of their group cohesiveness and identity. To do so would seem to confirm what the Nazis were saying—the Jews were unassimilable, an ineradicably alien racial element wherever they dwelt. For Jews even more than others, Nazism utterly discredited racism and, in doing so, also discredited related forms of collective consciousness, including what came to be called ethnicity in the 1960s. We must remember that the term and concept *ethnicity* had not yet been introduced in the 1930s. People spoke much more inclusively in those days of "racial groups" and "race feeling," or of immigrant "nationalities." The kind of group consciousness later benignly characterized as "ethnic" was then associated with "ethnocentrism," and was regarded as an unalloyed social evil.[33] In these circumstances, "ethnicity" as a way of defining Jewish group identity was simply not an option. Jews could perhaps have insisted on calling themselves a nationality rather than a religion, but that would have created problems of its own. To stress the religious quality of Judaism was a far more appealing policy because it entailed none of the "loyalty" problems implicit in the terminology of nationality, and at the same time made the struggle against anti-Semitism part of America's historic commitment to religious toleration.

Besides discrediting all forms of descent-based group feeling, Nazism was part of broader phenomena—totalitarianism and world war—that lent new intellectual respectability to traditional religious beliefs about the reality of evil, suffering, and the demonic potentialities inherent in projects to remake the world. Although dismissed by secular Jews like Sidney Hook as a "new failure of nerve," the intellectual revival of religion was a reality sufficiently consequential to require from liberals a vigorous counterattack on the "authoritarianism" of the "absolutists."[34] Louis Finkelstein, provost of the Jewish Theological Seminary of America, was the leading promoter of its most important institutional expression, the Conference on Science, Philosophy and Religion in Their Relation to the Democratic Way of Life. This body, organized shortly after the outbreak of war in 1939, sponsored annual symposia for two decades; its religious orientation was so pronounced at first that a group of prominent secular thinkers, including John Dewey, seceded in protest.[35]

We might plausibly assume that this kind of intellectual revitalization would make the "religious strategy" all the more appealing to American Jews. Another factor that enters the picture in this connection is the introduction of the term *Judeo-Christian tradition*, which was popularized in the wartime crisis by those who wished to emphasize that the values threatened by totalitarianism were deeply rooted in the spiritual traditions of the West.[36] Although later commentators tend to treat the term ironically, consideration of the wartime circumstances suggests a more generous interpretation of the outlook and thinking of those who put it into circulation. In any case, popularization of the expression clearly reinforced the tendency to emphasize the religion dimension of Jewishness.

These war-related factors, along with the reasons mentioned by Montalto and Herberg, operated to bring out and to underline the religious element in Jewishness—which surely helped to make the Jewish "return" to religion seem the natural, almost inevitable, way of reaffirming and maintaining the identity and coherence of the group. In the postwar era, observers like Oscar Handlin began to insist that Jews were better understood as an ethnic group than as a religious body. But Handlin also made the same point as Glazer, Gans, and Herberg: Jewish ethnicity was increasingly coming to expression in the form of more active participation in Judaism as a religion.[37] It was this complex relationship between religion and ethnicity among American Jews as the group entered its third generation stage that made the rediscovery of Hansen's essay so opportune. The intensity with which Jewish students of ethnicity developed his ideas testify to the brilliance of Hansen's insight and make the rediscovery of the Augustana lecture an important landmark in the historiography of American religion.

NOTES

1. Marcus Lee Hansen, "The Problem of the Third Generation Immigrant," republication of the 1937 address with introductions by Peter Kivisto and Oscar Handlin (Rock Island: Swenson Swedish Immigration Research Center and Augustana College Library, 1987). Aside from the present volume, the most recent discussion of Hansen's essay is to be found in Werner Sollors, *Beyond Ethnicity: Consent and Descent in American Culture* (New York:

Oxford University Press, 1986), pp. 214ff. It is part of a brilliantly provocative book, but Sollors errs in ascribing to Hansen himself sentiments that Hansen attributed to spokesmen for the first generation. For the place of the Augustana Synod in the history of Swedish immigration, see George M. Stephenson, *The Religious Aspects of Swedish Immigration* (Minneapolis: University of Minnesota Press, 1932), chaps. 13, 16, 22–25; for the establishment of the Augustana Historical Society, p. 379n.

2. Hansen, "The Problem of the Third Generation," pp. 15–18.

3. Ibid., pp. 18–21.

4. Ibid., pp. 21–23.

5. This talk, "Who Shall Inherit America?" was not included in the printed proceedings of the 1937 meeting of the National Conference of Social Work, but it appeared in single-space typescript format as vol. 14, no. 34 of *Interpreter Releases* (July 6, 1937):226–33. Moses Rischin first called attention to it in "Marcus Lee Hansen: America's First Transethnic Historian," in *Uprooted Americans: Essays to Honor Oscar Handlin*, ed. Richard L. Bushman, Neil Harris, David Rothman, Barbara Miller Solomon, and Stephan Thernstrom (Boston: Little, Brown, 1979), pp. 319–47.

6. Marcus Lee Hansen, *The Immigrant in American History*, ed. Arthur M. Schlesinger (Cambridge: Harvard University Press, 1940), pp. ix–xi; C. Frederick Hansen, "Marcus Lee Hansen—Historian of Immigration," *Common Ground* 2 (Summer 1942):87–94.

7. Margaret Mead, *And Keep Your Powder Dry: An Anthropologist Looks at America* (New York: William Morrow, 1942), chap. 3. Peter Kivisto's mention of Mead in his introductory remarks to the 1987 reprint version of Hansen's Augustana lecture leaves the impression that Mead knew Hansen's work. Rischin's review essay of the *Harvard Encyclopedia of American Ethnic Groups* (Cambridge: Harvard University Press, 1980) notes the divergence between Mead's and Hansen's views on the third generation; see *Journal of American Ethnic History* 2 (Spring 1983):74–75.

8. William Carlson Smith, *Americans in the Making: The Natural History of the Assimilation of Immigrants* (New York: Appleton-Century, 1939), which devotes almost half its space to the second generation, has only one index reference to the third generation. There (p. 350) Smith observes: "Even if members of the third generation may be found using more of the parental practices than some of the second generation they may be much further along in the assimilative process, since these traits have been selected on the basis of deliberation."

9. Francis J. Brown and Joseph S. Roucek, *Our Racial and National Minorities* (New York: Prentice-Hall, 1937). For the citation to Hansen's "The Minor Stocks in the American Population of 1790," which appeared in American Historical Association, *Annual Report, 1931*, see p. 680. Brown and Roucek, *One America: The History, Contributions, and Present Problems of Our Racial and National Minorities* (New York: Prentice-Hall, 1946), pp. 471–85 (Koenig essay), pp. 661, 680 (bibliographical citations).

10. Edward N. Saveth, ed., *Understanding the American Past* (Boston: Little, Brown, 1954), pp. 472–88.

11. Edward N. Saveth, "The Immigrant in American History," *Commentary* 2 (August 1946):180–85; Saveth, *American Historians and European Immigrants, 1875–1925* (New York: Columbia University Press, 1948), pp. 217ff. For Saveth's connection with the AJS, see *Commentary* 14 (September 1952):296.

12. Marcus Lee Hansen, "The Third Generation in America: A Classic Essay in Immigrant History," *Commentary* 14 (November 1952):492–500. Nathan Glazer described the background of the essay's republication in a conversation with the author.

13. Hansen, "The Third Generation," pp. 492–93.

14. Saveth, *Understanding the American Past*, p. 473.

15. Nathan Glazer, "Ethnic Groups in America: From National Culture to Ideology," in *Freedom and Control in Modern Society*, ed. Monroe Berger, Theodore Abel, and Charles Page (New York: Octagon Books, 1978; orig. pub. 1954), pp.158–73; the earlier version, entitled "America's Ethnic Pattern," appeared first in *Commentary* 15 (April 1953): 401–8, and then in *Perspectives USA* no. 9 (Autumn 1954): 137–52.

16. Will Herberg, "The 'Triple Melting Pot': The Third Generation, from Ethnic to Religious Diversity," *Commentary* 20 (August 1955):101–8; Herberg, "America's New Religiousness: A Way of Belonging or the Way of God?" *Commentary* 20 (September 1955):240–47; Herberg, *Protestant-Catholic-Jew: An Essay in American Religious Sociology* (Garden City: Doubleday, 1955). The book also appeared as an Anchor paperback in 1960. For a discussion of this work in the context of Herberg's life, see Harry J. Ausmus, *Will Herberg: From Right to Right* (Chapel Hill: University of North Carolina Press, 1987), chap. 8.

17. The quotation is from Charles F. Marden, *Minorities in American Society* (New York: American Book, 1952), p. 394. For other evidence (besides chap. 3. of *Protestant-Catholic-Jew*), see Alfred McClung Lee, "Sociological Insights into American Culture and Personality," *Journal of Social Issues* 7, no. 4 (1951): 10–11; and Oscar Handlin, *The American People in the Twentieth Century*, rev. ed. (Boston: Beacon Press, 1963; orig. pub. 1954), p. 223.

18. Nathan Glazer and Daniel P. Moynihan, *Beyond the Melting Pot: The Negroes, Puerto Ricans, Jews, Italians, and Irish of New York City* (Cambridge: MIT Press, 1963), pp. 314–15; Milton M. Gordon *Assimilation in American Life* (New York: Oxford University Press, 1964), chap. 7.

19. Nathan Glazer, "Religion without Faith," *New Republic* 133 (November 4, 1955):18–20; Glazer, "The Jewish Revival in America: I," *Commentary* 20 (December 1955):493–99; Glazer, "The Jewish Revival in America: II, Its Religious Side," *Commentary* 21 (January 1956):17–24; Marshall Sklare, review of Herberg, *Commentary* (February 1956):195–96; Herbert Gans, "American Jewry: Present and Future, Part I: Present," *Commentary* 21 (May 1956):422–30; Herbert Gans, "The Future of American Jewry, Part II," *Commentary* 21 (June 1956):555–63 (esp. p. 561n for Hansen); and C. B. Sherman, *Jews within American Society: A Study of Ethnic Individuality* (Detroit: Wayne State University Press, 1961), pp. 207–8.

20. *Christian Century* 73 (May 30, 1956):662–63.

21. Gustave Weigel, "Religion Is a Good Thing," *America* 94 (November 5, 1955):150–54. See also Weigel's review in *Theological Studies* 16 (1955):651–53; Joseph Fitzpatrick's review in *Thought* 30 (Winter 1955):595–600; and C. J. Nuesse's review in *Catholic Historical Review* 42 (July 1956):214–15.

22. Fitzpatrick, *Thought*, p. 596.

23. See Philip Gleason, *Keeping the Faith: American Catholicism Past and Present* (Notre Dame: Notre Dame University Press, 1987), pp. 181–87.

24. Erich Rosenthal, "Acculturation without Assimilation: The Jewish Community of Chicago, Illinois," *American Journal of Sociology* 66 (November 1960):275–88, quotation on p. 287. For Glazer's and Gans's arguments, see the articles cited above in note 16. See also Herberg, *Protestant-Catholic-Jew* (paperback ed.), pp. 186–90, and the literature cited there, including Marshall Sklare, *Conservative Judaism: An American Religious Movement* (New York: Free Press, 1955).

25. In an authoritative discussion, Arthur A. Goren states that east European immigrants and their children constituted five-sixths of the Jewish population in 1920. See the *Harvard Encyclopedia of American Ethnic Groups*, ed. Stephan Thernstrom (Cambridge: Harvard University Press, 1980), p. 579.

26. See Nathan Glazer, *American Judaism*, 2d ed. (Chicago: University of Chicago Press, 1972), pp. 3–8; Charles S. Liebman, *The Ambivalent American Jew: Politics, Religion, and Family in American Jewish Life* (Philadelphia: Jewish Publication Society of America, 1976), esp. chaps. 1, 3.

27. In discussing this development, Glazer calls attention to its practical similarity to Mordecai Kaplan's view that Judaism expressed, but did not exhaust, Jewishness as a "civilization." See Nathan Glazer, "The Jewish Revival in America: I," *Commentary* 20 (December 1955):499; see also, Liebman, *Ambivalent American Jew*, pp. 73–77.

28. Herberg, *Protestant-Catholic-Jew* (paperback ed.), pp. 186–87.

29. Nicholas V. Montalto, "The Forgotten Dream: A History of the Intercultural Education Movement, 1924–1941," Ph.D. diss., University of Minnesota, 1978, pp. 188ff for discussion of NCCJ; pp. 200–1, for funding issue. Herberg, *Protestant-Catholic-Jew* (paperback ed.), pp. 242–44, discusses the NCCJ, but makes no particular mention of Jewish support.

30. Montalto, "Forgotten Dream," pp. 199n, 188, where the subheading for the discussion is "Cementing 'American's Religious Triangle': The AJC and the National Conference of Christians and Jews."

31. Ibid., pp. 185, 186, 204–5. Montalto quotes the phrase about "ethnic separatism" from Naomi W. Cohen, *Not Free to Desist: The American Jewish Committee, 1906–1966* (Philadelphia: Jewish Publication Society of America, 1972), p. 193.

32. A general work and guide to the literature is David A. Gerber, ed., *Anti-Semitism in American History* (Urbana: University of Illinois Press, 1986). See also Donald S. Strong, *Organized Anti-Semitism in America: The Rise of Group Prejudice During the Decade 1930–1940* (Washington: American Council on Public Affairs, 1941); Charles Herbert Stember et al., *Jews in*

the Mind of America (New York: Basic Books, 1966), esp. pp. 110ff., 237–58, 259–72; Cohen, *Not Free to Desist*, chaps. 8–9; and Richard Weiss, "Ethnicity and Reform: Minorities and the Ambience of the Depression Years," *Journal of American History* 66 (December 1979):571–72, 574–75.

33. Sollors, *Beyond Ethnicity*, pp. 21ff.; Philip Gleason, "Americans All: World War II and the Shaping of American Identity," *Review of Politics* 43 (October 1981):493–95, 513–14.

34. Sidney Hook, "The New Failure of Nerve," *Partisan Review* 10 (January–February, 1943):2–23; Edward A. Purcell, Jr., *The Crisis of Democratic Theory: Scientific Naturalism and the Problem of Value* (Lexington: University Press of Kentucky, 1973), pp. 203–4, 218ff.; Philip Gleason, "Catholicism, Pluralism, and Democracy in the Era of World War II," *Review of Politics* 49 (Spring 1987):208–30.

35. This group has not been studied; for a brief description and citation of relevant documents, see Philip Gleason, "World War II and the Development of American Studies," *American Quarterly* 36 (Bibliographical Issue, 1984):347.

36. Mark Silk, "Notes on the Judeo-Christian Tradition in America," *American Quarterly* 36 (Spring 1984):65–85.

37. Oscar Handlin, "Group Life within the American Pattern," *Commentary* 8 (November 1949):411–17; and Handlin, *American People*, p. 223.

6

Hansen's Hypothesis and the Historical Experience of Generations

We each approach Hansen's fertile hypothesis from the perspective of our own work, the ethnic groups with which we are familiar, and the problems that concern us. And for each of us, the hypothesis proposes a question, or an answer to a question, that we might not have thought of otherwise. The question that my own work has raised concerns the relationship between the way a generation approaches its past and the specific and unrepeatable historical experience that has marked that generation. Hansen's essay suggests a more placid time in the historical experience of ethnic groups in the United States, one in which a regular generational sequence primarily determined how a group related, or wished to relate, to its homeland, its culture, its historical memories. And the thesis made excellent sense. There are permanent elements in the relationship between parent and child and grandchild that transcend specific historical experience. And yet a problem I have dealt with—American Jews' relationship between the passage of generations and the degree of allegiance to the group and its religion—sharpens for me the importance of the contrast between specific and unrepeatable historical experience versus the general and always repeated passage of the generations.[1]

Consider one historical example. Hansen's essay presents a fact to demonstrate the central thesis, one that, reread after fifty years, sharply reminds us of the importance of a differentiated history. As one example of the German-American community's revival of historical interest in its past, some sixty years after the mid-point of heavy German immigration, Hansen cites the establishment by German Americans of a Theodore Roosevelt professorship at the University of Berlin.[2]

Fortuitously, the story of this professorship is discussed in detail in Harold Wechsler's fascinating and meticulously researched *The Qualified Student*, which deals with quite another topic.[3] The professorship was endowed by a German-Jewish banker, James Speyer, whose principal objective in establishing the professorship was to reflect credit on American Jews. As we learn from Wechsler's account,

Speyer wanted the chair to be filled by a Jew on some regular basis. Nicholas Murray Butler, president of the committee that oversaw the chair, assured Speyer that he need make no specific provision in this respect; the committee would see that the chair was filled on occasion, without any formal requirement, by a Jew. Alas, after Felix Adler, the founder of Ethical Culture and a professor at Columbia University, filled the chair, the committee evaded its part of the agreement. During this same period, regular efforts by the Jewish community of New York (whose leaders then were almost exclusively German Jews) to get a Jew appointed to the board of trustees at Columbia University were thwarted. The point of this story is to indicate the degree that historical context may affect any piece of evidence on the third generation hypothesis.

Hansen's thesis was sociopsychological. It describes a process that takes place between parents and children and is presented relatively independently of a sequence of specific, external historical events. To be sure there is no implication that these have no influence on the sequence. The immigrant wants to adapt to a country that demands acculturation, but also wants to retain connection with his or her church, language, and culture of the homeland. All these elements seem to recur because of fixed circumstances: the United States regularly demands acculturation, the immigrant want regularly to adapt, but does not want to surrender his or her culture and group connections totally. The second generation experience changes and is different from the immigrant generation. It is concerned with the adolescent peer group, intolerant of any deviation from conformity. The third generation, more at ease in America, has no psychological hang-ups about exploring its past and its heritage.

This is a remarkably powerful insight. But the historical changes that affect the country that the immigrant has left, and the country that he or she has come to, are left out. Not completely, of course: Hansen tells us that the revival of interest in German-American history was snuffed out by World War I—as was Speyer's Theodore Roosevelt professorship at the University of Berlin.

The addition one must make to the hypothesis is that each generation is located within a specific time period. Its fate is determined not only by the relationship between the generations—immigrant and second, second and third—but also by what was happening in the world outside this relationship at the key moments when a generation was growing up, attending school, entering the job market, or getting married.

It was one of Hansen's important points that we can fix the generations that follow the immigrant in a specific period because of the concentration of immigrants from any country in only a few decades. If immigrants from each country arrived in equal numbers, each year and each decade, we could not do this. The second generation would then not have any location in a specific historical period, nor the third generation: each generation would be equally distributed over time and would thus not be marked by any distinctive historical experience, only by a distinctive sociopsychological experience in relationship to parents and children. But as we know, that is not the way it happened. Immigrants from each major source were concentrated in given historical periods. The second generation of the various Asian groups, who date in substantial number only from the late 1960s because of the adoption of new immigration legislation in 1965 and the fact that North Vietnam conquered South Vietnam, Laos, and Cambodia a few years later, will have the distinctive experience of growing up in the 1980s and 1990s. Of course, what their specific historical experience will be is unknown. Suppose German immigration had peaked twenty or thirty years later than it did and World War I had occured while the German-American second generation was dominant. Following Hansen's hypothesis, we would have seen an avoidance of involvement in German culture. Could we have attributed that to the typical second generation pattern of a push to total Americanization—or to the impact of the fierce anti-Germanism of World War I, which swept even the teaching of German from public schools?

The reason that I see the impact of specific historical experience on a generation as so important is that I deal with the history and experience of American Jews. There is great concern among American Jews over the connection between the passage of the generations and how this affects Jewish identity and commitment to Jewish religion and Jewish interests, in particular Israel. This concern undoubtedly played some role in my original interest in Hansen's essay at a time when I was an editor of the Jewish monthly *Commentary* and contributed to my interest in bringing it to the attention of a new audience. I came across it in 1952, when I was working in the field of immigration, and arranged for its republication in *Commentary*. At that time, American-Jewish institutions were not worrying much about the third generation: they worried about the second generation, whose major intellectuals were then very distant from Jewish interests. This second generation was the second generation of the mass immigration of Jews from eastern Europe. Second generation Jews of that immigration came to leadership in American-Jewish institutions during the 1950s. My own parents had come to this country in 1912 and 1914. I was born in 1923. In 1952, I could consider myself somewhat at the younger end of the second generation of this mass immigration, which began in the 1880s but reached its heaviest rate of flow in the first decade and a half of the twentieth century, in the years up to World War I. The great majority of today's community of five or six million Jews dates from this immigration. There were only 250,000 Jews in the United States in 1880, primarily of German origin. Substantial immigration then began from eastern Europe, but the peak period of immigration was concentrated in 1900–14. It was cut off by the war, and after resumption in 1920s, by the restrictive legislation of 1924. Further flows—from Germany in the 1930s, the survivors of East European Jewry after World War II—were very modest indeed compared to the mass immigration of East European Jews between 1900 and 1914.[4]

The reprinting of Hansen's essay in 1952 was occasioned by the concern of a second generation Jew (and a journal edited by second generation Jews) about the coming third generation. If indeed our relationship to the Jewish people and to Judaism was dominated primarily by our distance from immigrant origins, then we might expect almost nothing in the way of Jewish identity and commitment in the third generation. But Hansen's essay threw a new light on the question of acculturation and assimilation: it suggested that not only was there no historical inevitability in the steady and monotonic decline of identity, allegiance, interest, commitment, but there was also reason to expect a change in direction in some of these features in the third generation.

It is intriguing to perform some exercises with the history of American Jews following the pattern of Hansen's illustrations in his essays. He seems to take sixty years from the peak of an immigration stream to the time when one may detect a "third generation return." He does not justify this period but—considering that most immigrants come as young adults, already married, or soon to marry in this country—in some thirty years after the immigration peak one may expect a second generation to be entering into full maturity after schooling, entry into the labor market, marriage, and child-bearing. One may also expect a third generation to follow thirty years later. Or so I would interpret the sixty years that regularly seem to recur in Hansen's examples of third generation return.

It is possible to relate those points in the Hansen sequence to American-Jewish history, and see how it might have affected American-Jewish generations. One may take 1907 as the midpoint of the period when East European immigration was at its height, from 1900 to 1914. The midpoint of the more extended period of East European Jewish immigration that runs from 1881 to 1925, when the effect of the immigration restriction act finally cut off any substantial volume of East European Jewish immigration, came in 1903.

If we take 1907, consider what historical experience was affecting the second generation thirty years after, and the third generation sixty years after that. Thirty years after 1907—1937—saw a generation that gained much of its formative experience in the depression. It was a generation that married late, had children late, and had very few children. It was a generation concentrated in the very large cities, in particular New York, and which Jewish organizations and congregations were not effective in reaching. We can attribute this variously to the effects of assimilation, the American public school, the impact of the depression, the strong hold of radical institutions and movements in the Jewish community (socialist, communist, anarchist), the fact that most Jews were workers and influenced by Jewish labor organizations unsympathetic to religion and to Zionism, and to other factors as well. It was a generation that aroused in committed Jews and Jewish organizations fears for the survival of Jewish organizational life in the United States, religious or secular.

This is of course a crude exercise. The second generation of a migration that spread over almost fifty years cannot easily be localized in a specific historical period. But if we concentrate on the years of peak immigration, we come to a much more restricted period. If we take into account such features as the characteristic ages of immigrants when they married and had children, we will be able to describe a rather distinctive historical experience for a second generation. The second generation would have been born in number in the years of World War I and the twenties, gone to school in the twenties and thirties, entered the labor market in the depression, would have married and had children late—the characteristic experience of the 1930s. And we could perform the same exercise for a third generation with even greater accuracy because it was bunched in the years of the baby boom between 1945 and 1960, going to school in the fifties and sixties, and entering the labor market in the 1970s. These attempts to localize within specific decades the experience of a given ethnoreligious group lean on the experience of my own family. My parents immigrated between 1912 and 1914 with two young children born in Poland, and had five more in the United States; I was the youngest. My elder brothers and sisters married relatively late, and the entire third generation of the Glazer family dates from the period beginning with World War II. My own children were born in 1950, 1952, and 1955, and two have already contributed to a fourth generation.

If the preceding example is considered too personal, I will point out that good social surveys of Jewish communities regularly divide a community by generation and by age. I will also show that what I have tried to argue from the dates of the immigration peak works: each generation is concentrated in certain age ranges that correspond to distinctive historical experiences.[5] If we can do this for Jews, we can do this for other groups. All have been affected in their immigration flows by specific events—American immigration laws, depression, wars, massacres, famines, revolutions in Europe or Asia or Mexico—which have concentrated an immigrant generation in certain years, and, by the same token, concentrate a second and third generation in specific time periods.

To return to the story of the East European Jewish generations: Should one attribute the second generation's indifference or hostility to ethnic and religious identification to the second generation effect, or to a 1920s' and 1930s' effect? And consider the experience of the third generation. If we take the sixty-year period that Hansen uses to account for two generations and add it to the mid-point of Jewish immigration of 1907, we come to the year 1967, an *annus mirabilis* in postwar American Jewish history.[6] This was the year of the six-day war between Israel and the Arab states, a war preceded by a month of terrible fear among American Jews that Israel would be annihilated and the Holocaust repeated. It is irrelevant that these fears turned out to be unfounded. They were real and led to an outpouring of support for Israel that had never been seen before—one of the formative experiences of the third generation.

Other things were happening that added up to something of a Jewish revival, for example, the great move of Jews as well as non-Jews to the suburbs. For Jews, this move meant leaving dense Jewish neighborhoods in which any specific involvement in, or commitment to, Jewish organizations and causes was paradoxically relatively low as measured by such indexes as synagogue affiliation and percent of children receiving Jewish education. In the suburbs, these indexes zoomed. There was a specific suburban effect. More of social life was organized along church lines. There was a class effect: suburban Jews were more middle-class and upper-middle-class.

Combined with these changes was the impact of the war of 1967, and later of 1973. The demonstration of the permanent danger to Israel was accompanied by a revival of Jewish interest in the Holocaust. What explains that is another problem, the answer to which may well have its generational aspect. Perhaps the generation that experienced the Holocaust, either as victims or as bystanders who did not or could not do enough, wishes to forget it; the children insist on remembering it. The sequence of the generations with their characteristic sociopsychological orientation combines with the historical events that impinged on each generation, it seems to me, to create a third generation effect in American Jewish life that contradicts the expectation of straight-line decline with successive generations in identity, commitment, interest, and affiliation.

Other characteristics of the 1920s and 1930s versus the 1950s and 1960s might explain these generational differences. The 1920s and 1930s were decades of widespread anti-Semitism that had great consequences for Jews. It was difficult to get into elite colleges, to enter medical schools, to get professional and white-collar jobs. This anti-Semitism was a reason for avoiding Jewish identification. There was a great deal of name-changing, most undoubtedly simply an adaptation to anti-Semitism, but some of it also reflecting a desire to assimilate. The 1950s and 1960s by contrast constituted a period of relative prosperity when anti-Semitism declined sharply. This might be a reason for greater willingness to accept the burden of Jewish identification, which was in any case no longer very burdensome. Thus, historical change, in the United States, as well as in the homeland (for American Jews, Israel is a kind of homeland), may have consequences for identification, pride, and ethnic cohesiveness.

The identification of generations with specific historical epochs directs us to other issues in immigration history. Although I have emphasized only one major period of Jewish immigration to this country, immigration did not of course end with the immigration restriction act of 1924. It resumed after 1933 when Hitler came to power. There was a burst after 1945 as the survivors of the Holocaust emigrated to this country and Israel. And there was a burst of immigration of Russian Jews in the late 1970s and early 1980s. These groups did not go through their generational experiences isolated from the experience of the Jewish generations that preceded them. We can see some interesting interactions. The German-Jewish immigrants and the survivors of the Holocaust came to a country in which the Jewish community and its attitudes were dominantly second generation. One's experience of America as an immigrant is not only of America in general: it is also of the city to which one has come, as well as the ethnic and religious community that offers aid and of which one may become a part. Whatever the generic first generation traits of German and East European survivor immigrants, the attitudes of the relatives and the community that had preceded them by a generation or two affected them. These later immigrants were first generation who became in many ways not very different from the dominant American-Jewish second generation.

And yet there is another case of generational interaction: the typical generational sequence of German Jews occurred of course in a different historical period from that of East European Jews. Fourth and fifth generation German Jews coincide in time with second and third generations of East European Jews. Matters are less neat than that because people marrying may be of different generations, and of different Jewish subgroups (leaving aside the impact of the substantial degree of marriage outside the Jewish group). But what dominates in Jewish institutional life are the attitudes and orientations of the largest group, the East Europeans, and thus when one describes a third generation pattern among American Jews, one should not be surprised to find fourth and fifth generation German Jews—insofar as they are still part of the Jewish community—showing the same pattern, a third generation return characterizing a fourth and fifth generation.

Other groups have gone through their own history, and their experience too has been shaped by history as well as by generation. It was, of course, never Hansen's intention to create a rigid and mechanical interpretation in which generation became an iron framework to be imposed on ethnic phenomena. I hope that this discussion suggests how generation interacts with history, and how the master experience connected to a generation will for a period, shape the outlook of the ethnic group.

NOTES

1. Nathan Glazer, "New Perspectives in American Jewish Sociology," in *American Jewish Year Book* (New York: American Jewish Committee, 1987).

2. Marcus Lee Hansen, "The Problem of the Third Generation Immigrant," republication of the 1937 address with introductions by Peter Kivisto and Oscar Handlin (Rock Island: Swenson Swedish Immigration Research Center and Augustana College Library, 1987), p. 18.

3. Harold Wechsler, *The Qualified Student: A History of Selective College Admission in America* (New York: Wiley Interscience, 1977), pp. 141–44.

4. The overall pattern of Jewish immigration to the United States is given in a table in Jacob Lestschinsky, "Jewish Migrations, 1840–1956," in *The Jews: Their History, Culture, and Religion,* ed. Louis Finkelstein (New York: Harper and Brothers, 1960), p. 1554:

Jewish Migrations		
Years	Jewish Immigrants	Immigrants per Year
1840–80	200,000	5,000
1881–1900	675,000	34,000
1901–14	1,346,400	96,000
1915–20	76,450	15,000
1921–25	280,223	56,000

Continued

Jewish Migrations

Years	Jewish Immigrants	Immigrants per Year
1926–30	54,998	5,500
1931–35	17,986	3,600
1936–39	79,819	20,000
1940–42	70,954	27,000

As is clear from this data, the heaviest flow of immigrants was in the years of 1901–14, when almost three-fifths of the immigrants of the period of East European Jewish immigration (1881–1925) entered. It is on this basis that I would take 1907 as the modal date from which one might calculate the periods of the second generation and third generation.

5. See, for example, Marshall Sklare, *Jewish Identity on the Suburban Frontier* (New York: Basic Books, 1967), pp. 31–38; and Steven M. Cohen, *American Modernity and Jewish Identity* (New York: Tavistock, 1983), chap. 3, "From Generation to Generation," and tables therein.

6. Nathan Glazer, *American Judaism* 2d ed. (Chicago: University of Chicago Press, 1972).

Marcus Lee Hansen and the Swedish Americans

When Marcus Lee Hansen presented his paper, "The Problem of the Third Generation Immigrant," May 15, 1937, he did so before a group of Swedish Americans, members of the Augustana Historical Society, established in 1930. Throughout, his presentation was largely tailored to this particular clientele, which raises some questions about the applicability of the ideas he expounded to the ethnic group his listeners represented.

How much did Hansen know about the Swedes in America? He was, to be sure, himself the son of Scandinavian immigrant parents—a Danish father and a Norwegian mother—and grew up in Scandinavian communities in the Upper Midwest. He visited parts of Scandinavia during the 1920s while doing research on emigration elsewhere in Europe. He could read the Scandinavian languages. Yet, up to 1937 Hansen had not given much specific attention to Scandinavian emigration or the Scandinavians in America.[1]

At the time of his early death in 1938, he had written only the first part of a planned trilogy on the European Atlantic migration; published posthumously in 1940, it covered the period from 1607 to 1860.[2] By the latter date, Scandinavian emigration was still both recent and relatively modest in scale, and therefore Hansen gave it only brief and somewhat cursory treatment. There can be no doubt that had he lived, Hansen would have given a great deal of attention to the Swedes and other Scandinavians during the time they began to comprise a considerable element in the great migration. His Rock Island speech from 1937 would seem to place the modal point, from which he reckoned Swedish-American generations, around 1870.[3] Much of what he has to say specifically about the Swedes and other Scandinavians in "The Problem of the Third Generation Immigrant" thus seems rather oversimplified and categorical.

In that address, Hansen offered a generational hypothesis on the relationship between assimilation and cultural retention among immigrants and their descendants in the new land. In essence, the first or foreign-born generation naturally remained attached to their native culture and traditions; the second, American-born generation sought to escape "the strange dualism into which they had been born" by disassociating themselves as much as possible from their ethnic roots.[4]

This hypothesis was of particular interest as it offered an alternative to—or perhaps more accurately a synthesis of—the ostensibly opposed views of the melting pot and cultural pluralist theories of ethnicity. Although he envisioned an ebb and flow during the first three generations following migration, Hansen recognized that ethnic interest would become "gradually thinned out as the third generation merges into the fourth and the fourth shades off into the fifth," and considered it "the ultimate fate of any national group to be amalgamated into the composite American race. . . ."[5]

If in this presentation Hansen seemed to lean toward a deterministic view, in another address, "Who Shall Inherit America?," given in Indianapolis only ten days later, he stressed the importance of deliberate efforts to preserve America's various ethnic heritages, as Rudolph Vecoli has pointed out. Hansen was both a sober historian and by this time an "advocate and evangelist," in Moses Rischin's words, concerned with the survival of ethnic values.[6] He had evidently not yet worked out to his own satisfaction the dilemma of free will versus determinism in ethnic life.

The "Hansen thesis" is a striking one. Oscar Handlin has described a two-phase reaction on the part of Jewish readers that may be taken as characteristic for essentially all American ethnic groups: astonishment that so much of what seemed unique to one's own group was common to the immigrant experience as a whole, followed by an intensive search for all "the possible ways" in which one's own people were "exceptional and distinctive" and might "carry forward their unique identity." Repeated attempts have been made, Peter Kivisto reminds us, to test Hansen's thesis pragmatically for varying ethnic elements in America, generally with at least partially negative results.[7] Such findings would apply also to the Swedish Americans, as will be seen.

There are above all two basic weaknesses to Hansen's hypothesis. The first is simply the bewildering complexity of the concept of generation as such, as Robert Wohl, for example, has demonstrated in his penetrating study of the European "Generation of 1914."[8] In particular, the continuous flow of births and deaths tends to make any effort to single out distinct generations problematical and at best arbitrary. Most commonly, historical "generations" are defined in relation to major historical events, but the sociologist Nathan Glazer identified the second underlying weakness of Hansen's thesis when he pointed out that the one thing the historian Hansen left out of it was history. As Glazer observed, a generational theory appears to work well for certain ethnic groups, but for largely fortuitous reasons based on concrete historical circumstances.[9]

It was Hansen's basic assumption that the first, foreign-born generation of immigrants was deeply attached to its native culture and language. This is a view, however, which can only be taken with some important reservations about both historical circumstance and individual dispositions.

Cultural Swedish America passed through its own particular life cycle, involving at least three distinct phases, between the beginning of Swedish immigration around 1840 and the present. Before the middle 1860s, the relatively high cost and the hardships of the ocean crossing under sail made migration an almost irrevocable commitment, while the small numbers, dispersal, and general lack of formal education of Swedish immigrants placed formidable obstacles in the way of organized ethnic life. The earliest Swedish pioneers were thus outspokenly assimilationist and strove, even in the first generation, to Americanize as quickly and completely as possible. Heavy Swedish immigration between 1865 and 1914 thereafter created both the will and the critical mass for organized ethnic activity, reinforced both by the lower price and increased ease of Atlantic travel and by the arrival of potential leaders with higher levels of educational attainment and a commitment to the higher culture of the homeland. A third phase has involved the elective and selective preservation of aspects of a distinct identity and culture—which is no less Swedish American than Swedish as such—by an increasingly American-born group, following the end of the great migration in the 1920s.[10]

If, then, Swedish ethnic pride and commitment varied considerably within the first generation as a whole during the period of the migration—which for the Swedes lasted longer than for many other immigrant nationalities—it varied no less on the basis of differences in individual attitudes. Contemporary evidence makes clear that while some first generation immigrants never felt at home in the new land and sought as best they could to return to Sweden, others, apparently more numerous, expressed a high degree of animosity against the land of their birth, based on grievances they held responsible for the circumstances of their leaving. The latter often went to ridiculous lengths to appear as "American" as possible and to disassociate themselves entirely from their Swedish origins. Hansen himself admitted as much in discussing those immigrants who abandoned their ancestral faith to join new denominations in America: "When they said that they passed from the old world to the new many of them meant that the world should be new in all respects."

Swedish visitors to the United States were frequently offended by the lack of attachment, if not downright disdain, toward the homeland they encountered among their emigrated compatriots. The younger women, it was noted, appeared to be particularly enthusiastic Americanizers. Many immigrants, moreover, arrived as children and grew up, to a greater or lesser degree, as Americans, thus belonging more to the second than to the first generation, according to Hansen's classification. For example, my own paternal grandfather changed his surname to Barton, rather than the original Svensson.[11]

It is meanwhile apparent that there may be cycles of interest within the lifetimes of individuals as well as within generations or periods. "Thousands of our countrymen," the Lutheran pastor Lars Gustaf Abrahamson wrote in 1903, "have only here rediscovered their love for Sweden. . . . We have found that even if immigrants come here filled with prejudices against the land of their fathers, even if they have forgotten the Swedish language before they have learned English, even if they have been determined to break all the bonds that tie them to the land from which they have emigrated, when they have lived here a while they can once again speak Swedish and begin to feel an ever-growing love for their fatherland."[12]

John Higham, in describing Hansen as a representative of the "Old," as opposed to the "New Social History," maintains that his unit of analysis was the "unencumbered individual." In "The Problem of the Third Generation Immigrant," however, it seems to be precisely the missing individual factor, at least in the ways I have discussed here.[13]

In considering the ethnic attitudes of the Swedish Americans, especially of the first generation, another important factor needs to be taken into account: the prevailing attitudes in the Old Country at any given point toward the United States, the emigration, and the emigrants, and the extent to which these attitudes tended to encourage among the immigrants a separate sense of identity, based upon their own group in America, rather than upon the homeland. From the 1870s onward, articulate Swedish Americans tended to stress their own uniqueness. The concept of a distinctive "Swedish-American nationality" found a particularly influential spokesman in the patriarchal Johan A. Enander, editor of the newspaper *Hemlandet* in Chicago for nearly thirty years following his arrival in America in 1869.[14]

What then of the second generation? That it was frequently rebellious against its parents' alien ways is clear. "Youth is the future," the visiting Swedish journalist Ernst Beckman wrote as early as 1883, but the ways of the youth among the Swedish Americans were such "that their future is surely not going to be Swedish." They adopted American speech and customs, "often in caricatured form," although significantly they were often encouraged in this by their Swedish-born parents who were ambitious for their futures—a factor Hansen failed to take into account. The American ideal of education, moreover, sought above all to foster independent judgment. "One must deal carefully with a free citizen in a free country," as Beckman put it. Still, life tends to improve upon education, he added, and most Swedish-American young people grew up to be "both capable and pleasant, once they had passed their problem years." In 1925, another Swedish visitor, Lydia Hedberg, found it painful to note how prosperous Swedish Americans of the second generation sought "with panicky anxiety to conceal the fact that they were of Swedish origins." In lightly fictionalized form, John Wahlborg, who traveled in the United States in 1915, described a visit to a Swedish-American home in New Jersey, where the father explained: "We may thank God, for our children have given us no grief. But the thing is, we are Swedes and can never be anything else, and our children are Americans in their whole way of thinking and hereafter can hardly be otherwise. Swedish demands for children's obedience and children's respect for their elders do not fit in with the American life philosophy."[15]

How universal a phenomenon was the second generation revolt? Swedish visitors also reported meeting young persons who took pride in their background. Will Herberg, who perhaps more than anyone else popularized the Hansen thesis from the 1950s onward, pointed out that some members of the second generation "saw in their position 'at the boundary' an opportunity to mediate between the two cultures and societies, and to build their lives, though obviously not their children's, upon this vocation."[16]

Swedish America offered its own notable examples of such second generation ethnic leadership. A conspicuous case would be that of Pastor Carl Aaron Swensson, born in Pennsylvania in 1857, who recalled how he grew up staunchly Swedish in America, to the point where in his younger years he felt no little contempt for "all that could be described as American." At Augustana College in the later 1870s, he encountered, among his classmates—most of whom had come to America as youngsters or like himself were born in America—a wave of enthusiasm for the ancestral land and its culture recalling what Hansen would later describe as "third generation interest." This spirit had spread so that by the 1890s it was "almost modern among Swedes in America to be Swedish and to show their pride in this. Otherwise

I can well remember the time during my childhood when many considered it good tone to have forgotten Swedish. . . ." Perhaps a high point was when young Swensson defended, in one of the college's lively Swedish literary societies, the proposition that "Little Sweden is the greatest land on earth." Before his untimely death in 1904, he became one of Swedish America's most revered leaders.[17]

Many older members of the second generation of today experience nostalgia for the Swedish-American world in which they grew up and against which they may in their time have rebelled. Such persons presently form the backbone of most traditional Swedish-American organizations, and as editor for a good many years of the *Swedish-American Historical Quarterly* (before 1982 the *Swedish Pioneer Historical Quarterly*), I can report that their fond childhood recollections constitute a substantial proportion of the articles submitted for consideration. There is also plentiful evidence of thriving Swedish-American organized activities among residents of retirement communities in the Sun Belt, most of whom must by now belong to the second generation. Like many in the first generation itself, much of the second is evidently more "Swedish" at age seventy than at age twenty, or even fifty.[18]

Hansen was speaking in Rock Island not only to a group of Swedish Americans, but also to a historical society; he defined "the problem of the third generation immigrant" in terms of the latter's responsibility to record the history of its nationality in America in sympathetic yet objective fashion. "As a broad generalization," he meanwhile claimed, "the second generation is not interested in and does not write any history. That is just another aspect of their policy of forgetting." In this regard, Hansen, the son of immigrant parents, would have to regard himself as an exception. Significant exceptions would likewise be such second generation Swedish-American historians as Andrew A. Stomberg or George M. Stephenson. Stephenson—along with Hansen, Theodore C. Blegen, and Carl F. Wittke—is recognized as one of the fathers of immigration history in the United States.[19]

The first ethnic historical organizations, according to Hansen, were "pioneer societies," in which grizzled old-timers "told one another of the glorious deeds that they had seen and sometimes performed and listened to the reading of the obituaries of the giants that had fallen." When the last of them "joined his ancestors," such organizations automatically disbanded, leaving "a conglomerate mass of literature, much and often most of it useless."[20]

How does this scenario fit the Swedish Americans? Hansen held that it would have been predictable that a Swedish-American historical society would come into existence around 1930—the very year in which the Augustana Historical Society was established—because the Swedish Americans were "fast approaching the third generation stage." This timing was certainly arbitrary, considering the long Swedish presence in the United States. Hansen meanwhile noted that the leaders of the Augustana Historical Society, which he was addressing, included persons of both the first and second generations, although he explained this by describing them as "third generation in spirit." They would, moreover, succeed only if the grandchildren of the pioneers were prepared to follow them.[21]

The Augustana group was, however, not the first Swedish-American historical society. It had been preceded a quarter century earlier by the Swedish Historical Society of America, established in Chicago in 1905. Although its founders belonged mainly to the first generation and it propounded to begin with a staunchly filiopietistic version of the Swedish-American past, in the style of the day and under the initial leadership of Enander, it cannot be dismissed as simply a pioneer society such as Hansen later described. It lasted until 1934, when it went under due to economic difficulties caused by the Great Depression and to personal conflicts. The extensive materials that the society published remain highly valuable to research. By the 1920s, its dominating figures, Stomberg and Stephenson, were committed to high standards of objective scholarship. Their principal rival at this stage was Amandus Johnson, also an academically trained scholar, who had come to America as an infant and thus himself belonged essentially to the second generation, the new champion of the filiopietistic tradition.[22]

If the Augustana Historical Society were to follow certain guidelines that he set forth in his lecture, Hansen held that "the product would be a history of the Swedes in America that no one could accuse of being tainted with partiality. Perhaps not all the passages would be read with a glow of pride but there would be no humiliation and the pride of achievement of what no other ethnic group in America has been willing to do would soon overcome regrets that arose out of what truth made it necessary to say."[23]

In retrospect it seems surprising that Hansen could claim that such objectivity had not yet been attempted considering not only the later work of the Swedish Historical Society of America under Stromberg's and Stephenson's guidance, but also what should have been even more apparent to Hansen, given his own background: the high scholarly standards set from its beginning in 1925 by the Norwegian-American Historical Association under Blegen's leadership.[24]

What Hansen called the "principle of third generation interest" has by all odds been the most widely noted and influential part of his

Rock Island presentation: "What the son wishes to forget the grandson wishes to remember."[25] Both for Hansen himself and for many others it has represented both a hope and a prediction. If Hansen has enjoyed a considerable vogue in recent decades, it is thanks in no small measure to the so-called "new ethnicity" of the 1960s and 1970s, which bore all the marks of "third generation interest."

Those active in the study of Swedish America are well aware of the effects of the new ethnicity upon their own group, even though, in characteristic Swedish fashion, it may not have been as demonstrative as that shown by some others. Hansen wrote, moreover, that the third generation, if it recognized its opportunity in time, could "not only do a good job of salvaging but probably can accomplish more than either the first or the second generation could ever have achieved."[26] There can be no doubt that Swedish culture as comprehended by the descendants of Swedish immigrants in America today is more broadly inclusive and nationally Swedish than the local provincial cultures familiar to their far less educated and sophisticated immigrant forebears. Swedish culture today, for those who are interested, means Tegner, Strindberg, and Martinson, Bellman and Alfven, Zorn and Milles, as well as ring dances and gingerbread cookies.

Swedish cultural activities in America now involve persons of all generations. As Nathan Glazer has put it, we have perhaps by now become a "third-generation country." This, in turn, may be the same thing as saying that Hansen's "generations" are best understood as states of mind, through which individuals may pass within their own lifetimes, as well as alternating between one biological generation and the next.[27]

If a widespread second generation reaction against an alien parental background was generally recognized long before Hansen described it in 1937, the question naturally arises, How original was his idea of "third generation interest"? The whole basis for Hansen's Rock Island address is a more or less deterministic belief that a particular idea will arise when the time is right. Concerning Frederick Jackson Turner's celebrated Frontier Thesis, Hansen (once a student of Turner's) wrote: "Turner or no Turner the frontier hypothesis was bound to come and to appear in the very decade during which he wrote his famous essay."[28]

One might say much the same thing about Hansen's third generation hypothesis. Within the Swedish-American community there are signs that such a concept was evolving at least a decade before Hansen enunciated it before his Swedish-American audience in 1937. That this should be so should not be surprising, considering the wealth of generational theories that had flourished in the Western world since before the turn of the century.[29]

In 1923, Johannes Hoving, a leading champion of Swedish cultural preservation in America, discerned an "encouraging up-swing" in Swedish-American sentiment. "He, who through the whim of fate has been born in another land or part of the world other than Sweden," Hoving maintained, "need not be regarded as less Swedish, as long as he is of Swedish blood and has Swedish interests." In 1933, Hoving declared: "What was so shamefully neglected by that generation of immigrants which came here 40 or 50 years ago, the present culturally interested American generation is doing everything to make good."[30]

The question of cultural maintenance was, by the 1920s and 1930s, tied intimately to the language question. To cultural conservatives like Hoving, language, culture, and ultimately ethnic identification were inseparable. "To claim that a sense of Swedishness could be preserved if the Swedish language disappears is pure nonsense," Hoving declared in 1928: "That would mean the end of a Swedish identity [*svenskheten*] within two generations." By 1933, Hoving was engaged in a spirited controversy with Vilhelm Berger, editor of the New York Swedish newspaper *Nordstjernan*, who, although himself one of America's more notable Swedish-language authors, was prepared to accept the younger generations' complete shift to English. Berger belittled the idea that "Swedish culture and the Swedish language are like a pair of Siamese twins, who must hang together to survive," and urged, "Why not let the language question resolve itself naturally? The mouth speaks that which the heart is filled with. Let each one speak that language in which he or she is best able to express his or her thoughts."[31]

Despite the admirable efforts of Hoving and others, Swedish has, with rare exceptions, not survived as a venacular language in America. Yet the pragmatic divorce between language and ethnic sentiment doubtless cleared the way for a new kind of elective ethnicity. In 1927, the Swedish journalist Anna Lenah Elgström discussed the question of Swedish-American interest in the Old Country with an unidentified Swedish-American newspaperman:

> The third generation! It has often received a university education, he explained. Its members have often traveled to Europe and learned the value of having an old cultural tradition to build upon. They come home and speak as enthusiastically of their origins as the Dutch Americans do of theirs. . . . No, it is not just snobbery, in any case not from the Swedish Americans' side, he continued. Usually the Swedish American of the third generation no longer speaks Swedish or even understands the language. But his higher education nonetheless gives

him a better basis for comprehending and appreciating Swedish cultural values than his more half-educated, although Swedish-speaking, parents had—they who wished only to forget what their parents in turn had told them about Sweden. "Herring and potatoes and red cottages—much more than that they probably could not remember!" But for Swedish Americans this was often *all* there was to Sweden. . . .[32]

In 1933, another visiting Swedish journalist, Oscar Rydqvist, heard much the same message from the Swedish consul general in New York, Olof Lamm, who told him, "we must not stare ourselves blind at the language question," and assured him that "often out here I have encountered perhaps the strongest sense of Swedish identity among Swedish Americans who only with great difficulty could express themselves in their ancestral tongue." Rydqvist also found Oliver Linder, the veteran editor of *Svenska Amerikanaren* in Chicago, cautiously optimistic: "The third generation is now proud of its Swedish origins, Editor Linder continues. That is something that can have its psychological significance in the future, even if the third generation of today is not itself Swedish-speaking. . . ."[33]

Similar ideas may well have been current during the same period among certain other ethnic groups in America; the extent to which— and ways in which—different ethnic groups picked up ideas and impulses from each other remains one of the most neglected aspects of American ethnic history.

It nonetheless remained for Marcus Lee Hansen to conceive of and enunciate the concept of "third generation interest" as a principle affecting ethnic life as a whole. Taking into account the reservations set forth herein, Hansen's thesis has proven remarkably useful in seeking to understand the Swedish experience in America.

NOTES

1. Cf. Oscar Handlin's introduction to the 1961 paperback edition of Marcus Lee Hansen, *The Atlantic Migration, 1607–1860: A History of the Continuing Settlement of the United States*, ed. Arthur M. Schlesinger (New York: Harper Torchbooks, 1961; orig. publ. Cambridge, Mass.: Harvard University Press, 1940), pp. x, xi, xiv–xv.

2. Hansen, *The Atlantic Migration*.

3. Marcus Lee Hansen, "The Problem of the Third Generation Immigrant," republication of the 1937 address with introductions by Peter Kivisto and Oscar Handlin (Rock Island: Swenson Swedish Immigration Research Center and Augustana College Library, 1987), pp. 18, 19. Hansen's other published writings, including *The Mingling of the Canadian and American Peoples* (New Haven: Yale University Press, 1940), co-authored by John B. Brebner,

and *The Immigrant in American History,* ed. Arthur M. Schlesinger (Cambridge, Mass.: Harvard University Press, 1940), likewise gave little specific attention to the Scandinavians.

4. Hansen, "The Problem of the Third Generation," esp. pp. 12–15.

5. Ibid., esp. pp. 21, 24. Cf. Peter Kivisto's introduction, "Hansen's Classic Essay After a Half Century," ibid., p. 5.

6. Rudolph Vecoli's commentary at the symposium, "Hansen's 'Classic Essay' Revisited," Augustana College, April 24, 1987, Rock Island, Ill. (hereafter referred to as Symposium 1987). I am indebted to Vecoli for sending me a copy of "Who Shall Inherit America?" Cf. Kivisto in Hansen, "The Problem of Third Generation," p. 5, for Rischin's description.

7. Oscar Handlin's introduction, "A Classic Essay in Immigrant History," in Hansen, ibid., p. 10; Kivisto, ibid., p. 6.

8. Robert Wohl, *The Generation of 1914* (Cambridge: Harvard University Press, 1979).

9. Commentary by Nathan Glazer at Symposium 1987. Other commentators at the symposium, including John Higham and Victor Greene, also reflected on the concept of generation versus period.

10. H. Arnold Barton, "The Life and Times of Swedish America," *Swedish American Historical Quarterly* 35 (July 1984): 282–96.

11. H. Arnold Barton, "Who Is a Swedish American?" *Swedish Pioneer Historical Quarterly* 31 (April 1980):83–85; Barton "Scandinavian Immigrant Women's Encounter with America," *Swedish Pioneer Historical Quarterly* 25 (January 1974): 37–42; Hansen, "The Problem of the Third Generation," p. 22. H. Arnold Barton, *The Search for Ancestors: A Swedish-American Family Saga* (Carbondale: Southern Illinois University Press, 1979), esp. chaps. 9–10, discusses the case of my paternal grandfather. The evidence of Swedish travel accounts is too voluminous to cite here, but a good idea of immigrant hostility toward the Old Country may be gained from the anonymous testimony assembled by the Swedish government Inquest on Emigration [*Emigrationsutredningen*] in 1907–8, excerpts of which are given in translation in H. Arnold Barton, *Letters from the Promised Land: Swedes in America, 1840–1914* (Minneapolis: University of Minnesota Press, 1975), pp. 276–92.

12. L. G. Abrahamson, "Licentiat C. L. Sundbeck och betydelsen af hans resa i Förenta Staterna," *Prärieblomman 1903* (Rock Island: Augustana Book Concern, 1903), p. 113. See also H. Arnold Barton, "Becoming Swedish-American," *Swedish-American Historical Quarterly* 38 (October 1987):145–46, written after Symposium 1987 and drawing upon insights gained from it.

13. Higham, commentary at Symposium 1987.

14. Enander is discussed briefly in Victor R. Greene, *American Immigrant Leaders, 1800–1900* (Baltimore: Johns Hopkins University Press, 1987), pp. 78–80, but he calls for a full-scale study. His ideal of "Swedish-Americanism" is expounded not only in *Hemlandet*, but also through the speeches, essays, and poems contained in his *Valda skrifter af Joh. A. Enander*, vol. 1 (Rock Island: Augustana Book Concern, 1892); no second volume was published.

15. Ernst Beckman, *Från nya verlden* (Stockholm: Norstedt, 1877), p. 197, and *Amerikanska studier*, 2 vols. (Stockholm: Z. Haegström, 1883),

I:142, 151–52; Bergslagsmor [Lydia Hedberg], *Reseminnen från U.S.A.* (Skövde: Isakssonska boktryckeri, 1925), p. 81; John Wahlborg, *Stjärnbaner i blågult* (Gefle: Berättelseförlaget, 1915), pp. 62–63.

16. Will Herberg, *Protestant-Catholic-Jew: An Essay in American Religious Sociology* 2d ed. (Garden City: Doubleday Anchor Books, 1960), pp. 16–17.

17. C. A. Swensson, *I Sverige* (Stockholm: P. Palmquist, 1891), pp. 13–18, 25–29. Cf. Daniel M. Pearson, *The Americanization of Carl Aaron Swensson* (Rock Island: Augustana Historical Society, 1977), esp. pp. 5, 12.

18. Barton, "Becoming Swedish-American."

19. Hansen, "The Problem of the Third Generation," pp. 16, 19–21. Cf. O. Fritiof Ander, "Four Historians of Immigration," in *In the Trek of the Immigrants: Essays Presented to Carl Wittke,* ed. O. Fritiof Ander (Rock Island: Augustana College Library, 1964), pp. 15, 17–32.

20. Hansen, "The Problem of the Third Generation," p.16.

21. Ibid., pp, 18, 19.

22. H. Arnold Barton, "Clio and Swedish America: Historians, Organizations, Publications," in *Perspectives on Swedish Immigration,* ed. Nils Hasselmo (Chicago: Swedish Pioneer Historical Society, 1978), pp. 3–24, and "Swedish-American Historiography," *Immigration History Newsletter* 15 (May 1983):1–5; Ulf Beijbom, "The Historiography of Swedish America," *Swedish Pioneer Historical Quarterly* 31 (October 1980):257–85. Also Roy Swanson, "Our Predecessors," *Swedish Pioneer Historical Quarterly* 1 (January 1950): 12–20. The next such organization—following the Augustana Historical Society, which is also still in existence—would (almost ironically) be called the Swedish Pioneer Historical Society, established in Chicago in 1948. This not withstanding, it has maintained high standards of scholarly objectivity and in 1983 changed its name to the Swedish American Historical Society, for reasons Hansen would have appreciated. See H. Arnold Barton, "The Society's Change of Name," *Swedish-American Historical Quarterly* 34 (July 1983):235

23. Hansen, "The Problem of the Third Generation," p. 23.

24. On the NAHA, see Lloyd Hustvedt, "The NAHA and Its Antecedents," in *Americana Norvegica* 3, ed. Harald S. Naess and Sigmund Skard (Oslo: Gyldendal, 1971), pp. 294–306; Franklin D. Scott, "Controlled Scholarship and Productive Nationalism," *Norwegian-American Studies and Records,* 17 (Northfield: Norwegian-American Historical Society, 1952); H. Arnold Barton, "Historians of the Scandinavians in North America," in *Scandinavians in America: Literary Life,* ed. J. R. Christianson (Decorah: Symra Literary Society, 1985), esp. pp. 48, 50.

25. Hansen, "The Problem of the Third Generation," p. 15. Hansen introduces the same idea in "Who Shall Inherit America?"

26. Ibid., p. 15.

27. Commentary by Glazer at Symposium 1987. Cf. Kivisto in Hansen, "The Problem with the Third Generation," p. 6.

28. Ibid., p. 25.

29. Cf. Wohl, *The Generation of 1914.*

30. Johannes Hoving, *I svenskhetens tjänst,* 5 vols. (Stockholm: Skandinaviska släkt studie samfundet, 1944-53), vol. 2, p. 184; vol. 3, p. 126.

31. Ibid., vol. 3, p. 34; see also vol. 3, p. 125; Vilhelm Berger, *Svensk-Amerika i målbrottet* (New York: Published privately, 1933), esp. pp. 13–17. The essays in Berger's booklet appeared first in *Nordstjernan.*

32. Anna Lenah Elgström and Gustaf Collijn, *U.S.A. Liv och teater* (Stockholm: Bonniers, 1927), p. 432. I have been unable to identify the Swedish-American journalist in question, even though the views he expressed might seem to suggest Vilhelm Berger.

33. Oscar Rydqvist, *En handfull amerikanskt* (Stockholm: Holger Schildt, 1933), pp. 194, 197, 199–200.

Hansen's Theory and America's Black Birthright: The Historical Novel as History and Collective Memory

In 1938, the Augustana Historical Society published what, almost a half-century later, Werner Sollors declared to have become the "best known modern formulation of generational succession among immigrants . . . to the United States"[1]—Marcus Lee Hansen's "The Problem of the Third Generation Immigrant."[2] In that essay Hansen put forward an addition to the laws of history, a generalization that he elevated to a principle: "the principle of third generation interest." Hansen insisted that this principle "is applicable in all fields of historical study," that it "explains the recurrence of movements that seemingly are dead," that "it is a factor that should be kept in mind particularly in literary or cultural history," and that "it makes it possible for the present to know something about the future." Referring to his principle as a theory, Hansen presented it as a virtually universal phenomenon: "what the son wishes to forget the grandson wishes to remember."[3]

Although Hansen exemplified his thesis chiefly in reference to the history-recovering activities carried out by the grandchildren of European immigrants to America, he clearly meant his "law" to apply to third generation legatees of any historically significant event. His citation of *Gone With the Wind* as a third generation product evinces his intention.

A moment's reflection will reveal that every generation (except that of the Biblical first couple and their children) is a third generation, as well as being one that is first, second, or fourth. Generations are measured in relation to a fateful event.[4] The second generation that Hansen criticizes so harshly for aggressively and intentionally "forgetting" its parental heritage is also a third generation when counted from the time and condition of the latter generation's parentage. And the premier generation is a third generation in relation to its own grandparents. Thus, the third generation offspring of America's slaves is also a second generation, one that has come after that of the first freeborn parents and of slave-born grandparents. Hence, the actual intention of Hansen's law, and certainly its vital spirit, is embodied in its calling attention to the temporal dimensions that circumscribe the historicity of significant events: it describes a cycle of experience, forgetfulness, and remembering that occurs over a period of three generations. It is a statement about a particular kind of time-track.[5]

"Time," Maurice Halbwachs once observed, "is like a blank sheet on which an indefinite number of parallel lines may be drawn."[6] Along one set of these lines, Hansen has singled out certain moments of intense and significant experience and demarcated these as historical. And from these moments he has counted generations and observed the generational period in which the original "historical" moment of experience is erased from the collective mind and, later, in another generational period, remembered. The latter process restores the experience to its eventful place, making it the central part of the heritage of the group as well as a source of its collective identity. Hansen's law describes, thus, a process of pure sociology—a denotation of how it is that groups and group consciousness come to rise, fall, and rise again.

Reconstruction, Redemption, and White Collective Memory

After the fashion of Halbwachs, consider remembering. Critical to the formulation "what the son wishes to forget the grandson wishes to remember" is the thesis that the memory of the grandchild is turned toward recalling experiences that are not his or her own. Even more significant, one example of the living's appropriation of the experiences of their dead ancestors is the reawakening of Southern patriotism among third generation descendants of the Reconstruction Era. Discussing the historiography that developed after the Civil War, Hansen writes, "The Southerners who survived the four years of that struggle never forgot." But, the "second generation made little effort to justify the actions of their fathers." However, Hansen goes on to rejoice in the fact that "now the grandsons of the Confederates rule in the place of the sons and there is no apologizing for the events of 1861; instead, there is a belligerency that asserts the moral and constitutional justice of their grandfathers' policy."[7]

In Hansen's descriptions of third generation activities, there is entailed a creative employment of the intellectual imagination as well as a redisciplining of the passions. It is thus appropriate that he cites a work of fiction as a crowning achievement of third generation interest by the grandchildren of the Confederacy: "The great novel of the Civil War and Reconstruction era was not written by one who had participated in the events or witnessed the scenes. It did not come from the pen of one who had listened to a father's reminiscences. *Gone With the Wind* was written by a granddaughter of the Confederacy, in the year 1936, approximately sixty years after the period with which it dealt had come to an end."[8] An aroused collective memory had transposed an earlier generation's experience first into a new history[9] and then into an imaginative tale. From both the history and the tale, the white legatees of the Confederacy could take on a new and proud identity and employ that identity in the pursuit of their own current interests.

The revival of interest in the history and mythology of the antebellum South, the Civil War, and Reconstruction presents a fine example of the attendant processes. Of all the divisions among Americans, that between white Southerners and all others has had a marked noticeability. The eleven states that make up "the South" have constantly struggled to effect a solution to the pushes toward sectional or national independence from—and the pulls back to regional recognition and absorption within—the United States.

The historical conflict that was supposed to settle the issue was fought between 1861 and 1865, but, rather than ending the matter, the Civil War and its aftermath created a new and perhaps permanent course of irresolution. In the six decades that separated the ending of Reconstruction and the publication of Margaret Mitchell's classic of redemptionist thought, the South found itself trapped between the prideful claim that it was ever-enduring and the doleful lament that it was slowly vanishing.[10] Caught in the flux of these contradictory perspectives, white Southerners found it difficult to become Americanized in Hansen's sense of the term, that is, to make a "treaty of peace with society."[11] Understood in this light, the founding of the Southern Historical Society in 1934[12]—an event Hansen hailed as an important instance of nonethnic third generational return—is also an example of the South's continuation of the war by another means. Publication of *Gone With the Wind*, together with its selection for the Pulitzer Prize in 1936 and its widely acclaimed film version in 1939, constitute important victories in that war. Advertised in the *American Historical Review* as the greatest historical novel ever written by an American,[13] the book, and the film that followed, provided popular literary legitimation for the "moonlight-and-magnolia school of history."[14]

In a generational sense, Mitchell's novel was the lineal descendant of Thomas Dixon's negrophobic 1904 treatment of the same era, a melodrama entitled *The Clansman*;[15] whereas David O. Selznick's film version was a later generation's screenplay of the theme that D. W. Griffith had explored two decades earlier in his film translation of Dixon's novel, retitled and released as *Birth of a Nation*.[16] Indicative of how much the Confederacy had won in its seven-decade struggle since Appomattox are the facts that until the making of *The Old Soldier's Story* (1909), the first film sympathetic to the Confederacy, Civil War movies had favored the Union; that Griffith had pioneered the filmic mystique of the "Lost Cause" in three films made in 1909 and 1911; and that the National Association for the Advancement of Colored People, which had pressed for banning Griffith's film, after persuading Selznick to cut some of the most offensive scenes from his screenplay,[17] did not join in the fight against the showing of *Gone With the Wind*.[18] The latter was left to such dissident groups as the National Negro

Congress and the Communist party. Yet, some "critics felt that where *Birth of a Nation* ended, *Gone With the Wind* began." However, by 1936–39, sympathy for the "lost cause" of the Confederacy and indifference toward the plight of blacks had so penetrated American social consciousness that Mitchell's novel and Selznick's film version of it "completed the job of wiping out of the public mind the 'Northern' view of slavery, Civil War, and Reconstruction, replacing it with the traditional 'Southern' view."[19] What justification the Confederacy had lost in 1865, its third generation descendants had recovered seventy years later.

Despite his warnings about excessive pride and false filiopietism, there is no air of criticism in Hansen's designation of the revived Southern attitude as "a belligerency that asserts the moral and constitutional justice of their grandfather's policy," nor does he evince any apprehension about his own conclusion on the matter: "The South has been revived. Its history is taught with a fervid patriotism in the universities and schools."[20] But, as was surely evident then, that revived and fervidly patriotic history exemplified so well in Margaret Mitchell's novel was partial and one-sided. Moreover, although it spawned several intriguing internal disputes, much valuable research, the discovery of previously overlooked facts, and some imaginative interpretations of particular aspects of the era, it subjected blacks either to distorted and demeaning stereotypy or to a less than benign neglect. As James Temple Kirby has observed, "Margaret Mitchell's Scarlett O'Hara . . . , macho beau Rhett Butler, frail-noble Melanie, sensitive-romantic-tragic Ashley Wilkes, and Hattie McDaniel's Mammy—were stark stereotypes. . . . House servants are toms, mammies, and pickaninny types. Tara's overseer is a rogue, later a scalawag, implying a direct link from slavery's own sinister side to Reconstruction."[21] Hansen's selection of *Gone With the Wind* as an exemplar of his "law," however unintentionally, gave historical credence to the Southern stereotype of blacks.

Hansen's Vision of Black Americans

Supposedly, Hansen's law enhances individual self-esteem by identifying the third generation descendants of an identifiable people with some positively valued activities carried out by their grandparents' generation. In some cases, if a third generational identification is to be effective it must obviate a stigma discrediting the acts in question and demeaning those who committed them. The Southern school of thought associated with U. B. Phillips and his disciples constitutes a case in point; it seeks to justify slavery and exonerate the slaveholders from any moral defaults.[22] In opposition to that school is one espousing revisionism. Associated with such contemporary historians as Kenneth M. Stampp,[23] John Hope Franklin,[24] and their colleagues and followers, its perspective represents a counterreaction to the whitewashing of a sorry chapter of American history.[25] However, Hansen, not himself a party to the debates over the meaning and implications of slavery in American history, contributed, if only in an incidental way, to the exclusion of blacks from self-enhancing ethnic history and from a positive sense of group identity.

Blacks are not treated as migrants or settlers in Hansen's two books on the settlement of America. Indeed, Afro-Americans hardly appear at all in this work. "Negro," "African," or "slavery" are not to be found in the index of Hansen's *The Atlantic Migration, 1607–1860*. Yet, readers of that important study will learn in passing that "many Negro slaves belonged to the households of the prosperous [New Netherlanders], and free blacks and mulattoes already formed a special class";[26] and, in a discussion of the connections that bind the population history of the North American mainland to that of the islands of the Caribbean, that the introduction of sugar cane in the latter led to "large plantations and slaves [taking] the place of white servants." In Hansen's interpretation, blacks exist as a servile people who once elbowed out white smallholders: "The Negroes, numbering sixty-four hundred in 1643, totaled over fifty thousand in 1666, and for nearly every one who came, an Englishman, Scotchman or Irishman had to depart." Blacks are next mentioned as bloody rebels, forcing whites to flee, in Hansen's brief description of how French refugees from strife-torn Haiti reached the United States: "The Negroes of the French colony of Haiti rose in revolt, spreading bloodshed and destruction in their wake. The whites who fled . . . landed in Charleston, Norfolk, Baltimore, Philadelphia or New York . . . Americans were amazed at the ease with which these Frenchmen accommodated themselves to their new life."[27]

In Hansen's version of the settlement patterns of eighteenth-century Maryland and Virginia, blacks are mere objects of economic history, never its subjects. Hence, the ending of the head rights system of labor recruitment enhanced "the institution of slavery, which had taken possession of the tobacco areas and was now bringing in the first large influx of Negroes. . . ."[28] Without mentioning the plight of the new class of freedmen and women, or describing the many and varied roles that the people who crossed the Atlantic from Africa had played in the social, cultural, economic, aesthetic, and political construction of the United States, Hansen confines the analytic conclusion of his study of the first 250 years of the Atlantic migration to pointing out the effect of the Civil War on the European immigrants: "The four years of bloody strife destroyed not only the old South, but also, in a less obvious way, the varied immigrant America of the North. . . . When the war ended, foreign languages and foreign customs had not disappeared, but ideals had changed. All who lived in America, alien-born and native-born, were resolved to become one people."[29] The nation-building that Hansen envisions does not seem to extend itself across racial lines or in a racially democratic fashion.

Hansen took brief but significant notice of the moral aspects of black life in America, North and South, and of their relation to the subordination and social control of the black population. In an essay entitled "Immigration and Puritanism in America" (1936),[30] he wrote that "In a history of Puritanism in America slavery deserves a special chapter because, from the definition that has been adopted, slavery was Puritanism raised to the nth degree."[31] Hansen conceives American Puritanism to be a religiopolitical philosophy that has as its most distinctive feature "the regulation of the morals and actions of those whom the regulators deemed dangerous to society because they were unable to take care of themselves."[32] Blacks belonged to such a class: "When the labor class (or it may be designated the lower class) consisted of slaves, no code of moral behavior was necessary. The upper ranks of society curbed the lower, not by state law but by personal decree. Every master established the standards of morality to which his Negroes must submit and he determined the punishment to be meted out in case of infraction."[33] In effect, Hansen incorporated into his vision of slavery the thesis that had been advanced in 1854 by America's first sociologist—Henry Hughes's ideal of "warranteeism": Slaves lived under a stern but paternal regime of watchful superintendence, governed according to a reciprocity of obligations and subsistence and presided over by a Puritanically minded seigneurial aristocracy.[34]

However, Hansen was at pains to point out that the very same Puritanism that deemed it absolutely necessary to maintain magisterial watchfulness over the dangerous and dependent classes of Americans had also inspired the movement to abolish slavery. "The Civil War (which in many ways was an attempt of the South to escape this [Puritan] domination) was a great victory for the [Protestant] ministers and, elated by success, they persisted in their efforts until at last morality was written into the fundamental law of the land in the Eighteenth Amendment."[35] The transition from the privately enforced morality of a slavocracy to the democratic state's surveillance over its citizens' vicious habits had called for special police regulation of both the newly emancipated blacks and the newcomers from Europe. As Hansen conceived of the matter, "What the immigrant was in the North, the Negro was in the South—a laborer whose daily life and mental attitude encouraged overindulgence in the cup that cheers."[36] But, while the bulk of Hansen's writing exonerates the European immigrant from blanket accusations of tippling, vice, and immorality, his silence on the actual condition of black life in America leaves their alleged immorality unchallenged. To this limited extent, uncritical acceptance of Hansen's own historical writings on the matter would very likely lead third generation black historians to a less than flattering imagery of their forebears, and white

historians to making a moral distinction between the first generation of
European immigrants and that of black freedmen and women.

Of all the many statuses blacks occupied, none seemed so incapable of
refuting the still operant demeaning stereotypy than that summed up in the
ethnophaulism *sambo*, a term that identified blacks with a supposedly de-
served status as bond servants. "Slavery," wrote Allan Nevins and Henry
Steele Commager, "brought manual labor into contempt."[37] Worse, to some
historians, it seemed to fasten onto the Negro a docile, childlike character
and an only occasional unwillingness to submit to menial servitude, rude
surroundings, a poor diet, a virtually familyless existence, and an intermin-
able future of craven servility. In the film of *Gone With the Wind*, the
female variants of this stereotype are essayed by Hattie McDaniel (who won
an Academy Award for her performance) and Butterfly McQueen. In 1942,
three years after the release of Selznick's version of Mitchell's novel, Henry
Steele Commager and Samuel Eliot Morison included the following statement in volume 1 of their *Growth of the American Republic*: "As for
Sambo, whose wrongs moved the abolitionists to wrath and tears, there is
some reason to believe that he suffered less than any other class in the
South. . . . Although brought to America by force, the incurably optimistic
negro [sic] soon became attached to the country and devoted to his white
folks."[38] Commager and Morison went on to describe antebellum blacks as
members of "a race with exasperating habits" and to depict the typical slave
as "childlike, improvident, humorous, prevaricating, and superstitious."[39]
Although by 1950 these statements were sufficiently controversial to evoke
an unsuccessful call from the City College of New York's chapter of the
National Association for the Advancement of Colored People to remove
Growth of the American Republic from the list of approved texts, and, one
year later, for the history department at Queens College to ban the book
altogether from its curriculum,[40] the demeaning of the historical black was
not so easily erased from either the black or white collective mind of the
mid-twentieth century. From 1932 through 1939, the black historian
Charles Harris Wesley had labored mightily to show that, in direct response
to their enslaved condition, "Negroes worked to improve their own status
and to advance the cause of emancipation." Wesley demanded that "In light
of . . . historical facts no one . . . say . . . that the Negroes . . . did nothing
for the emancipation of themselves and the group to which they belonged."[41]
Although a new era, criticizing and revising the historiography that Hansen
had praised in 1938, was beginning to dawn in the late 1940s, blacks would
continue to suffer for years thereafter the lack of esteem that the previous
era's conceptions had loaded onto them.

The collective memory of blacks in the twentieth century draws, as it
must, on the psychological fact that the individual's as well as the group's
sense of identity establishes itself by relating and referencing the self with

respect "all other individuals, *known and unknown*, who have the same defining features."[42] When, in 1959, Stanley Elkins attempted to find some truth value in the "sambo" imagery and to attribute the existence of a psychosocial sambo personality to the infantilizing effects that American slavery's total institutionalization had on both the black psyche and morale,[43] a chorus of critics accused him of reinvigorating a pernicious stereotype that generations of black scholars had struggled so valiantly to overcome.[44]

For this reason there would appear to be at least an incentive for some blacks to retreat from history, to embrace forgetfulness rather than revival of the historical memory, should the latter prove capable only of deepening stigmatization and reinforcing degradation. By couching his criticism of the second generation's rejection of its own history in terms of an escape from its potential for humiliating both the individual and the generational group with which he or she is identified,[45] Hansen pointed to the possibility that the reactivation of the group's collective historical memory could inflict harm on both the remembering individual and on the living members of the common descent group whose grandparental history is thereby recalled. In the case of the American blacks, three or more generations removed from slavery and a heritage of stereotypy and oppression, there is a painful choice: to forget heritage altogether, and, like Mircea Eliade's mythical "archaic man" abolish history altogether and begin life anew;[46] or, as in fact has been the case with four generations of black historians, to plunge into that heritage not merely to gather and order its data, but to arrange its interpretation so that guilt, shame, embarrassment, and any other degrading sensibility is removed from its interpretation. However, accepting the latter mission carries its own dilemmas and contradictions, not the least of which is encountered in establishing a sound basis for integrating black history into general American history.

Genitors and Myth-history: American Blacks and the Founding Fathers

When the collective memory of one group is reconstituted as part of that of already assimilated Americans, it finds powerful expression in claiming a symbolic inheritance from the Founding Fathers. That the American nation-state claims to have been "born" by a bellicose Caesarean section from the womb of another entails the symbolic transfiguration of the Revolutionary Era's leading men. Present and participating at the creation, these men have become genitors in a supremely important myth-history of national procreation. As America's Founding Fathers, they are invested with a posthumous charisma that tends to convert them from ordinary mortals into supramundane monuments. Among such figures perhaps none is more important to the beginnings of the United States and to the fact that its value system emphasizes both liberty and equality than Thomas Jefferson. Author of the Declaration of Independence and *Notes on the State of Virginia*, third president of the United States during the period when the slave trade came to an end, and an uneasy holder of slaves, Jefferson's life and thoughts are so riddled with ambivalence and anxiety about matters of race and civil order that he may well embody what Gunnar Myrdal later termed the "American Dilemma." Later generations of settlers, immigrants, and immigrant descendants are invited to be legatees to the heritage of Jefferson, to become virtual scions of this and the other Founders. By willingly accepting this new paternity, they renounce the national patriarchic claim of any other fictive mythohistorical parentage group. They merge *civitas* with *patria*.

In the case of American blacks, however, this form of mythohistorical repatriarchalization takes on a special poignancy. Black citizenship had been conferred on the ex-slaves and their descendants by the post-Civil War amendments; yet their civic and symbolic heritage from the Founding Fathers is haunted by the possibility of a real matriarchy that threatens to disinherit them as descendants of a morganatic union. Since 1802, Thomas Jefferson and his family, friends, admirers, and biographers attempted to stave off the accusation that he maintained an illicit relationship with one of his slaves, Sally Hemings, and that the paternity of the several children born of this affair was never acknowledged by Jefferson.[47] Although it is quite likely that the truth of the matter will never be proven to the satisfaction of any of the disputing parties,[48] Nathan I. Huggins points out, "It does not matter whether or not it was *actually* true. It is *symbolically* true. The story, like so many legitimizing myths, symbolically ties a people (through Sally Hemings) to the founding of the nation."[49] The story links blacks to America's beginnings as a birthright.

As a literary treatment of history this relationship was first presented in William Wells Brown's novel, *Clotel; or, The President's Daughter: A Narrative of Slave Life in the United States*, published in 1853.[50] In terms of its generational situs, *Clotel* appeared in the era marking the third generation of America's independence and thus deserves comparison with the Margaret Mitchell novel. As a third generation novel, *Clotel* breaks new ground, not only serving the cause of abolition, but also identifying eighteenth-century blacks with America's national procreation myth and contrasting their ignominious status with that accorded to white European newcomers.[51] Conceived as a result of the illicit union of a slaveholder and a slave, Brown escaped his situation and later novelized a tale of the tragic death of a person similarly situated—only the eponymous fugitive slave woman in his book is identified as the illegitimate daughter of Thomas Jefferson and a black female bondservant. Unacknowledged by her father, Clotel grows up in the shadow of his steadily advancing career. Fleeing from the desolation that has become her lot in life, Clotel finds herself trapped by slave-catchers on a bridge over the Potomac and in sight of the Capitol and her father's presidential mansion. Clasping her hands in front of her and raising her eyes to heaven, she begs "for that mercy and compassion *there*, which had been denied her on earth; and then with a single bound, she vault[s] over the railing of the bridge, and [sinks] for ever beneath the waves of the river!"[52]

Brown's novel returns its readers to the situation affecting the first generation of blacks in the new republic. The fundamental distinctions of race that, on the one hand, excited most Americans' sympathy for the oppressed European immigrant but, on the other, evoked hostility toward the African slave and indifference to the plight of the black freedom-seeker were not lost on William Wells Brown. He contrasted the tragedy that befell the fugitive slave Clotel with what would have happened had she been a white woman in flight from Europe:

> Had Clotel escaped from oppression in any other land . . . , no honour within the gift of the American people would have been too good to have been heaped upon the heroic woman. But she was a slave, and therefore out of the pale of their sympathy. They have tears to shed over Greece and Poland; they have an abundance of sympathy for "poor Ireland"; they can furnish a ship of war to convey the Hungarian refugees from a Turkish prison to the "land of the free and the home of the brave." They boast that America is the "cradle of liberty"; if it is, I fear they have rocked the child to death.[53]

Margaret Mitchell's novel made the cruelties inflicted by slaveholders and the depredations carried out by the Ku Klux Klan into acts of paternal benevolence and quests for righteous justice, in effect justifying the actions of historical and present-day protagonists of white supremacy. Brown's novel was far less successful. Whereas *Gone With the Wind* was elevated to the place of a modern American classic, Brown's was consigned to that special oblivion reserved for Afro-American fiction. It occupies no place in the American canon.[54] Until a wave of black consciousness revived interest in neglected masterworks of black fiction, it existed outside both collective memory and literary history.[55]

Conclusion

Another celebratory event occurred in the same period as the fiftieth anniversary of Hansen's great speech. June 30, 1986 marked the half-century since Macmillan Publishers first released Margaret Mitchell's *Gone With the Wind*—the book that Hansen singled out as an instance of Southern white third generation interest and that had already sold two million copies by the time his essay was published. By 1986, Mitchell's book was still selling at the rate of 250,000 copies per year, and the eponymous film made from the novel had been seen by more movie-goers than make up the total population of the United States. In his introduction to the book's fiftieth-anniversary edition, Tom Wicker attempts to defend the racist imagery found throughout the book by pointing out that "Margaret Mitchell was born in 1900, when the Civil War was barely 35 years in the past and Reconstruction was even more recent," that she "began work on her novel in 1926 . . . when first generation descendants of the war and the post-war years were all about her and the South itself was by no means economically or politically recovered from those years . . . , [and when the] modern civil rights movement was 25 years in the future." Wicker asserts that "Margaret Mitchell was a child of her time, not ours, and is unfairly judged by the current view of racism."[56] However, with the understanding available from Hansen's essay, we may critically evaluate Mitchell's racism as a feature of a particular group's third generation return—her novel is not properly described as a product of her time; it is rather a presentiment of her generational group's last stand in behalf of white supremacy.

Although Carter G. Woodson had founded the Association for the Study of Negro Life and History and the *Journal of Negro History* in 1915–16, fifty years after the Civil War had ended and two decades before Mitchell published her novel, the disciplinary gatekeepers of official American history looked askance at the subject and confined its teachers and practitioners to black colleges. Although professional American historians relegated black history's expression to arenas outside the mainstream;[57] the need to revive black history seemed urgent. In 1916, the noted black historian, Charles Harris Wesley, exhorted his compatriots: "An interest should be awakened among colored America in its history, and encouragement should be given to its general reading, study and investigation."[58] Nevertheless, with perhaps a few exceptions, black history did not achieve the goal that Hansen had envisioned for third generational historiography—becoming accepted "as one chapter in the larger volume that is called American history . . . , [its] historical [society's] activities . . . merged with the activities of other societies of the same nature and finally within the main line of American historiography itself."[59] Assessing the struggle of Woodson's and Wesley's generation to crack the color line in America's historical disciplines, John Hope Franklin pointed to its peculiar character, one that required blacks first to establish that they had a history worth recognizing, and then to convince their white colleagues that it might be accepted as a significant part of Americans' history of themselves: "Their fight to integrate Afro-American history into the mainstream was part of the fight by Afro-American students to break into the graduate departments of history in every predominantly white university in the southern states and in very many such institutions outside the South. . . . They also did so in order to support their argument that Afro-American history should be recognized as a centerpiece—an adornment if you will—of the history of the United States."[60]As late as 1970, at least one popular historian of Afro-Americans claimed that that people's history still remained either lost, stolen, or strayed.[61] But, more recently, Vincent Harding has wondered whether acceptance and integration might have come too late. He asks how and in what sense successor generations should remember black Americans at all, if the more important task for present-day scholars is to work, not merely for racial understanding, but to prevent a worldwide nuclear annihilation, one that threatens to end the very continuity of all human history and of its memorable subjects.[62]

When it is exemplified in a racially divisive work like Margaret Mitchell's *Gone With the Wind*, Hansen's law tends not only to impose a concrete and binding tie on its particular generational racial group, but also to spread out and incorporate other whites, who, although not of the same descent group, nevertheless see in its thesis an expression of their own race-referential ideal and selfish social interest. But within any generation, as Karl Mannheim once pointed out, "there can exist a number of differentiated, antagonistic generation-units." In the case of the black and white third generation descended from the eras of Emancipation, Reconstruction, and Redemption, there is in fact constituted what Mannheim calls "an 'actual' generation precisely because they are oriented toward each other, even though only in the sense of fighting each other."[63]

Since Hansen presented his thesis as an historical law, historians have pointed out its falsification in the failure of some third generations to make a return to their grandparental roots. However, Mannheim observed that "not every generation location—not even every age group—creates new collective impulses and formative principles original to itself and adequate to its situation." Hansen's law speaks to those generations that do realize the potentialities inherent in their location, that are capable of forming a particular center of configuration around their common descent group and around all who would identify with it. Mannheim calls this capability one that fosters "a new *generation entelechy*."[64] Perhaps blacks and whites are at last in a position to establish such an intellectual formation—to look back honestly to their history of unhappy antagonisms so that they can look forward to, if not a consensus historiography, at least one that recognizes that racial justice is to be sought as the fruit that has long been ripening on the common American family tree.

NOTES

1. Werner Sollors, *Beyond Ethnicity: Consent and Descent in American Culture* (New York: Oxford University Press, 1986), p. 214.

2. Marcus Lee Hansen, "The Problem of the Third Generation Immigrant" (Rock Island: Augustana Historical Society, 1938).

3. Hansen, "The Problem of the Third Generation."

4. See, for example, Stanford M. Lyman, "Generation and Character: The Case of the Japanese Americans," in Lyman, *The Asian in North America* (Santa Barbara: American Bibliographic Center-Clio Press, 1977), pp. 151–76.

5. For the concept, see Stanford M. Lyman and Marvin B. Scott, "On the Time Track" in Lyman and Scott, *A Sociology of the Absurd* (New York: Appleton-Century-Crofts, 1970), pp. 189–212.

6. Maurice Halbwachs, *The Collective Memory*, trans. Francis J. Ditter, Jr., and Vida Yazdi Ditter (New York: Harper and Row, 1980; orig. French pub. 1950), p. 93.

7. Hansen, "The Problem of the Third Generation," pp. 9–10.

8. Ibid., p. 10.

9. See E. Merton Coulter, "What the South Has Done About Its History," address to the Southern Historical Association, Birmingham, Ala., October 25, 1935. Reprinted in *The Pursuit of Southern History: Presidential Addresses of the Southern Historical Association*, ed. George Brown Tindall (Baton Rouge: Louisiana State University Press, 1967), pp. 163–214.

10. See Dewey W. Grantham, *Southern Progressivism: The Reconciliation of Progress and Tradition* (Knoxville: University of Tennessee Press, 1983).

11. Hansen, "The Problem of the Third Generation," p. 6.

12. George B. Tindall, "Introduction," in *The Pursuit of Southern History*, pp. xi–xxi.

13. October 1936, p. vii.

14. Wyn Craig Wade, *The Fiery Cross: The Ku Klux Klan in America* (New York: Simon and Schuster, 1987), pp. 9–10.

15. Thomas Dixon, Jr., *The Clansman: An Historical Romance of the Ku Klux Klan* (Phoenix: Associated Professional Services, 1965). For the political and psychohistorical elements of Dixon's novel, Griffith's subsequent film of it, and the racial politics of Woodrow Wilson, see Michael Paul Rogin, " 'The Sword Became a Flashing Vision': D. W. Griffith's *The Birth of a Nation*," in Rogin, *Ronald Reagan, the Movies, and Other Episodes in Political Demonology* (Berkeley: University of California Press, 1987), pp. 190–235.

16. See Bosley Crowther, "The Birth of *Birth of a Nation*," in *Black Films and Film-Makers: A Comprehensive Anthology from Stereotype to Superhero*, comp. Lindsay Patterson (New York: Dodd, Mead, 1975), pp. 75–83; William K. Everson, *American Silent Film* (New York: Oxford University Press, 1978), pp. 72–89; Thomas Cripps, *Slow Fade to Black: The Negro in American Film, 1900-1942* (New York: Oxford University Press, 1977), pp. 41–69; Peter Noble, *The Negro in Films* (London: Cornhill, 1948; repr., Port Washington: Kennikat Press, 1969), pp. 33–43; Edward Mapp, *Blacks in American Films: Today and Yesterday* (Metuchen: Scarecrow Press, 1972), pp. 18–20; James R. Nesteby, *Black Images in American Films, 1896-1954* (Washington: University Press of America, 1982), pp. 27–42; Donald Bogle, *Toms, Coons, Mulattoes, Mammies and Bucks: An Interpretive*

History of Blacks in American Films (New York: Viking Press, 1973), pp. 10–18; Richard Schickel, *D. W. Griffith: An American Life* (New York: Simon and Schuster, 1984), pp. 212–302.

17. Richard A. Maynard, ed., *The Black Man on Film: Racial Stereotyping* (Rochelle Park: Hayden Book Co., 1974), pp. 25–40.

18. Evelyn Ehrlich, "The Civil War in Early Film: Origin and Development of a Genre," in *The South and Film*, ed. Warren French (Jackson: University Press of Mississippi, 1987), pp. 70–82; Lawrence Reddick, "Of Motion Pictures," in *Black Films and Film-Makers*, comp. Patterson, pp. 14–15.

19. Reddick, "Of Motion Pictures," p. 15.

20. Hansen, "The Problem of the Third Generation," pp. 9–10.

21. James Temple Kirby, *Media-Made Dixie: The South in the American Imagination* (Baton Rouge: Louisiana State University Press, 1978), pp. 72, 73–74.

22. See four works by Ulrich Bonnell Phillips: *American Negro Slavery: A Survey of the Supply, Employment and Control of Negro Labor as Determined by the Plantation Regime* (Gloucester: Peter Smith, 1959; orig. pub. 1918); *Life and Labor in the Old South* (Boston: Little, Brown, 1963; orig. pub. 1929); *The Slave Economy of the Old South: Selected Essays in Economic and Social History*, ed. Eugene D. Genovese (Baton Rouge: Louisiana State University Press, 1968); *The Course of the South to Secession: An Interpretation*, ed. E. Merton Coulter (New York: Hill and Wang, 1964; orig. pub. 1939).

23. See Kenneth M. Stampp, "The Historian and Southern Negro Slavery," *American Historical Review* 57 (April 1952):613–24.

24. See seven works by John Hope Franklin: *The Free Negro in North Carolina, 1790–1860* (New York: W. W. Norton, 1971; orig. pub. 1943); *The Militant South, 1800–1861* (Boston: Beacon Press, 1964; orig. pub. 1956); *Reconstruction After the Civil War* (Chicago: University of Chicago Press, 1961); *The Emancipation Proclamation* (Garden City: Doubleday-Anchor, 1963, 1965); *Racial Equality in America: The 1976 Jefferson Lectures in the Humanities* (Chicago: University of Chicago Press, 1976); *From Slavery to Freedom: A History of Negro Americans*, 5th ed. (New York: Alfred A. Knopf, 1980); and *George Washington Williams: A Biography* (Chicago: University of Chicago Press, 1985).

25. See Thomas J. Pressly, *Americans Interpret Their Civil War* (New York: Free Press, 1965); and Kenneth M. Stampp and Leon F. Litwack, eds., *Reconstruction: An Anthology of Revisionist Writings* (Baton Rouge: Louisiana State University Press, 1969).

26. Marcus Lee Hansen, *The Atlantic Migration, 1607–1869: A History of the Continuing Settlement of the United States,*ed. Arthur M. Schlesinger (New York: Harper Torchbooks, 1961; orig. pub. 1940), p. 39.

27. Hansen, *The Atlantic Migration*, pp. 39–40, 59.

28. Ibid., p. 44.

29. Ibid., p. 306.

30. Marcus Lee Hansen, "Immigration and Puritanism," *Norwegian-American Studies* 9 (1936):1–28. Reprinted in Marcus Lee Hansen, *The Im-*

migrant in American History, ed. Arthur M. Schlesinger (New York: Harper Torchbooks, 1964; orig. pub. 1940), pp. 97–128. All quotations are from the reprint edition.

31. Hansen, "Immigration and Puritanism," p. 125.

32. Ibid., p. 111.

33. Ibid., pp. 125–26.

34. Henry Hughes, *Treatise on Sociology, Theoretical and Political* (Philadelphia: Lippincott, Grambo, 1854; repr., New York: Negro Universities Press, 1968); Stanford M. Lyman, ed., *Selected Writings of Henry Hughes: Antebellum Southerner, Slavocrat, Sociologist* (Jackson: University Press of Mississippi, 1985).

35. Hansen, "Immigration and Puritanism," p. 101.

36. Ibid., p. 126.

37. Allan Nevins and Henry Steele Commager, *A Pocket History of the United States,* 7th ed. (New York: Washington Square Press, 1981), p. 38.

38. Samuel Eliot Morison and Henry Steele Commager, *The Growth of the American Republic,* vol. 1 (New York: Oxford University Press, 1942), p. 537.

39. Morison and Commager, *The Growth.*

40. *Time Magazine,* February 26, 1951, pp. 48–49; Otto Lindenmeyer, *Black History: Lost, Stolen, or Strayed* (New York: Avon Books, 1970), p. 15.

41. Charles Harris Wesley, "The Negroes of New York in the Emancipation Movement," *Journal of Negro History* 24 (January 1939):103.

42. Harold Proshansky and Peggy Newton, "Colour: The Nature and Meaning of Negro Self-Identity," in *Psychology and Race,* ed. Peter Watson (Chicago: Aldine, 1974), p. 181. Emphasis added.

43. Stanley Elkins, *Slavery: A Problem in American Institutional and Intellectual Life* (Chicago: University of Chicago Press, 1959), pp. 81–139; 2d ed. (1968), pp. 81–139, 239–44; 3d ed., rev. (1976), pp. 81–139, 223–302.

44. Ann J. Lane, ed., *The Debate over Slavery: Stanley Elkins and His Critics* (Urbana: University of Illinois Press, 1971); Kenneth M. Stampp, "Rebels and Sambos: The Search for the Negro's Personality in Slavery," in Stampp, *The Imperiled Union: Essays on the Background of the Civil War* (New York: Oxford University Press, 1980), pp. 39–71.

45. Hansen, "Immigration and Puritanism," pp. 6–9.

46. See Mircea Eliade, *The Myth of the Eternal Return,* Bollingen Series 462, trans. Willard R. Trask (New York: Random House-Pantheon Books, 1954).

47. For the most comprehensive account of a real Jefferson-Hemings affair, see Fawn M. Brodie, *Thomas Jefferson: An Intimate History* (New York, W. W. Norton, 1974); for a typical example of the polemical denial, see John Chester Miller, *The Wolf by the Ears: Thomas Jefferson and Slavery* (New York: Free Press, 1977), pp. 148–76.

48. On this matter see the bitter exchange of letters to the editor of the *New York Times,* pitting Justice Bruce McM. Wright against John J. McCartney, February 7 and 15, 1987.

49. Nathan I. Huggins, "Integrating Afro-American History into American History," in *The State of Afro-American History*, ed. Darlene Clark Hine (Baton Rouge: Louisiana State University Press, 1986), p. 163.

50. See William Edward Farrison, *William Wells Brown: Author and Reformer* (Chicago: University of Chicago Press, 1969), pp. 215–32.

51. In the tradition of one seeking the legitimation of his people's American identity, Brown would later write *The Blackman, His Antecedents, His Genius, and His Achievements* (Miami: Mnemosyne Publishing, 1969; orig. pub. 1865); and *The Negro in the American Rebellion: His Heroism and His Fidelity* (New York: Citadel Press, 1971; orig. pub. 1867).

52. Brown, *Clotel*, p. 219.

53. Ibid. p. 220.

54. Even Robert Bone, the important contemporary critic of black American literature, dismisses *Clotel* as a melodrama whose "intended irony depends upon Brown's allegation that Clotel was the illegitimate daughter of Thomas Jefferson," and whose ironic point is blunted when, in the first American edition of 1867, "an anonymous senator is substituted for Jefferson, and the plot . . . altered accordingly." Robert A. Bone, *The Negro Novel in America*, rev. ed. (New Haven: Yale University Press, 1965), pp. 29–30, n30.

55. By the late 1930s, critics had recognized Brown's importance. See Sterling Brown, *The Negro in American Fiction* (Washington: Associates in Negro Folk Education, 1937), pp. 39–40; Sterling A. Brown, Arthur P. Davis, and Ulysses Lee, eds., *The Negro Caravan: Writings by American Negroes* (New York: Citadel Press, 1941), pp. 138, 145–51. For the later recognition see Herbert Hill, "Introduction" to *Anger and Beyond: The Negro Writer in the United States* (New York: Harper and Row, 1966), pp. xix–xx; Philip Butcher, ed., *The Minority Presence in American Literature, 1600–1900*, vol. 1 (Washington: Howard University Press, 1977), pp. 421–27.

56. Tom Wicker, "Introduction," in Margaret Mitchell, *Gone With the Wind*, 50th anniversary ed. (New York: Macmillan Publishing, 1986), p. xii.

57. August Meier and Elliott Rudwick, *Black History and the Historical Profession, 1915–1980* (Urbana: University of Illinois Press, 1986), pp. 1–160.

58. Charles Harris Wesley, "Interest in a Neglected Phase of History," *AME Church Review* 32 (April 1916):268.

59. Hansen, "The Problem of the Third Generation," p. 17.

60. John Hope Franklin, "On the Evolution of Scholarship in Afro-American History," in *The State of Afro-American History*, ed. Hine, p. 21.

61. Lindenmeyer, *Black History*.

62. Vincent Harding, "Responsibilities of the Black Scholar to the Community," in *The State of Afro-American History*, ed. Hine, pp. 277–84.

63. Karl Mannheim, "The Problem of Generations," in *Essays on the Sociology of Knowledge*, ed. Paul Kecskemeti (London: Routledge and Kegan Paul, 1968; orig. pub. 1952), pp. 306–7.

64. Mannheim, "The Problem of Generations," p. 309.

Old-time Folk Dancing and Music Among the Second Generation, 1920–50

In his lecture in Rock Island and his talk a short time later entitled "Who Shall Inherit America?," Marcus Lee Hansen offered his thoughts on one of the most important social issues of the day, how ethnic grandparents, parents, and children, in a variegated pattern of persistence and rejection, relate to their ethnic heritage and to one another. The aim of this discussion will be to evaluate Hansen's conclusions in light of research on America's ethnic cultures in the interwar era. In particular, I will examine Hansen's contention that in response to heavy outside Anglo-American—or *Yankee* in Hansen's term—pressure, the American-born second generation, the offspring of adult immigrant arrivals, rejected its group artistic culture. Although such a judgment has an obvious and in some cases verifiable plausibility, it is more fruitful to consider the matter from the standpoint of American culture as a whole. From that larger perspective, the student finds cultural continuities or a modification of ancestral traditions in the ethnic arts, not the rejection that Hansen suggested. More surprisingly, immigrant children (in some cases working together with Yankees) by mid-century helped integrate those ethnic art forms into a new American national culture. The whole process was not one of first generation persistence, second generation alienation, and third generation reattachment, but a gradual transformation through generations.

The criticisms of Hansen's remarks herein will not alter or detract from the distinquished place he holds in the historical profession. Current scholars rightly view him, as Peter Kivisto noted in his republication of the Third Generation address, as the first academician to highlight the salience of the multiethnic phenomenon in American history.[1] Hansen had the great insight to raise the entire complex issue of this nation's pluralistic origins and character. In addition, he addressed a very real and human conflict that often erupted in immigrant households. As he put it, subjected to the taunts of parents and peers, American-born children were "uncomfortable at both school and home," wanting to lose as many evidences of foreign origins as they could. . . ."[2] That intimate tension and struggle was in fact a classic emotion within the family, a source of much of our finest creative literature. The strained ties between foreign-born parents and native-born children have been a common theme in fiction, films and theater. One confession of a young Italian-American writer, John Fante, illustrates that generational conflict. He writes that at school he began:

> to loathe his heritage. I avoid Italian boys and girls who try to be friendly . . . I choose my companions by the Anglo-Saxon ring of their names. . . . [But] I am nervous when I bring [those] friends to my house; the place looks so Italian. Here hangs a picture of Victor Emmanuel, and over there is one of the cathedral of Milan, and next to it, one of St. Peter's, and on the buffet stands a wine-pitcher of medieval design; it's forever red and brilliant with wine. These things are heirlooms belonging to my father, and no matter who may come to our house, he likes to stand under them and brag.
>
> So I begin to shout at him. I tell him to cut out being a Wop and be an American once in a while. Immediately he gets his razor strop and whales the hell out of me, clouting me from room to room and finally out the back door. I go into the woodshed and pull down my pants and stretch my neck to examine the blue slices across my rump. A Wop! that's what my father is! Nowhere is there an American father who beats his son this way. Well, he's not going to get away with it; some day I'll get even with him. . . ."[3]

Any reader of such sentiments would have to agree that many immigrant children probably felt a similar shame and ethnic inferiority. However, although that embarrassment was familiar to writers and scholars, we have surprisingly little empirical evidence on the matter. Current immigration scholarship has concentrated on the first generation; it has shed little light on the condition of its children.[4] The entire issue of the generational response to the conforming pressures of the majority culture still merits our scrutiny.

Hansen offered two views on the subject of the persistence of ethnic cultures in a dominant Anglo-American milieu. The first, his Rock Island address, was a dispassionate observation about the revived interest he detected of immigrant grandchildren in the musical and artistic heritage of their ancestors after their parents, the second generation, had rejected it. Those assimilationist parents had been "entirely aware of the contempt in which such [ethnic cultural] activities were held [by Yankees] and they hastened to prove that they knew nothing about casts, symphonies or canvas. Nothing was more Yankee than a Yankeeized person of foreign descent."[5]

He developed the idea of more civilized but neglected ethnic cultures in a more subjective and editorialized address a month later in

Indianapolis before the National Conference of Social Work. There Hansen condemned Yankee society for pressuring immigrant children to assimilate when that second generation ought to be instructing Americans in their varied cultural treasures. Hansen appealed to his audience to help build a national museum of American culture that would recognize, honor, and preserve the aesthetic endowments of our ethnically pluralistic society.[6]

My research into two of those very characteristics, ethnic dance and music, indicates that Hansen overlooked the great impact that ethnic cultures had on Yankee America. Those artistic activities in the foreign-born communities flowered, helping to bind the foreign and native-born generations. Immigrant community members of the various generations, along with certain other Americans, were in fact ethnicizing the dominant culture by the late 1940s.

Yale sociologist Maurice Davie offered a clue regarding the process of culture change that occurred when Yankee and immigrant cultures encountered one another. He insisted that in most cases when two cultures met, they interacted. One did not do away with the other. Cultural change occurred not simply because it was imposed by the majority upon the minority; the minority also affected the majority. This "syncretism" suggested a mutual modification.[7]

Observers of immigrant life, from the most enthusiastic filiopietist to the most sober historian, have described the artistic heritage that all ethnic groups brought with them to America. Unfortunately, most writers have referred to these aesthetic attributes as "gifts," essentially static "contributions" added to the older American stock. They have not see those attributes as influencing the native culture, modifying and altering it. This discussion is a tentative effort to illustrate some of those ethnic influences on the majority culture in the three decades after World War I. Not only did various native-born ethnics appreciate, cultivate, and disseminate their traditional culture, but also the new technologies of the era (phonograph records and radio) along with an emerging international folk-dance community all combined to produce a new, ethnically flavored American culture by 1950.

Folk Dancing

The first ethnically induced modification of our national culture was the emergence of an international folk-dance movement, popularized when immigrant dancers and others displayed traditional steps at large urban festivals and parks. This transfer of ethnic dance from the communities to intergroup functions began at the start of this century and became common in American metropolitan centers by the end of the 1930s. Hansen would be surprised to learn that many of the promoters of international folk dancing included Yankees, as well as members of the groups' second generations.

Nongroup, native-born Americans initially promoted ethnic folk dancing beyond the individual groups. They saw the activity as being for all Americans, or at least all female Americans. Before 1914, these promoters were Progressive reformers like Luther Gulick, head of the Playground Association of America, and his aide, Elizabeth Burchenal.[8] They and their playground reformers believed that there were considerable moral and physical advantages for young women and young men in learning the polka, cardas, and tarantella in public school.[9]

Additional support for dance exercise came from the YWCA. The person most responsible for encouraging the dances there was Edith Terry (later Edith Terry Bremer). Reacting to the mounting nativist pressures on immigrant newcomers, she sought to show the value of their arts and crafts by display and performance.[10] Her efforts in the 1920s were modestly successful even though intolerance continued to grow. By the end of the decade the YWCA had created more than fifty International Institutes around the country to foster the ethnic arts at various metropolitan festivals.[11]

In that postwar decade two other reasons for promoting these metropolitan events appeared: the desire to boost civic sentiment and to combat the very problem Hansen observed, the alienation of the second generation. Probably the best example of the former was the serious effort of a Cleveland daily newspaper to display that city's cosmopolitan character in a very successful Festival of Nations. With the depression's deleterious impact on the American family, social workers reemphasized the need for community sanction of the ethnic arts as a way to ease the generational conflict in the the immigrant home. They sought to build the children's respect for their parents' traditions. As a YWCA publication entitled *Second Generation Youth* put it, foreign-born parents would be less authoritarian and their American-born children more considerate of their parents when the total community recognized the artistic expression of the parents' ethnic group.[12]

This concern of social workers about generational alienation might have been lessened had they been aware that certain ethnic group leaders were laying the groundwork for an international folk-dance movement. These ethnic dance leaders would later join the social workers in a more formal framework and establish the symbolic birthplace of international folk dancing—the American Common—at the 1939 New York World's Fair.

Probably the earliest major group dance leader to instruct young people in dances of their own and of other nationalities and one of the most important founders of international dancing in America was the young Lithuanian immigrant, Vytautas Beliajus of Chicago.[13] Having arrived as a youth with his grandmother in 1923, he conveyed his enthusiasm for Lithuanian and other ethnic dances to his group's young people—the American-born. By 1930, he was teaching Lithuanian adolescents a variety of folk dances in Chicago's Lithuanian center, the Bridgeport neighborhood. After officials of the Chicago World's Fair of 1933 invited him and his dancers to perform at the exposition, he organized students into a dance ensemble called the Lithuanian Youth Society.[14] Later the Chicago Park District engaged Beliajus to conduct folk-dancing classes at parks around the city.[15] For the next ten years he edited a newsletter on ethnic folk dance, helped form a confederation of ethnic dance groups, the Folk Dance League, and by the beginning of World War II established the nation's foremost international folk-dance periodical, *Viltis*, which has continued for almost a half-century.[16]

Other promoters of international dance in the 1930s also helped establish this new American cultural activity and provided the ethnic self-confidence that social workers had sought for second generation participants. Among the promoters were the Swedish-American Linnea Osman of St. Paul; "Mama" Gravender of San Francisco; the Ukrainian-American Michael Herman of Cleveland and New York; the Italian-American Elba Farabegoli (Gurzau) of New York and Philadelphia; and the Polish-American Alfred Sokolnicki of Milwaukee.[17]

The most important agency for promoting international folk dancing, as it drew social workers and ethnic dance instructors together in a long-lasting formal association, was the New York Folk Festival Council. The council began in 1931 as an offshoot of the Foreign Language Information Service, and its major intellectual founder was a Chicago dance leader, Mary Wood Hinman.[18] She envisioned the variety of ethnic folk dances as dynamic and a vital part of the changing American culture. For the rest of the decade she insisted that "no [ethnic group] can be considered to have a corner on folk dancing of any kind. The folk material of any country is not to be appropriated or possessed by anyone or any group else it becomes static and loses its special quality."[19] Hinman and the council put these principles of shared performance into effect by means of dance festivals and instructional parties led by Elba Gurzau and Michael Herman.[20] These international folk-dance activities were not peculiar to New York; they served as a model for at least two other cities, Boston and Buffalo, by the end of the decade.[21]

The final establishment and symbolism of these ethnic dances as a part of American culture came in 1939 at the New York World's Fair. When officials expelled the Russians from the site and dismantled their pavilion in retaliation for Russia's invasion of Finland, a fair vice president, Robert D. Kohn, decided to use the space to honor America's ethnic pluralism. He helped design this new area—called the American Common—like a New England town square surrounded by an ethnic "Wall of Fame" with inscribed names of prominent personalities. The space within was used as an ethnic dance plaza. It was a place where Michael and Mary Ann Bodnar Herman of the Folk Festival Council regularly instructed crowds in the steps of the various groups.[22]

This discussion of the forces that brought about international folk dance as a new element in American culture is not a full refutation of Hansen's second generation thesis. As we have seen in John Fante's statement and the observations of social workers of the time, conflict between foreigners and their American offspring did exist and was common. Yet this sense of embarrassment and shame among ethnic adolescents and young adults was not universal. Some evidence of the ethnic reassurance of dance festivals does exist. It suggests that dancing in colorful costume to the folk music of a group that the performer's family had a connection with overrode any feeling of inferiority. For example, a New York high school freshman who participated in one of the early New York Festival Council pageants in 1932 said that "I used to feel ashamed of everything 'old country', but we have had so much fun at the festival and it was so beautiful that now I am proud of the things my mother tells me about the old country and I love my costume."[23]

Folk dancing, then, helped to combat the superiority complex of Yankees; it may even have been a manifestation of a hostile anti-Yankee attitude. Thus, in a 1935 YWCA publication entitled *What It Means to Be a Second Generation Girl*, a Ukrainian American, Mary Ann Bodnar, told of encountering Yankee denigration of her heritage at school. She responded, not as Fante did, but by condemning her peers. Instead of blaming her parents for their foreign ways, she criticized her teachers and fellow students for their ignorance of her ancestral home. As a result she decided "to spread as much information [about her old country] as possible." She then resolved to learn Ukrainian folk dancing and found it satisfying, taking "much joy in the colorful costumes and whirling figures."[24] She later married Michael Herman and contributed substantially to the folk-dance community. Although her expressed self-confidence may be unusual, it is not unique. Certainly, from her example one may conclude that personal security in, or dissatisfaction about, one's ethnic heritage depends not only on the response of outsiders, but also on how well immigrant parents were able to give their native-born children a sound understanding of their group culture before peer influences became effective.

Ethnic Music

My contention that some members of the second generation had sufficient ethnic awareness of their heritage to enrich our national culture in dance is pertinent to another area of popular artistic expression. At the same time that international folk dancing was emerging, a transformation was taking place in American popular music for which immigrant children were also partly responsible: the growing popularity of "old-time" music, immigrant-based tunes that broke onto the national charts by the late 1930s and early 1940s. This period, the "golden age" of polka-style old-time music, extends roughly from the "Beer Barrel Polka" of 1938 to Frankie Yankovic's 1948 hit, "Blue Skirt Waltz."

Music historians have been well aware of the various changes occurring in American popular music in the three decades before mid-century: the emergence of jazz and big-time swing, the rising appeal of musical comedy, and the shift from hillbilly to country music.[25] Through it all, authorities tell us that music publishers and Tin Pan Alley promoters maintained their hold over popular music culture, catering especially to the American middle-class. Still, scholars have neglected one important element of popular music that also became prominent during that era: polka-style old-time.

Like international folk dancing, this musical genre was rooted in the traditions of most of America's immigrant communities. It consisted of tunes that appealed both to parents and children. With the aid of other factors such as ethnic musicians, band leaders, music store owners, arrangers, and leading American record companies and radio stations, this new musical form became an integral part of mainstream popular culture. Germans, Poles, Scandinavians, Jews, and others certainly knew and cultivated polkas, laendlers, schottisches, obereks, kolomykas, tarantellas, and the like in their colonies. Later, certain popular entertainers from those communities, individual musicians like Lawrence Welk, "Whoopee John" Wilfahrt, and Frankie Yankovic, commercialized and broadcast those pieces nationally.

Of course, traditional music was altered in the process of popularization. Folk instruments like the Norwegian Hardanger violin and the Italian stornella (bagpipe) gave way to the more widely accepted brass and reed instruments of the jazz-swing era. Peasant dance pieces became English-language songs, but the melodies and rhythms of the polka and waltz remained the same. Most important, some of the second generation not only welcomed old-time music, but they were also its practitioners.

The popularity and transformation of old-time music can be traced from within and without immigrant communities by examining examples at both the local and national level. The reference herein must be to particular localities or regions, which may appear to make such designations exceptional rather than representative. Although the illustrations are isolated in rural and urban Wisconsin, Utica, New York, and in east Texas, that geographical diversity itself suggests a certain universality in the cultivation of traditional music. In this sense American music itself consists of the sum of music from local and regional areas.

One example of the wide appeal of a particular group's traditional music across generational lines was the Norwegian house party of central Wisconsin, common in the 1920s and 1930s. This cultural practice was based on immigrant themes but was cultivated solely by members of the group's second generation. Held at a time when Norwegian immigration was declining, the house party combined both work and recreation. Norwegian-American farmers from a district— they might well include others from the area—would come together in both warm and cold weather to help a family with a major task such as quilting, building a barn, or some similar activity. They would reserve the evening for their own entertainment, clearing the barn or house for dancing. The instruments used were the fiddle and button accordion. The dances were not all the peasant variety, but rather the ones that could be danced more easily, particularly the polka, waltz, and schottische. Finally, the tunes themselves would be hybrid, somewhat altered traditional melodies.[26]

A similar experience was that of the small community of Slovaks in Milwaukee during the same period. This group was not large; many more of them lived in Chicago, Cleveland, and Pittsburgh. But a recent publication of the Slovak Historical Society of Wisconsin expressed commonly felt sentiments of American-born members who grew up in the jazz age and took part in both the majority and minority cultures. Readers were reminded of the pleasure of learning both the fox trot at school and the czardas and polka at the Slovak dance hall. By the 1930s, the Milwaukee city directory listed sixteen Slovak bands (there well may have been more) that performed at both private and public community functions. This amazing number was only a part of the musical organizations performing; other ensembles came from Slovak communities elsewhere.[27]

Another recorded case of the vitality of old-time music in a multi-generational ethnic community at this time was Polish polka music in Utica, New York. Like Milwaukee, this small upstate city was essentially a manufacturing center that had drawn the new immigrants of the late nineteenth and early twentieth centuries. Utica's most prominent foreigners were the Italians of East Utica and the Poles of West Utica and nearby New York Mills. According to a folkloric field study, traditional music was very popular among several generations of Poles around 1930. Many small bands performed at private as well as the more public occasions.[28] At least two second generation Polish American musicians who played as teen-agers in small community bands in the 1930s did so because they found they could earn some extra money. One said that he was a member of a musical family, and that both the foreign-born and some of their children comprised their enthusiastic audiences.[29]

A final example of the popularity of old-time ethnic music was the orchestral tradition of the Baca Family Orchestra of Fayetteville, Texas. In the mid-1800s, Joseph Baca of Austria, a dulcimer player, had settled in a region of German and Bohemian farming families, the eastern Texas grasslands. He taught music to his several sons, one of whom, Frank, in 1892 established the band, which became a regional institution. The high point of the Baca Band was probably its fortieth anniversary celebration held in Fayetteville in 1932. The occasion drew four other bands and a huge audience, indicating the significance of its repertoire among Central and Eastern Europeans of different ages.[30]

These examples suggest that this traditionally based music played a significant part in the lives of both immigrants and their children in the years before World War II. Sources suggest that such popular music tended to unify families rather than divide them. A similar kind of ethnic music and musical performance, with a similar impact on a group, was that of the Italian band. This ethnic musical genre however, differed from that of other immigrants because it soon achieved a distinctively high place among the general Yankee public. A number of Italian band leaders became well-known in America, but one leader stands out as the most famous: Giuseppe Creatore, who rivaled John Philip Sousa in artistry and reputation.

Band music had emerged by the 1880s as a widely accepted form of entertainment for many Americans. One estimate is that by 1889 as many as ten thousand bands performed across the country. Normally, local merchants and occupational groups provided the financial support and sponsorship as part of their civic obligation as well as for more practical reasons. It was often clear that the Italian-born instrumentalists, generally the players of wind instruments, were among the more talented members of these American bands. By the turn of the century a few all-Italian bands had begun touring and establishing a wide reputation for quality performance. Their repertoire would be eclectic, to be sure, but they would include specifically Italian ethnic pieces, marches, and arias from Italian opera. Some scholars contend that the Italian band tradition originated in the Old World ritual of the *festa*, where on certain religious occasions Italian villages would honor a patron saint.[31] Italian bands performed the same function as German, Scandinavian, and Polish bands did for their neighborhoods, and Italian bandmasters provided excellent musical entertainment. In receiving the acclaim of their Anglo-American listeners, these musicians simultaneously built individual self-esteem.

Songs such as "Beer Barrel Polka" and "Blue Skirt Waltz" were polka-style tunes that sold a million records during the thirties and forties. The reasons for this national enthusiasm for polka music are suggested by Albert Maisel, who comments on the extraordinary popularity of polkas among the younger generation. Maisel refers to the effect of the phonograph records and radio and the stylistic modifications of ethnic pieces.

> The performers who recently have exercised the greatest influence—among the juke box set at any rate—are the leaders of polka bands. For many years while such groups provided Polish language radio programs with traditional mazurkas, polkas, and obereks, they attracted only a Polish audience. Then they changed their style, added a batch of hot licks, put in a Gene Krupa beat (he too is a Pole), translated old lyrics into English, and wrote a batch of new ones. Suddenly low power radio stations found themselves capturing network audiences as millions of high school live wires began arguing the merits of Frank Wojnarowski's pressing of "Broke But Happy Polka" versus Bernie Witkowski's "Wa, He Say Mambo." In Chicago recently one disc jockey casually asked his listeners to name their favorite polka band. Within three days he had received 22,000 postcards.[32]

Maisel was writing at the height of the enthusiasm for old-time polka music; it would soon decline in the face of the emerging rage for rock.[33]

The reference to phonograph records and the changing forms of disseminating popular music highlight the significance of the new entertainment technology in the interwar era. Records did not neglect, but rather promoted, ethnic music. Along with radio, the new technology did much to educate its audience about old tunes. Almost from their very start, American recording companies highlighted traditional music and conveyed it beyond its original group in America. Most important, by regenerating tradition, records aided in the assimilation of ethnic members: one could even say that the new discs took some of the native-born back to their roots. A brief review of the phonograph industry and its sensitivity to ethnic music illustrates that conclusion.

Until the 1930s, record companies had no real competition in broadcasting popular songs and other musical pieces. After Edison invented the phonograph in 1877 and Berliner and Johnson perfected the disc record around the turn of the century, records became the most common and accepted form of listening to musical entertainment. The industry continued to expand; record production increased from about 325,000 in 1909 to more than 100 million by 1919, a number maintained until the depression. The medium was an integral part of the lives of Americans of all classes. Phonographs were in 250,000 homes in 1919, and in probably half of our households by 1930. Records cost a few cents; the machine on which to play them, a few dollars.[34]

The phonograph industry, it is true, suffered serious reverses because of the depression, competition with radio, shortages of material, and strikes during World War II. Record output, for example, plummeted 90 percent with the coming of the depression. But record companies recovered by the late 1930s with the help of the jukebox. Further, radio became less a competitor and more an aid to record sales thanks to disc jockeys. Thus, by 1945, sales were again up to about $100 million, with about two hundred million records sold.[35]

One must conclude that even with the setbacks, the impact of this musical medium was pervasive over the first half of the century. But one ought not to assume that because this was an American industry, its overall affect would be to homogenize its audience culturally, forcing majority Anglo-American influences upon particular immigrant colonies. The general impact was probably the opposite. In the early years, a majority of the pieces recorded were foreign, not domestic. The industry's philosophy from the very beginning was to meet the musical tastes of all its customers, not just the Anglo-Americans.[36] They found a fertile market among the immigrant communities in America; by 1919, Victor was heavily promoting ethnic records, and Columbia followed.[37] By the early 1920s, these leading record companies set up long catalog lists of the more popular ethnic pieces.[38]

The outpouring of records designed specifically for ethnic consumption was sizable in scope and sales. For example, Victor cut 15,000 between 1923 and 1952; Columbia issued more than 1,300 Italian, almost 800 Polish, and hundreds of others for each of many smaller groups, and the other companies followed suit. Victor's "V" International Series of the 1920s and 1930s consisted of records for twenty-three different groups, including small ones like Albanians and Syrians.[39]

A list prepared by Richard Spottswood indicates the full extent of ethnic records in the entire industry. This discography enumerates all ethnic records made between 1893 and 1942, with about 150,000 entries.[40] Clearly, a popular American medium through the first half of this century was recognizing the traditional although modified musical heritage of almost every one of our immigrant groups. That fact alone could have forced Hansen to revise his generational hypothesis about the Yankee destruction of immigrant culture.

From a review of one type of ethnic record and the functioning of three major immigrant music firms, Sajewski and Vitak and Elsnic (both of Chicago) and Surmach of New York City, we can get a general impression of the business of making ethnic records.

Unquestionably the most popular kind of recording in the late 1920s was not the simple song, dance, or tune, but rather a skit or short playlet concerning the immigrants' most treasured life event, the wedding. It memorialized the one moment in their lives during which many traditional customs were cultivated. The piece that sold the most copies was the Okeh-Columbia recording, "Ukrainske Wesele [Ukrainian Wedding]," a twelve-inch platter led by the well-known folk fiddler Pawel Humeniak. Recorded late in 1925, it was a traditional account, with the most familiar Ukrainian songs and dances, of the relationship between marrying ethnic families. The record sold an amazing 125,000 copies, purchased by many non-Ukrainians from Central and Eastern Europe. In fact, Columbia realized its success and had Humeniak record another version, almost as popular, in Polish.[41]

Of course Humeniak's success was unique only in its superior sales; many other ethnic artists did well with similar traditional pieces. The most popular Swedish accordionist, for example, was Eddie Jarl. One of his records sold close to a hundred thousand copies.[42] Humeniak, Jarl, and a host of other ethnic musicians, artists, and singers helped to reinforce traditional values and customs, providing a bond between immigrants and their children in the interwar era.

How these American recording companies found such musical talent in the ethnic communities reveals the manner of music promotion inside these groups. Agents were usually ethnic businessmen who operated music stores. Some retailers turned to selling musical instruments, later publishing and selling sheet music and records. In fact, some of these businessmen did more than just engage in the trade, they actively promoted it. They located talent for recordings and helped put on radio programs.

Three of the leading ethnic music promoters in America in the interwar period were the Polish Sajewskis of Chicago, father Wladyslaw and son Alvin; the Czech uncle and nephew, Louis Vitak and Joseph P. Elsnic of the same city; and the Ukrainian Myron Surmach of New York City. For their own profit and self-interest they sought to dispel cultural inferiority. These three firms were representative of businesses in other locales.

Wladyslaw Sajewski had opened his store in 1897 on the famous Polish north side of Chicago in the most Polish neighborhood of the most Polish American city. He began offering musical and cultural wares when he noticed the growing demand for them. In the years leading to World War I, the firm began publishing sheet music after it found someone to write out and arrange the more popular Polish folk songs and *koledy* [Christmas carols]. The business prospered when Wladyslaw's son, Alvin, joined him around World War I. It was to the Sajewski firm that Columbia records turned to when it wanted Polish artists for its ethnic green label series. The Sajewski firm had by then become the leading nationwide purveyor of Polish sheet music.[43]

Myron Surmach provided the same service for Ukrainians and other Slavic and East European Americans. He became much more involved than Sajewski in the new medium of radio. Surmach became an agent and talent scout for Columbia, Victor, and Okeh records in the 1920s and promoted the music on ethnic radio.[44]

The most important old-time musical firm in America was Vitak and Elsnic of Chicago. The company had begun before World War I as Georgi and Vitak, selling musical instruments, particularly the traditional button box concertinas and accordions. However, with the appearance of Joseph P. Elsnic as a partner in 1924 and the retirement of Vitak in 1926, the business turned more to publishing, arranging, and selling the familiar Central and Eastern European folk music. By the depression it became the largest distributor of old-time ethnic sheet music in the United States.[45]

The existence and the success of these three music firms in the middle of the depression certainly suggest the strong appeal of old-time music among their customers. One also must remember that while much of their sales were in-person transactions, other profits came from a sizable mail order business, making the impact of their sales national rather than just local. One might also speculate about the similar function and financial condition of ethnic music firms in other immigrant centers at this time, as the ones among the Greek community in Chicago, the Slovenian in Cleveland, the Scandinavian in Minneapolis, the German in Milwaukee, and the Irish in Boston.

While the ethnic colonies themselves continued to listen to the old tunes, such ethnic persistence also had an impact on American popular culture. Old-time music was breaking the confines of the immigrant enclaves and becoming a part of mainstream American culture, largely because of the work of ethnically rooted but nationally known entertainers. These personalities originally had been a part of the internal group band network. But with ambition for success and stardom, a willingness to go on the road and tour widely, and, most important, with a repertoire that would appeal to a multiethnic, multigenerational audience, these musicians helped remake American popular music. Three of the best known bands and their leaders were "Whoopee John" Wilfahrt of New Ulm, Minnesota; Lawrence Welk of Strasburg, North Dakota; and Frankie Yankovic of Davis, West Virginia and Cleveland.

The success of this trio was not wholly their own doing. The timing of their appearance was favorable. Even before World War I, historians have referred to a shift in societal values that made entertainment, especially music and dancing, a much more important part of people's lives. Americans became more concerned with individual needs and desires, consumption, recreation, and personal fulfillment.[46] An especially appealing element of old-time music was the fast-growing rage for social dancing. With the onset of the depression, a particularly inexpensive form of recreation was an evening in a ballroom or dance hall dancing not only an American fox trot, but also the more ethnic polka and waltz. As accounts of these three old-time leaders show, the late 1920s and the 1930s were the heyday of the dance ballroom.

While widely popular in the region he performed, the Upper Midwest, "Whoopee John" Wilfahrt had a national following due, in large part, to the more than a thousand records he made for Decca. The full dimension of his appeal is probably best indicated by the fact that he was third in Decca sales, after Bing Crosby and the Andrews Sisters. His standard repertoire was German-style polkas, but his audience derived from many ethnic backgrounds.

It is important to note in light of Hansen's "law" that Wilfahrt's second generation parents strongly encouraged him to play the traditional pieces. The grandson of German immigrants, he was born in Sigel Township near New Ulm, Minnesota in 1893. His mother played a significant role in fostering her son's musical interest in old-time tunes. The town's array of German bands created an atmosphere favorable to his playing; indeed, New Ulm's continual claim of being the nation's polka capital has considerable merit.[47] He mastered the concertina as a youth, and by the time he was fifteen Wilfahrt had formed a small band that performed at various local occasions. Shortly thereafter, he adopted his mother's favorite piece (possibly in gratitude for her support), the traditional "Mariechen Waltz," as the theme tune he kept the rest of his career.[48]

Wilfahrt's playing became very popular, and he expanded his group to a ten-piece orchestra around 1918. His break into wider popularity came in 1924 when he went on radio in Minneapolis on WLAG, later WCCO. This appearance may have been the first time that an old-time polka-style band appeared on a major metropolitan radio station. He stayed on WLAG for six years and remained on Twin Cities' radio until his death in 1961. Wilfahrt left New Ulm permanently in the late 1920s and played regularly at the major German and American ballrooms in the Midwest for the next three decades. He also was a pioneer in recording, making his first record in 1927. His music was not exclusively ethnic, but multiethnic pieces that were Scandinavian, Bohemian, and Polish in origin, and had an American instrumentation.[49]

During the depression, Whoopee John Wilfahrt's band and its distinctive yellow Dodge bus with blue lettering and red wheels were a familiar sight on the roads of Wisconsin, the Dakotas, Iowa, and Minnesota. He had two million-selling record hits: his theme and the better known Polish "Clarinet Polka."[50] Wilfahrt achieved national visibility when he signed with Jack Kapp of Decca Records in 1938, four years after the firm had begun.[51] The height of his popularity was immediately after the war, the high point during the golden age of old-time music.[52]

While Whoopee John Wilfahrt had promoted old-time and had been a beneficiary of its multigenerational popularity, a more popular bandleader with a similar background from the Upper Midwest shared in that music. Lawrence Welk differed from Wilfahrt in his more burning desire to lead a nationally popular big band. He tempered this assimilationist drive by including old-time and found phenomenal success.[53]

Welk's example also qualifies Hansen's generalization because Welk was a member of the second generation. He was born to immigrant parents in 1903 near Strasburg, North Dakota. Like the Wilfahrts, his family provided an appropriate musical atmosphere; his father taught him to play the accordion, and Lawrence was often engaged to perform at family affairs, neighbors' weddings, and barn dances.[54] The young German American hated farm life, so he decided to leave home in 1924 to make his way as a musician. He traveled widely until he gathered a small band and got a permanent engagement in 1927 with a radio station, WNAX in Yankton, South Dakota. Welk's Novelty Orchestra played primarily popular pieces on the air, as well as some old-time tunes, and continued to tour the many ballrooms in the region.

By 1940, Welk's Champagne Music, as it was called, became familiar to dancers in the East as well as the West after extended engagements in hotels in Pittsburgh and Boston. But the Midwest remained the more supportive audience into the 1940s, after Welk was established at the palatial Trianon Ballroom in Chicago. He appealed to a youthful audience who liked his mixture of old-time with some swing pieces such as the fox trot and rhumba. He described a typical Trianon evening, when most of his patrons were of East European descent: "It was the custom . . . for groups of boys and girls to come separately as well as on dates, and many a lifetime romance began with a . . . dance at the Trianon. Some nights we had a predominately Polish audience, and how that big room would come to life then! The Polish polka is very fast, very quick and requires tremendous endurance. Watching from the stage as the dancer bobbed up and down [sic], it used to look to me as if the whole floor was on springs."[55]

Welk responded to critics of his novel combination of old-time and swing music mixture by insisting that he played what his audience wanted. As he put it, "The prime purpose of entertainers is to entertain and give the audience what it wants, always consistent with basic moral standards."[56] Unlike more famous jazz and swing leaders, Welk was not trying to educate his audience, only entertain them, and he met a felt need of his dance-mad listeners. But with his modernized polka and waltz, he remained a regional figure and did not achieve national stature until later in the 1950s, after moving to California. One of his major limitations was that he had no hit record until 1961.

The band leader who did the most in winning national acceptance for polka music was an ex-foundry worker from Cleveland, Frankie Yankovic. Yankovic was much younger than his two other old-time colleagues. But like Welk, he, too, was of the second generation and played in part for his age cohort. Just after his birth, in Davis, West Virginia, in 1916, his musically minded Slovenian family moved to their group's major colony in Cleveland. Yankovic played the button box accordion by the time he was eight. His playing had the enthusiastic blessing of his mother and father, like that of Wilfahrt and Welk. Like them also, he found part-time employment at neighborhood social occasions and weddings.[57]

By the early 1930s, Yankovic had won a good regional following through touring the Midwest and appearing on a Slovenian radio program in Cleveland. The city had a rich ethnic radio schedule for its nationalities by 1935; station WJAY and two of the city's other four stations had widely available ethnic programs.[58] Ethnic programming was common in many American cities by the mid-thirties; Cleveland's was unusual only in its vast coverage.

Yankovic was fortunate to be in a city whose people were both a resource and an enthusiastic audience for his music. Like Wilfahrt and Welk, he sought to modify his repertoire to appeal to the American working class in general. As he put it: "I always figured if I aimed my music at only one nationality I would be cutting down the market. So I tried to develop a sound that all nationalities could identify with."[59] Besides aiming at a multiethnic audience, he also wisely selected excellent musicians. After returning from service in World War II, he promoted an Americanized polka style by hiring a friend, Johnny Pecon, who had been known for his artistry on the chromatic accordion and for his arrangements.[60] For the next twenty-three years, Yankovic made more than two hundred records for Columbia, two of which, "Just Because" and "Blue Skirt Waltz," were his biggest hits.[61] He and his arranger borrowed and modified hillbilly, German, Czech, and Italian folk tunes.[62]

One final reason for Yankovic's national success was his readiness to travel all over the country to publicize his records. Unlike Welk, he was not interested in competing with the big bands; his group was small, without the kind of brass instrumentation of the large ensembles. Still, Yankovic booked his "Yanks" in Hollywood and New York nightclubs as well as the more common venues in the Midwest. By 1950, Yankovic had become the leading polka entertainer for all ages and generations. As one observer put it, Yankovic had "converted jitterbugging teenagers as well as their more sedate elders to enjoy polka music."[63] In several band contests held between 1948 and 1957, Yankovic's Yanks emerged as the audience's favorite by a wide margin.[64]

Yankovic's appeal peaked around 1955. Although he continued to get about three hundred bookings per year through the 1950s, he simply did not draw the crowds of young people that he did formerly.[65] Most likely the reason for his declining popularity was the music public's developing interest in rock. However, Yankovic still retained a part of his audience, probably the older segment, as he continued to make records for Columbia, RCA Victor, and others into the 1960s.[66]

Conclusion

The popularity of ethnic folk dancing, ethnic music, and old-time bands in the three decades after World War I clearly revises Hansen's notion that the children of the foreign-born fully rejected their parents' culture. One would have to admit, however, that some tension between the generations did exist. But the music and dance of the Old

World were attractive characteristics of that older way of life for immigrant children. The waltzes and polkas were accessible and enjoyable to nearly everyone. Great enthusiasm within the group for these elements of culture, even if modified, existed at the most intimate private family affairs, at large public occasions, and when listening and dancing to records and the radio. In essence, a new ethnic folklore was formulated from the old.

Some forms of traditional dance and ethnic music captivated members of several generations of ethnic and of nonethnic Americans. In a neglected essay, Nathan Glazer observed that it was the immigrants who pluralized American popular culture. To those agents I would add immigrant offspring, record companies, music firms, and radio stations.[67] If Hansen, one of our most distinguished historians, had carefully considered the popular music of his day, perhaps he would have agreed.

NOTES

1. Marcus Lee Hansen, "The Problem of the Third Generation Immigrant," republication of the 1937 address with introductions by Peter Kivisto and Oscar Handlin (Rock Island: Swenson Swedish Immigration Research Center and Augustana College Library, 1987), p. 6.

2. Hansen, "The Problem of the Third Generation," pp. 12–14.

3. Quoted in Wayne Moquin and Charles Van Doren, eds., *A Documentary History of Italian Americans* (New York: Praeger Publishers, 1974), pp. 368–69.

4. Note the lament of a president of one of the ethnic historical societies, Thaddeus Radzilowski, "The Second Generation: The Unknown Polonia," *Polish American Studies* 43 (Spring 1986):5–7.

5. Hansen, "The Problem of the Third Generation," p. 14.

6. Marcus Lee Hansen, "Who Shall Inherit America?," *Interpreter Releases* 14 (July 6, 1937):226–33, especially pp. 227, 231–32.

7. Maurice R. Davie, "Approaches to the Study of Nationality Groups in the United States," in *The Cultural Approach to History*, ed. Caroline F. Ware (New York: Gordon Press, 1940, repr. 1974), pp. 74–75, 78.

8. Elizabeth Burchenal, *Folk Dancing as a Popular Recreation: A Handbook* (New York: G. Schirmer, 1922), pp. 1–22; Betty Casey, "Elizabeth Burchenal," in *International Folk Dancing, USA* (New York: Doubleday, 1981), p. 13.

9. Pat Mooney Melvin, "Building Muscles and Civics: Folk Dancing and the Playground Association of America," paper given at the Organization of American Historians, April 1981, pp. 7–9, 17; Dominick Cavallo, *Muscles and Morals: Organized Playgrounds and Urban Reform, 1880–1920* (Philadelphia: University of Pennsylvania Press, 1981), pp. 1–5, 30.

10. Edith Terry Bremer, *The International Institutes in Foreign Community Work: Their Program and Philosophy* (New York: Woman's Press, 1923), especially p. 6. Raymond Mohl, "Cultural Pluralism in Immigrant Education. The International Institutes of Boston, Philadelphia, and San Francisco," *Journal of American Ethnic History* 1 (Spring 1982):35–38.

11. Dorothy G. Spicer, "The Folk Festival and the Community," *Foreign Born* 3 (August–September 1922):208–9. The basic Institute handbook for folk festival preparation and performance seems to have been Spicer, *Folk Festivals and the Foreign Community* (New York: Woman's Press, 1923).

12. Florence Gertrude Cassidy, *Second Generation Youth* (New York: Woman's Press, 1930), pp. 43–44.

13. Vytautas Beliajus, "To Keep the Record Straight," *Viltis* 30 (May 1980):7, 19; interview with Beliajus, Denver, June 17, 1983.

14. Vytautas Beliajus, "The Changing Scene of the Lithuanian Folk Dance in the United States," in "Laisvojo Pausalio Lietuviu Sestoji Tautiniu Sokiu Sventi: The Sixth Lithuanian Folk Dance Festival," Chicago, 1980, p. 74.

15. Vytautas Beliajus, "Folk Dancing in Chicago," *Recreation* (September 1936), reprinted in *Viltis* 39 (May 1980):10–11; Beliajus, "Changing Scene," p. 74.

16. See *Lore* (May 1936):1–2; (October 1936):2; (June 1939):9; Gretel Dunsing to author, June 27, 1984, May 10, 1984.

17. Interview with Lorraine McGrath, St. Paul, August 7, 1983; *St. Paul Pioneer Press*, June 20 and 27, 1920; Alice Sickels, *Around the World in St. Paul* (Minneapolis: University of Minnesota Press, 1945), pp. 75–76, 245, 248; Fern Kruse interview with author June 20, 1983; telephone interview with Alfred Sokolnicki, Milwaukee, November 26, 1984. For Mama Gravender, see Robert H. Willson and George and Emilia Hodel in a series of articles in the *San Francisco Chronicle*, November 5, 1932, p. 16; and Mary King to author, February 9, 1984; interview with George Shinn, Sausalito, August 6, 1984; Elba Farabegoli, "My Philosophy of Life and the Bearing of Religion on It," July 14, 1935, typescript in Elba Farabegoli Gurzau papers, Balach Institute, Philadelphia; interview with Gurzau, Philadelphia, May 10, 1984; Gurzau, *Folk Dances, Costumes, and Customs of Italy* (Philadelphia: Published privately, 1981), pp. 89–90.

18. Interview with Read Lewis, New York, February 23, 1984; Lynn Schweitzer, "Foreign Language Information Service," in *Social Service Organizations*, ed. Peter Romanofsky (Westport: Greenwood Press, 1978), pp. 311–13. I am deeply grateful to Selma Odom of York University, Toronto, for sharing her research on Hinman, especially her draft "Mary Wood Hinman" for the *International Encyclopedia of Dance*.

19. Mary Wood Hinman, "Educational Possibilities of the Dance," *Journal of Health and Physical Education* 5 (April 1934):15.

20. Mary Ann Herman, "Americans Dance Foreign Folk Dances," *Focus on Dance* 6 (1972):73; *Folk News* (publication of the Folk Festival Council), July 27, 1932.

21. Box 6, Boston International Institute Collection, Immigration History Research Center, University of Minnesota; *International Beacon*, November 15, 1936.

22. Interview with Michael Herman, Queens, N.Y. July 14, 1983; telephone interview with Mary Ann Herman, December 4, 1984; Richard Wurts, *New York World's Fair 1939–1940* (New York: Dover, 1977), p. xvii; *The Folk Dancer* (May 1942):n.p. and (March 1942):1.

23. From the *New York Herald Tribune*, May 8, 1932; see also February 26, 1933.

24. Mary Ann Bodnar, "The Pendulum of Percentage," in *What It Means to be a Second Generation Girl: Talks Given at the Second Generation Dinner at the National Board of the YWCA, April 10, 1935* (New York: Woman's Press, 1935), pp. 15–16, 19–21.

25. H. F. Mooney, "Popular Music since the '20s: The Significance of Shifting Taste," *American Quarterly* 20 (Spring 1968):68, 73.

26. From Phil Martin, *Across the Fields: Fiddle Tunes and Button Accordion Melodies* (Dodgeville: Folklore Village Farm, 1982), pp. 4–9.

27. "Muzicky . . . Muzicky, Muzicky," in *Wisconsin Slovak* 4 (Autumn 1983):2–4.

28. Susan G. Davis, "Utica's Polish Music Tradition," *New York Folklore* 4 (Autumn 1978):103–5.

29. Davis, "Utica's Polish Music," pp. 104–5, 114–5.

30. *Baca's Musical History, 1860–1968: An Old Texas Czech Band and Orchestra* (La Grange: La Grange Journal, 1968), pp. 4–7, 12–14, 27, 29; Clinton Machann, "Country Western Music and the 'Now' Sound in Texas-Czech Polka Music," *JEMF Quarterly* 19 (Spring 1983):3–7.

31. Emma Rocco, "Italian Bands: A Surviving Tradition," *Pennsylvania Ethnic Studies Newsletter* (Winter 1980):1–2.

32. Albert Q. Maisel, *They All Chose America* (New York: Thomas Wilson 1955), p. 217, quoted in *Ethnic Recordings in America: A Neglected Heritage* (Washington: American Folklife Center, Library of Congress, 1982), pp. 25–26.

33. Christine Ann Paton, "The Evolution of the Polka from 1830 to 1980 as a Symbol of Ethnicity and Disunity," master's thesis, Wayne State University, Detroit, 1981, p. 36.

34. My statistics are from Pekka Gronow, "The Record Industry: The Growth of a Mass Medium," in *Yearbook, Popular Music,* ed. Richard Middletown and David Horn (Cambridge: Harvard University Press, 1983), pp. 59, 62; Leroy Highbanks, *Talking Wax or the Story of the Phonograph* (New York: Hobson Book Press, 1945), pp. 7, 16, 34, 62, 113.

35. Highbanks, *Talking Wax*, pp. 114–7.

36. Gronow, "The Record Industry," p. 60.

37. Richard Spottswood, "Do You Sell Your Italians?" *JEMF Quarterly* 15 (Winter 1979):225–27.

38. Columbia had thirty-three different ones. Kathleen Monahan, "The Role of Ethnic Recording Companies in Cultural Maintenance: A Look at Greyco," *JEMF Quarterly* 14 (Autumn 1978):145.

39. Pekka Gronow, "Ethnic Recordings: An Introduction," in *Ethnic Recordings*, p. 23. See also *Victor International Records, "V" Series* (n.p., 1941).

40. Richard Spottswood, "Ethnic Music on Records: A Discography of Ethnic Recordings Produced in the United States, 1894 to 1942," manuscript, John Edwards Memorial Foundation, Folklore and Mythology Center, University of California, Los Angeles (in press, University of Illinois Press); Spottswood to author, March 1987.

41. Richard K. Spottswood, "Commercial Ethnic Recordings in the United States," in "Ethnic Recordings," pp. 60, 61, 63.

42. Gronow, "Recordings," p. 16.

43. Interview with Alvin Sajewski, Chicago, December 29, 1984.

44. Myron Surmach, The History of My "Surma": Memoirs of a Bookseller (in Ukrainian) (New York: Published privately, 1982), chap. 14.

45. It was Elsnic, for example, who brought the "Beer Barrel Polka" to America, and a sizable percentage of all polka music recorded in America were Vitak and Elsnic arrangements and compositions. Interview with Lawrence Musielak, Chicago, July 26, 1985.

46. Warren Susman, Culture as History: The Transformation of American Society in the Twentieth Century (New York: Pantheon Books, 1984).

47. "Bands Have Played Big Role in New Ulm," Historical Notes (New Ulm: Brown County Historical Society, 1982), pp. 184, 187–92.

48. From a scrapbook in the possession of Adeline Wilfahrt of New Ulm. I am deeply indebted to her.

49. Wilfahrt composed at least one hundred of the pieces he played and had the benefit of a superb arranger, Jim "Red" McLoed. Interviews with Vern Steffel, St. Louis Park, Minn., March 3, 1987, and Jim McLoed, Oshkosh, Wisc., June 14, 1987. McLoed wrote some of the pieces ascribed to Wilfahrt.

50. Clipping in Whoopee John file at the Brown County Historical Society, New Ulm, Minn.

51. Herbert Allen to Whoopee John Wilfahrt, January 10, 1931; Jack Kapp to Whoopee John Wilfarht, March 25, 1938, Dennis Wilfahrt Collection, St. Paul.

52. Louis Sebok to Whoopee John Wilfahrt, May 20, 1946, May 12, 1950; interview by Glen Reed of WMNE, all in Dennis Wilfahrt Collection.

53. The two best biographies are Lawrence Welk with Bernice McGeehan, Wunnerful! Wunnerful! (Englewood Cliffs: Prentice-Hall, 1971) and Ted Hilgenstuhler, Lawrence Welk (Los Angeles: Peterson, 1956).

54. Hilgenstuhler, Welk, p. 15.

55. Welk, Wunnerful!, p. 183.

56. George T. Simon, The Big Bands (New York: Macmillan, 1967, rev. ed., 1974), pp. 449–51; Welk, Wunnerful!, pp. 190–91.

57. Good biographical material is in Derek Van Pelt, "The Polka: The Dance that Refuses to Die," Cleveland Magazine 4 (April 1975):87; and Frankie Yankovic, as told to Robert Dolgan, The Polka King: The Life of Frankie Yankovic (Cleveland: D. L. Books, 1977), esp. pp. 14ff, 24.

58. Twenty-two programs were beamed at ten groups in 1935: Polish, German, Slovenian, Slovak, Czech, Hungarian, Croatian, Greek, Italian, and Jewish (Yiddish). John Mihal, "Radio Stations Here Lead in Old World Music Programs," The Cleveland News, March 30, 1935, p. 9B.

59. Yankovic, *Polka King*, p. 7.

60. *The Polka Journal* 3 (1952):1.

61. His total sales reached more than six million, some original compositions; Yankovic, *Polka King*, p. 15.

62. Newspaper article, "Frankie Yankovic, the Reigning King of the Polka," in the Fred Kuhar Collection, Clevland, Ohio. I am grateful to Kuhar and Jeff Pecon.

63. Gene Hersh, "The Revival of the Polka," *Cleveland Plain Dealer*, November 18, 1968.

64. Yankovic, *Polka King*, pp. 8–9.

65. Hersh, "Revival," n.p.

66. His touring never ended as he continued to appear in his seventies at engagements nationwide. Polka music experienced a minor revival as Yankovic received his first Grammy award by the National Academy of Recording Artists in 1986. It is significant that the record which won him the honor was a largely retrospective album.

67. Nathan Glazer, "The Immigrant Groups and American Culture," *Yale Review* 48 (Winter 1959):395–97. I disagree with his suggestion that the national culture was homogeneous before 1870.

PART THREE

Implications:
Hansen in Context

Paradigm Changes in Interpretations of Ethnicity, 1930–80: From Process to Structure

This discussion attempts to outline a major shift in ideal-typical interpretations of immigration and ethnicity by analyzing a sample of major works at approximately twenty-year intervals—the 1930s, the early 1950s, then the 1970s. It is concerned with the interpretive paradigms—the filters through which authors make sense of their data, built from assumptions about human nature, values, the direction and meaning of history—that can be detected in the literature of immigration and ethnicity at these moments. The literature of the 1930s reflected a pervasive view of life as process and (usually) progress, as a continuing interaction of individuals in perpetual motion given direction by secular tendencies toward the liberation of the individual from external constraint. Turning to the more voluminous and varied literature of the 1970s, a major trait of the most influential work can be called structural in that it views immigration (like other subjects) through filters that highlight the fixed, repetitive, limiting elements that contain experience, set limits to its potential for novelty, for creating new values and forms of organization unsanctioned by preexisting theory. The third historical moment, crystallized in Oscar Handlin's influential *The Uprooted*, marks the point of transition between the two ideal-typical interpretations.

An obvious caveat may need notice. The difference between "processual" and "structural" is always an ideal-typical one, and in specific works will always be one of degree and emphasis. Processual interpretations are not wholly unaware of persistent elements; structural interpretations usually are aware of the need to deal with change. The crucial difference lies in what is taken as axiomatically given or "natural," needing little explanation, and what is taken as novel, puzzling or "unnatural," hence needing explanation. Sometimes the theoretical presuppositions that underlie an interpretation will be so powerful that very little is left to seem problematic; the interpretive vision makes sense of everything all too neatly. Many will feel that such was the case with the optimistic emotional penumbra that usually accompanied the process interpretations of the 1930s; it is a matter of greater controversy whether this remained true of later interpretations. But it does seem reasonable to claim that the changing interpretations of immigration and ethnicity afford an excellent case study of a more general proposition: the values and assumptions about cause and meaning the scholar brings to the study of documents play a major if inconsistent role in molding the final interpretation.[1]

The interpretive filters through which professional sociologists and historians organized their study of immigration between the two world wars saw life as an endless series of interwoven processes. The unusual dynamism of these interpretations was in part a reaction against the earlier structural school that had seen ethnic differences and immigrant "problems" as unalterable givens, fixed by blood or racial inheritance. By the mid-twenties, such racialist theories were subject to strong critique, along with associated essentialist theories of human nature that postulated fixed instincts as the sources of behavior. The ascendant view rested on the theories of the Chicago School of sociology, whose professors and students wrote a large share of the immigration literature. Perhaps the most general statement of the process model was made by the influential Michigan sociologist, Charles Horton Cooley, who defined society as

> a complex of forms or processes each of which is living and growing by interaction with the others, the whole being so unified that what takes place in one part affects all the rest. It is a vast tissue of reciprocal activity, differentiated into innumerable systems, some of them quite distinct, others not readily traceable, and all interwoven to such a degree that you see different systems according to the point of view you take.

Cooley quoted Albion Small, the founder of the Chicago department of sociology: the larger social process was "a tide of separating and blending social processes, consisting of incessant decomposition and recomposition of relations within persons and between persons, in a continuous evolution of types of persons and associations."[2]

This version of society as patterned evolutionary process, stressing mutability, multiple perspectives, and dynamic interrelations, rested on the pragmatic philosophy of James and Dewey, with its rejection of fixed categories, structures of thought and judgment (except such processual norms as "growth"); at greater distance it codified broad assumptions of American thought since the early nineteenth century. The basic social unit was not the group or institution, but the individual human being. This individual was seen not as a preformed essence; although a basic human nature was assumed to exist, this nature was seen as malleable, open to influence, capable of making itself over without irremediable psychic damage. As its assumption suggests—that reality lay in transformation rather than fixity—process theory was an academic expression of a major theme of nineteenth-century romanticism filtered down through native gurus like Emerson and Whitman, and also via the European theories of society that influenced the founders of American sociology.

Like any theory that found eager consumers, these ideas could serve an ideological function in that they made sense of the pervasive, implicitly frightening change of the era between the Civil War and World War II in terms that made it seem constructive, not destructive. As words like *growth* and *evolution* suggest, the process was seen not as random or limitless, but as operating toward predictable and ultimately benevolent ends. It is in this vague area, the emotional penumbra where logically distinct ideas blur together, that the abstract model of process joined to American nationalism to produce a vision of a richer, more mature society that would emerge from the interwoven, often undeniably painful changes that characterized modernizing America.[3]

Many examples of the pervasiveness of this process model can be culled from the literature of sociolgy and history, at least through the watershed of the years after 1945. The assumption that radical change was inevitable and nondestructive because it released the full potential of the individual, and the derivative axiom that such group categories as ethnic identity were mutable without loss, were the premises that gave power to the work of Louis Wirth, the leading sociologist of ethnicity during the 1930s and 1940s. (Horace Kallen, the champion of ethnic persistence and plurality, was a philosopher by profession, not a historian or sociologist.) Wirth himself had emigrated from a German village to the Midwest, and his sense of personal liberation from the closed community of his childhood, his joy in the release of energy and talent he had experienced, were reflected in his sociological writings. To these feelings was joined the professional ideology of emotional neutrality toward his subjects that his Chicago mentor Robert Park insisted was a desideratum of the "scientific" as against the polemical approach to any topic. Chicago sociology encouraged empathy with subjects, thinking into their consciousness, but insisted that this must be separated from sympathy or championship. The intense recreation of the emotional horrors of migration that some later work displayed would probably have seemed to them an abandonment of objectivity for projection of anachronistic emotional states onto people who could not talk back.

Another Chicago-trained student of ethnic groups was William C. Smith, who wrote a monograph that was actually titled *Americans in Process*. Smith's work also reflects the interwar sociologists' stress on subjective experience, as captured through "personal documents," in the style pioneered by Thomas and Znaniecki's *Polish Peasant in Europe and America*. Subjective states of mind were, however, assumed to show a correlation to stages in the immigrant's progress through a variety of institutions and mileux toward the working relationship with others that constituted "assimilation" in the realistic definition of that loaded word given by Chicago sociology. Not only immigrants but also host societies were seen in process toward the secular, differentiated modern world; and as Park said, "assimilation" in such a society involved functional relations more than emotional ones. The sociologists of process (if not the historians) were already acquainted with European theories of evolution from primitive to complex, sacred to secular, gemeinschaft to gesellschaft. The transformation of attitudes around mid-century would involve not only novel theories, but also a radical shift of sentiment toward the relative value of enveloping community and secular society.[4]

It was in great part their theory of history as a general process of modernization that prevented the sociologists from treating assimilation merely as conformity to a preexisting Anglo culture. The America into which newcomers assimilated was the network of interacting processes expressed by Cooley, with no elements exempt from the pressure to redefine through interaction. The same assumption lies behind the fact-choked writings of interwar historians, with their tendency to fall into catalogs of the contributions of ethnic communities to the evolving American society. Later historians, eager to belittle their professional ancestors, have often viewed as atheoretical antiquarianism the lists of notable immigrants, societies founded, and musical works introduced that clutter even less filiopietistic works like Carl Wittke's *We Who Built America*. If one understands the process paradigm through which it was assumed these lists would be read, then they become illustrative examples of the process by which the interaction of ethnic groups reshaped and enriched the developing American culture. Wittke showed his awareness of Kallen's critique of assimilation as leading to vulgarity, noting his regret "that many immigrants conform so quickly and completely in all respects to 'American standards,' and become genuinely ashamed of their heritage. The man with two cultural homes is much less to be feared than the man who has none at all."

But the dominant paradigm was that of process in its optimistic form, which equated change with progress. Continuing immigration, over a long period, helped to keep American society open, fluid, generous, a place where all Europeans might share in peace and prosperity. The contrast between American peacefulness and European bellicosity and militarism was powerful in Louis Wirth as well, and indicates one source of the shift in attitudes that would soon come.[5]

Wittke stressed one trait of American society, obvious on reflection, which would sometimes become obscured by the later stress on ethnic groups as coherent communities carrying distant cultures. Citing Whitman, Bret Harte, and "nearly half the painters listed in John C. Van Dyke's *American Painting and its Tradition*," he pointed out that "the American stock is so varied that one man may be descended from a half dozen immigrant groups and from as many religious sects." For one who accepted the notion of America as a society in creative flux, with what Louis Wirth called a "crescive" culture, this was an opportunity not a calamity because elements of past cultures would enter the kaleidoscope of contemporary creativity to further enrich the process. It is a difficult question to what degree the emerging pluralist attitude reflected a greater sense of group consciousness among newer immigrants as against different emotional responses to the costs of change among those who wrote about ethnicity.[6]

It was Marcus Hansen who, after the posthumous publication of *The Atlantic Migration* and *The Immigrant in American History*, came to represent the most sophisticated and broadly researched work on immigration by a historian before the 1940s. As Peter Kivisto has noted, Hansen's writings, especially his seminal "Third Generation" essay, are capable of interpretation in more than one way. It may be read as an empirical proposition, to be tested by surveys of attitudes among the grandchildren of emigrants, or it may be taken as a metaphor of the loss of roots by all Americans during the process of modernization. It has been merged with persisting religious differences to postulate three long-term cultures based on religion, and it has been taken as an anticipation of the (allegedly) recent awareness that ethnicity is a subjective trait of identity that may wax and wane, be transformed in each generation as new needs arise in new situations. These multiple readings of "The Problem of the Third Generation Immigrant" are unsurprising, in part because Hansen may have been unaware of real ambiguities in his argument, but also because the variant interpretations are based upon theories that hardened into distinct entities after Hansen's death. Historians are prone to the fallacy of the blind men and the elephant, seizing upon one aspect of a complex whole in order to pigeonhole it into one or another category that was only defined later in time. The result is often to chop off the margins of subtlety that made the original provocative and still able to stimulate reappraisals of conventional categories.[7]

It does seem, however, when reading Hansen while attempting to keep later categorizations at bay, that his work, including the "Third Generation" essay, remained very largely inside the descriptive paradigm of process, and compared with what came later did not move far from the optimistic view of America as the land of progress that formed the interpretive penumbra around the descriptive model. Despite a glancing reference to the "bitterness" and "heart-breaking features" of the immigrant experience, his account of the reemergence of ethnic awareness and pride is not based on a sense of defeat, resentment, or injustice, nor on a loss of faith in the value of the experiment that immigrants joined. Quite the contrary, it was a sense of achievement and success that gave the third generation the security to look back with pride to the richness of the European heritage and the contributions of their ancestors to the new society. "Neoethnicity," to use a later coinage, was a function not of alienation but of "assimilation" in Robert Park's definition, of having made a name for oneself and one's group. Hansen's third generation are not alienated intellectuals, but solid burghers able to break bread amiably with George F. Babbitt.[8]

Hansen's hypothesis remains within the process paradigm in another sense. Although he sees it broadly, Chicago-style, as a "natural history" or predictable evolution, his account of the revival of ethnic awareness stresses the subjective, willed quality of such awareness, its responsiveness to changing context. The second generation had chosen to "forget" as a matter of "policy," and the new context of achievement and acceptance led the third generation to look back with pride. And, as a consistent process theorist would assume, further change was likely. Hansen noted that "resurgences of national spirit" were "periodic," and his example of the Scotch-Irish suggested that a decline of this spirit was also possible if the conditions for its intensity eroded. Hansen's two books, if we take them as representing his intentions, also seem to support the argument that he remained inside the process model on its descriptive side and never moved far from the valuational assumption that process had been linked to progress. Acknowledgments of the pain and suffering entailed by benevolent change were commonplace much earlier; Park loved to quote his teacher William James, that "progress is a terrible thing," but his overall model, like Hansen's, remained one of stoic acceptance if not simple affirmation. It would remain for the next generation to focus on the pain and question the value of what had been achieved.[9]

This challenge, delivered with a rich mix of sociological awareness and literary vividness, was the achievement of Oscar Handlin's *The Uprooted*, published in 1951. This widely read book has helped to mold attitudes toward immigration and America that would become stereotypical among millions of students over at least two generations. For all its simple surface and overall coherence of view, it is a complex book, incorporating elements of process theory along with an intensely felt personification of classic European social theory. Since it appeared in a new edition in 1973, with Handlin's account of its intellectual origins and his reflections on subsequent writings about immigration, *The Uprooted* has become a multilayered text whose afterthoughts help explain things left implicit. But it must also be read with care because Handlin's own viewpoint seems to have shifted, like that of so many New York intellectuals, between 1950 and 1970. The care is justified because the multiple layers of the book—recollection of influences, original text, and later reflections on how Americans viewed "the immigrant experience," to use a phrase Handlin helped to inspire—interact with each other and afford insight into the sources and consequences of the conceptual revolution in the study of ethnicity (as in other fields) that took place at midcentury. The special elements of *The Uprooted* can be summed up within three categories: the interpretation of data through concepts drawn from classic European social theory; the emotional and stylistic influence of imaginative literature mixed with the theoretical categories; and associated with both of these, the new sensibility generated in New York intellectuals by the traumas of the 1930s and 1940s as filtered through the newly popular literature of alienation. All these elements interacted to form a distinctively new approach, some of whose traits can be expressed through the suggestion that *The Uprooted* was the first history of immigration to express both the theoretical sophistication and the sensibility suggested by the noun *intellectual*.[10]

The reconceptualization of immigration in terms of classic sociological theory is vivid and obvious in general import, although elusive in terms of precise sources. In his Afterword in the 1973 edition, Handlin notes that as a junior member of Harvard's new social relations department, formed to unify the theory and methods of all the social sciences, he was commissioned to "compile a canon of social science classics," those written before 1920. No exact list of thinkers is given, although Handlin notes that earlier, following "the common hope of historians that others would absolve them of the necessity for original thought," he had read "MacIver, Marx, Durkheim, Sombart, Weber, Mannheim and Pareto." In the absence of a precise list, it seems a reasonable conjecture that the classic thinkers would have included those who dominate Robert Nisbet's delineation of *The Sociological Tradition*: Simmel and Toennies, he of gemeinschaft/gesellschaft fame, as well as Tocqueville, Marx, Weber, and Durkheim. And anyone familiar with *The Uprooted* will realize that to a remarkable extent it is a vivid, personified illustration of the basic transformation from traditional to modern forms of society that was the central theme for all these thinkers.

In *The Uprooted*, America serves the role Gertrude Stein had given it—as the first and oldest example of modernity. Wrenched out of the tight envelope of belonging and meaning that was "the community of the village," immigrants had lost a "precious sense of solidarity." "Seen from the perspective of the individual received rather than of the receiving society, the history of immigration is a history of alienation and its consequences." The immigrant experience was indeed a time of crisis, a word with emotional intensity in the 1940s: "while the old roots were sundered, before the new were established the immigrants existed in an extreme situation." In the traditionless new environment, responses could not be "easy, automatic." The transformation of sociological and moral context here is profound. What Wirth and his generation had seen as liberation was now seen as a stripping naked comparable to that undergone by prisoners. In an ingenious passage Handlin characterized the familiar conservatism of immigrants in terms that reflected the skepticism of post-Holocaust intellectuals toward the Enlightenment faith that had still molded the writings of people born a generation earlier: "Confronted with the prevalent notions of the inevitably of progress, of the essential goodness of man and his capacity to rule his own life, of the optimistic desirability of change, peasants and dissenters alike felt a chill distrust, a determination to resist, a threat to their own ideas." In the open American society, with its lack of rules and heirarchy, there was "no security of status...only money talked." There are echoes here of Tocqueville, whose work in the late 1940s was undergoing a major revival that would make him a basic source for the understanding of America. And the immigrants' distrust of American optimism recalls that most influential moralist of the same years, Reinhold Niebuhr; a plausible subtitle for *The Uprooted* might have been "The irony of immigrant history."[11]

The influence of classic sociological theory on *The Uprooted* seems clear. Handlin, however, has challenged the suggestion that he "applied social science theory to my data," because he "never declared allegiance to a coherent system. Nor did I test hypotheses." This statement seems to reinforce the interpretation offered here—while indeed not using sociological methods of verification, and indeed reducing a variety of

somewhat divergent theories to their common core, their root metaphor, he did project this single vision distilled from a complex tradition
onto a broad canvas where it made sense of details drawn from the
literary remains, the letters and newspapers, left by the immigrants. It
is the power of the basic vision, combined with the richness of detail,
that gave *The Uprooted* much of its special magic, the almost visual
intensity of a densely painted canvas like that of a painting by one of
the Old Masters.[12]

One problem remains in the attempt to clarify the relation between
The Uprooted and its theoretical sources. The older American sociologists explicitly, and the historians implicitly, had employed a version of what came to be called "modernization theory" in their efforts
to give meaning to the story of immigration. But, as noted previously,
this version stressed the individual as the basic unit of the ongoing
process, and usually also assumed the process of modernization to be
relatively benevolent. Its leading theoretical source was Herbert Spen-
cer, as modified in a voluntarist direction by James and Dewey, with
the liberal German sociologist Georg Simmel as an additional influence
on the Chicago School. The other great European theorists, like Toennies, Durkheim, and Weber, were not unknown but did not become
part of the basic interpretive paradigm until their championship by
Talcott Parsons at Harvard in the mid-1930s, followed by translations
and entrance into the newer canon of postwar social science.

One difference between the theorists influential on the earlier generation and those influential after 1945 is the relative stress placed on
the individual as against the group. For at least some of the later
influentials, notably Durkheim, the group was the basic ontological
reality; individuals were excrescences of the collectivity that had
molded them, and their personal reaction to situations were highly
typical and predictable. Without intending to imply any direct influence, such a view of individuals as predictably reacting in terms of an
older culture to new situations does characterize the anonymous, ideal-
typical people who populate *The Uprooted*. It had been their group
membership that gave meaning and direction, and when this was lost
in the breakup of community, they came close to losing a sense of
self. There is, at least, a certain congruity between the newer European
influences and the radically transformed view of the immigrant experience found in Handlin's seminal work.[13]

Further, as Nisbet notes in his classic history of social theory, the
concept of Community in continental European thought (but not in
the Anglo-American liberal tradition) stemmed from Edmund Burke's
polemics against the French Revolution and later antirevolutionary
writers like Maistre and Bonald. In these writers the polarity between

traditional and modern carried a built-in moral message: "legitimate society," made up of "kinship, class, religion, and locality, and cemented by tradition," was the healthy environment; the emerging modern society, resulting from "democratic leveling, unchecked commercialism, and rootless rationalism," carried the seeds of human destruction. Even those theorists, like Toennies and Durkheim, who denied a nostalgia for premodernity, tended to transmit such a nostalgia to the consumers of their ideas if the consumers had been sensitized to the argument that the horrors of the twentieth century stemmed precisely from the loss of traditional restraints on human aggression. And the educated audience of the 1940s had been steeped in this argument through such widely discussed works as Erich Fromm's *Escape from Freedom* and the work of popular psychiatrists and cultural anthropologists. By 1950, critiques of liberal modernity from both conservative and socialist sources had converged to express a new skeptical stance toward the older progressive confidence in change, and this intellectual context would tend to bring out elements in classic sociology that had previously been subordinated to the faith in process as progress.[14]

In *The Uprooted*, the pure theoretical influence was blended with the use of imaginative literature as a source of ideas, images, and literary strategies. Handlin noted in 1973 the persuasive power that novels of immigration had on him as he tried to put the materials of his project into coherent form. And certainly the emotional ambiance of the book, its stress on loss—loss of meaning and security, the terrible uncertainty of life in the volatile new America—echoes the emotional message of some of the most popular of the novels Handlin cited. In Ole Rolvaag's *Giants in the Earth*, the corpse of the progressive-minded immigrant, Per Hansa, who has been impatient with his traditionalist wife, is found, when the snows melt, staring emptily westward across the plains. And the Italian family in Pietro Di Donato's *Christ in Concrete* lives and dies around the all-important "Job," a reiterated term whose capitalization suggests the Biblical analogy. These are good people tormented by the unfair demands of an alien, exploitative society. Much of *The Uprooted*'s power stems from the fusion of the sociological types with the direct emotional statement and personalization of types into characters found in the novels. Intellectual penetration and emotional power are fused in a classic example of the truth that it is not density or precise fit of documentation that makes a seminal work of scholarship, but rather emotional power, clarity of conceptualization, and congruence with contemporary needs. And the fusion of ideal type with literary power was not idiosyncratic in American scholarship of the 1950s; one way to characterize *The*

Uprooted's achievement is to see it as a founding exemplar of the American Studies school with its use of imaginative literature to capture the subjective intensity, or as it came to be called, the "experience" of immigration, or of any novel milieu, as against the kind of broad but distant causal and consequential interpretation that drained the emotion from the older use of personal documents.[15]

The third context in which *The Uprooted* needs to be placed is the vaguest, the most difficult to pinpoint, but possibly the most important. The intellectual and emotional milieu of the New York intelligentsia of the 1930s and 1940s has been the subject of a phethora of books that stress its special quality as a close-knit network of children of recent immigrants. Educated in local public universities where standards were high, they had an unusual awareness of Europe and of the contemporary crisis of Western civilization that made political radicalism the norm. Some of the theoretical sources of the new realistic liberalism of the 1940s have been noted previously, but there were broader forces, stemming from the historical position of this group. Raised in East Coast metropolises, oriented toward continental Europe by their families and by contemporary events, they developed a mentality quite different from that of the midwestern children of immigrants who had been writing about their parents' experience until the 1940s. It has been said that Richard Hofstadter (who moved from Buffalo to New York City for graduate school) was the first professional historian to view American history from the standpoint of New York City; but Oscar Handlin, Hofstadter's almost exact contemporary who began publishing a few years earlier, was born and raised in New York City before going on to graduate school, the study of European social theory, and a distinguished career at Harvard, the old-line university most open to the latest intellectual trends. And this mix of East Coast metropolitan environment with close study of European rather than American theory is one functional definition of what was new in the New York intelligentsia of the 1930s and 1940s. Hofstadter's seminal work on the tradition and mentality of mainstream American politics achieved a creative break with that tradition, with the sense of continuity and membership with the past which had characterized American liberal historiography until the 1940s. Handlin's achievement in the study of ethnicity was exactly parallel, in arriving at a "mid-Atlantic" point of view that put into the spotlight of analysis the older American viewpoint from which his materials had previously been viewed.[16]

Appropriately, it was Hofstadter, in a brilliant review of *The Uprooted* that appeared (also appropriately) in *Partisan Review*, who pointed out that the central innovation of the book was its point of view. "Mr. Handlin has made of the immigrant's story a parable of alienation. Across the gulf that separates intellectuals from immigrants he has built a bridge founded on one thing that they unmistakably share: their estrangement from America, their experience of constant pressure to make them something other than what they are. . . ."

It is a sign of generational homogeneity of perspective that Hofstadter, like Handlin but unlike earlier historians, assumed that immigrants were "estranged." He did, however, note problems in the ideal-typical method of *The Uprooted*—its "exclusiveness," its concentration on just one typical career out of several, the difficulty of discerning its representativeness. Above all, he noted a problem that would echo down through the literature of immigration over the next generation. The book, he felt,

> also has a tendency to make of the immigrant's case a prototype of all suffering, appropriating to the immigrant several burdens that have been borne by others as well, and minimizing the immigrants' gains by failing to look at the poverty, famines, wars, and persecutions faced by those they left behind. This is a tale of *acute* poverty, *extreme* hardship, *severe* shame and agony. . . . The author has yielded, I believe, to a tendency which, as Lionel Trilling recently noted in these pages, has grown fashionable among us, to deal only in the strongest shades in the spectrum of emotion, with the consequence that moderate feelings, and shades of feeling, become devalued. It is as though the case of the immigrant could not command our sympathy if it were not set before us as a continuing agony. Mr. Handlin has, nonetheless, produced one of the most remarkable works of the historical imagination in recent years.[17]

To judge from his later comments, Handlin came to share some of Hofstadter's recoil from melodrama as younger scholars reinforced and hardened into an orthodoxy the view of "the immigrant experience" as one of overwhelming degradation and alienation. The theme of the neoethnicity of the late sixties and seventies, he felt, was: "*We have been made victims!*"

> America had created the void by the theft of their ancestors; now the victims needed the healing pride of ethnicity....The yearning to belong was already evident two decades before; the goal then however was a place in the gray-flanneled ranks which offered marchers the illusory security of homogeneity. Disabused, the ache not stilled, the men and women of 1970 were more likely to choose ethnicity as an anchor for life styles, values and tastes. . . . There now seemed an advantage to identification, just as earlier there had been an advantage to assimilation. . . . Therefore they huddled together, . . . seeking in the nest of the familiar the security lacking in the wide open spaces.

The insistence on a unique "experience" and sensibility for each group intensified—"only Catholics, only Jews, only Poles, only Italians. Then spread still further: only women, only youth . . . perhaps till finally: Only I, ME."[18]

It is a difficult question to what extent this protest represents a change of opinion from 1951. Certainly *The Uprooted* was a watershed volume in that the new sensibility it expressed was still combined with many elements of the process model—an awareness that immigrants did change, that the notion of distinct ethnic groups was to a degree a mental fiction, useful to intellectuals, and an open mind on the ultimate outcome of the long process of building a new society. Certainly there was no blaming in *The Uprooted*; it reflected the older view of objectivity as seeing large-scale processes in which people were pawns of progress, not of evil individuals. It may be that the audience interpreted the book in terms of a sensibility more stereotypically alienated than the one Handlin imagined; indeed, he may have gone for intensity of color from an assumption that a complacent audience needed the power of art to break down its defenses. But the audience, especially the student audience, was changing along with the writers of history. For example, having taught the literature of immigration to Canadian students for a generation, I can affirm the power with which *The Uprooted* speaks to the double alienation of many students—their estrangement as late adolescents from "a world they never made," but into which they must assimilate, and their distance as Canadians from the overbearing, exploitative elephant (i.e., the United States) that threatens to crush them. This is a context of consumers the author could not well have had in mind, and may point up the ironic importance of the audience in understanding the influence of scholarship as of other literature.

It may well be that this later reading of Handlin's great work is as important as any more recent work in explaining the most striking interpretations of immigration and ethnicity in the next generation. But a more abstract and conceptual treatment may also enlighten the change away from the optimistic processualism of the innocent 1930s. Here we encounter the problem of exponential prolificity—far more scholars and publicists have been producing, and far more relatively distinct points of view can be discerned, sometimes in the same volume. Some scholars, like Andrew Rolle, attempted direct replies to Handlin, stressing the variety of origins, careers, and achievements found among emigrants from Italy. Others, like Humbert Nelli, conceptualized their subject through a mix of Hansen with Handlin to provide a more rounded view of the career of one group, stressing the persistence of ethnic identity along with structural assimilation into a new American society. Some, like Philip Taylor, kept the broad questions raised by the polemics in mind as they assembled scrupulous factual accounts of the details of the process. These works may well last longer as secondary sources than the overt polemics; but the purpose of this discussion is to treat salient works as symptomatic of their own time. It is therefore concerned with those books that express attitudes toward ethnicity that echoed concerns of the 1960s and 1970s. Here, a certain parallelism appears to unite a number of responses to the older liberal view, which on the surface appear to be based on distinct theories of human nature and change. As noted previously, the common theme consists of a structuralist approach to psychology, sociology, and ethics, an approach that contrasts markedly with the older processual viewpoint.[19]

The various structural theories through which the American past, including ethnicity and immigration, were viewed employed diverse sectors of imagined experience as arenas in which structures ruled: the fixed structure of the psyche; the inner arrangement of emotional energy charges that could be nurtured or eroded by social values and strains; the long-term arrangement of society into a number of distinct units, called classes and institutions, which might be seen as harmful but are assumed to rule behavior and limit the possible; and the theory of ethics that sees a universal, knowable human nature as the basis for a structure of judgments on the events of experience that allows clear, definite categorization of them as good, bad, constructive, and harmful. Such structural theories are subjective in the sense of being mental constructs, but their believers think of them as objective in being given by the data of experience and confirmed by empirical analysis. They have in common the axiom that basic reality lies not in process, transitiveness, but in fixed entities and the recurrent relations among them. These structures contain events in two senses: they define their meaning, and they suggest the effect of their import on existing reality.

Whereas the inspirational thinkers for the process theory were men such as Emerson, Whitman, James, Dewey, and Simmel, the basic names underlying the structuralisms outlined here are (in order) Freud, Marx, and Aristotle as supplemented by Aquinas for the Catholic tradition of ethics. There are enormous differences among these three traditions, but in contrast to the older American liberalism they share the belief that there exists a basic, stable, and knowable reality, on the basis of which definitive judgments can be made of actions and types of society. The final standard is not something as vague as Dewey's "growth," but concrete norms prescribing the proper function of particular statuses. Taken together, they can be seen as a continuation of the conceptual changes signaled by the ascendancy of intellectuals such as Hofstadter and Handlin at midcentury. These are classic continental European thinkers, distinctly different from the Anglo-American tradition earlier dominant. Their stress on structural limits rather than endless possibilities may be seen to reflect a new awareness after midcentury of the superficiality of older, native types of thought.[20]

The most familiar type of structural interpretation is the one that postulates a relatively diverse society organized according to definable and relatively stable subcategories called classes, strata, or institutions. Such theories differ markedly in several dimensions, including the degree to which movement across subcategorical lines occurs or is desirable. Some social-structural theories, like Burkean conservatism, are approving; and one important theme in ethnic history has been the contrast between a golden age of stratified belonging and the naked competition of modern society. Other theories of social structure are analytical and judgmental, like the Marxian model, which postulates that everyone is held in a position inside an oppressive structure that limits opportunity, defines interest and consciousness. Marxian theory passes a negative ethical judgment on this structure and assumes its ultimate dissolution, but it merges with the sanctioning theories in postulating that position in a given social structure molds what the individual human being is and can aspire to.

In illustrating the effect of specifically Marxian categories on American historical writing one quickly trips over the problem of specificity and overlap. In a general way, the influence has been large, although often domesticated into a Beardian-Populist style of interpreting events as caused by conscious interest groups. Marxian theory is complex, and its influence on immigration history may be discerned in the insistence that ethnic consciousness either expressed class differences or served as superficial fault lines of conflict that prevented the natural solidarity of economic groups from expressing itself. This perspective is perhaps more common among British and European students. Barbara Ballis Lal, for example, raises questions about the tendency to see ethnic consciousness as an expression of coherent cultures rather than as "a stratification phenomenon, that is as a strategy for pursuing interests." Lal sees the assertion of common ethnic interests as a disguised expression of "class-related interests," which use an honorific language of cultural coherence as psychic necessity that is derived from the writings of social science.

From this perspective, the very language of ethnicity is a kind of false consciousness that employs the symbolism of "belonging" and "togetherness" to legitimate material interests. Accounts by native scholars in the Marxian tradition are more likely to accept the Handlinian process of deculturalization and enforced individuation, but add to it a concomitant depoliticization that may derive from thinkers like Gramsci and Herbert Marcuse. Elizabeth Ewen, in *Immigrant Women in the Land of the Dollar*, sees assimilation as the absorption of the second and third generations into a commercial culture where "patriotism, freedom and consumption become interchangable ideas." The capacity for corporate action to change society that had been based on ethnic consciousness is lost, and assimilation thus results in empty conformity and political helplessness.[21]

The most forceful and consistent radical account of the significance of ethnicity in modern America is in Gabriel Kolko's *Main Currents in Modern American History*. The "industrial reserve army" of immigrants was forced unwillingly out of Europe by "famine, overpopulation and sheer poverty," mechanization, "industrial stagnation," pogroms, and other external forces. Except the Jews, the "vast majority came with the explicit intention of remaining temporarily," raising enough money to improve their existence after returning home. "On this point there is no dispute, and it means that in terms of subjective orientation a large section of the de facto American working class was a transitional one." Thus, the aspiration of migrants to return meant they saw the indignities of the American workplace as "a transitional experience." One might say that they were premature Americans in the paradoxical sense that great expectations of a return to a premodern community undercut the solidarity needed for political action. For those who did have to remain in America, ethnic identity became a mask of belonging that hindered the emergence of real class consciousness. Statistics on the incidence of mental illness established the pathological effect of emigration to an exploitative society. The ethnic identity of the late nineteenth century was

> a kind of limbo ethnicity which left him with only slight knowledge of the most precious aspects of his own culture and only sufficient immersion in it psychologically to divide him from fellow workers who spoke other tongues. In the end, it produced a working class that was to a great measure both lumpen and insecure, accommodating but not assimilating in America, uncertain of its ultimate destination . . ., cut off from the larger society and even, to an increasingly remarkable and painful degree, his own ethnic community and family.[22]

The second type of structural theory is the psychological. A conception of human nature as composed of given, unchanging needs (with security and belonging central) was visible in *The Uprooted*'s statement of the nurturing qualities of the premodern community. And the 1951 edition's concluding assumption that a new coherence would appear to give meaning and security confirms this general psychological assumption. The degree to which this stable envelope of meaning could be combined with a society of self-defined, self-realizing individualists remains unclear. The fear Handlin expresses in the 1973 edition that the ethnic *we* would ultimately reveal the isolated, strident *me* suggests that Handlin's condemnation of the shriller versions of neoethnicity rested on the belief that it expressed a pathological rejection of bonds and responsibilities in general.[23]

Certainly such a fear of self-assertive individualism as a sign of psychopathology, of mental illness in the technical sense, has inspired a number of brilliant condemnations. The pioneer work was D. H. Lawrence's *Studies in Classic American Literature*, which had little influence on professional scholarship until after 1950. Echoing Lawrence, the most technically based indictment of American self-madeness as pathological is by another literary critic, Quentin Anderson. But *The Imperial Self* does not limit itself to pointing up infantile, regressive tendencies in stalwarts of American individualism like Emerson and Whitman. It stresses the social context that encouraged an immature individualism that promoted illusions of omnipotence over the clear perception of reality. Because of the repudiation of authority embodied in the Revolution, compounded by the rapid change of the expanding democracy, Emerson's generation failed to achieve the sublimations that led to an ability to distinguish between fantasy and external reality, and so projected this illusion of omnipotence and identity onto all experience. Anderson's is the most explicitly Freudian critique of American individualism, but there is a considerable literature of critical cultural history, elaborating at length Lawrence's remark that the archetypal American was a lonely, solitary killer. Combining Freudian and Marxian perspectives, this literature tends to see the United States as an aggressive and destructive society, a natural despoiler of more stable and coherent communities. Although most of this literature is not devoted primarily to immigrant groups, the analogy is clear: ethnic communities, like indigenous native peoples, are seen as virtuous victims, admirable because they are able to adjust to their natural environment in nondestructive styles. This is the worldview of large segments of the liberal intelligentsia, a mix of Freud, Marx, and Rachel Carson, forming a coherent critique of the American mainstream.[24]

There is a considerable overlap between this literature of condemnatory analysis and the most notorious, probably the most influential, writer on ethnicity in the 1970s, Michael Novak. Novak, however, is a distinctive and self-conscious thinker, writing through an elaborate set of assumptions about the structural needs of human beings that overlaps the Freudian and has some similarities to the Marxian, but which is explicitly rooted in classic and medieval European philosophy. Novak is a formally trained Roman Catholic theologian, and a very large part of his argument on many subjects is understandable in terms of his faithful application of the categorical givens of Aristotle and Aquinas about human nature and ethics. These thinkers share with Freud and Marx a traditional European assumption of fixed structures, subjective and objective, in terms of which American openness, fluidity, and transitiveness threatens meaning and morality.

Novak has written prolifically on many contemporary topics over twenty-five years. On the overt polemical level his views have certainly shifted, following many intellectuals who would be dubbed neoconservatives, shifting from indictments of mainstream America to defenses of its wisdom and resilience against radical critics. On the theoretical level, however, there is considerable continuity. Novak attacks his target of the moment in a predictable pattern of argument that rests on his theological view of human nature and the good society. The Aquinan view of society is similar to the Burkean one, an elaborate heirarchical structure in which each actor knows his or her place and function and collaborates fruitfully with others, treating them with proper courtesy and dignity. The damaging force, especially apparent in America, is the "protestant" principle, the tradition of defiance, transcendence, and perfectionism that destabilizes and leads to rashness, uncertainty, extremism, and aggression against the justified separateness of others.

This ethical stance is classic in its fear of romantic excess or enthusiasm; it bears a family resemblance to the social control interpretations popular among historians in the 1970s. And its targets have indeed shifted over the last generation. In the late 1960s Novak focused on the native American arrogance (rationalized by the faith in process-as-progress) that led to bulldozing urban neighborhoods at home and imperial aggression abroad. As the years passed, Novak's perception of threats to eternal values shifted to the "come-outer" rebels of the 1970s—feminists who demanded control over their bodies, gay rights activists, and champions of world revolution, all of whom shared the attempt to escape the objectively given constraints on infinite possibility laid down by the universal need for social and sexual differentiation. Indeed, while most neoconservatives are not theologians, Novak's explicit grounding in Aquinas reveals a common theme: a reaffirmation of universal structural constraints that limit the possibility of transcending all external barriers to realize radical dreams.[25]

Novak's explicit work on ethnicity, the influential *Rise of the Unmeltable Ethnics*, grows out of the earlier, apparently radical phase of his polemical life. It is, indeed, a good illustration of the argument that much modern radical writing employs the nostalgic image of a nurturing community lost to modernization, an image arising from the conservative tradition reviewed previously. Some commentators, myself included, have seen Novak's view as one that piles blame for all current evil onto a single ethnic group. This criticism neglects the extent to which the book is really a continuation of Novak's attack on the philosophical principles of Anglo-American liberalism and romanticism, now packaged in sociological form, with ethnicity as the objective correlative of belief. There are shrewd insights about the traditional subject of ethnicists, like the voluntarist, situational nature of neoethnicity; but the book's ambiguities stem from a premise that is clear in Novak's other works: the combination of political power with a dangerous pragmatic instrumentalism, lacking the protections of a fixed ethics, made America the world scourge. Paradoxically, Novak's ethical structuralism leads to a voluntaristic notion of ethnicity. As the book's title suggests, neoethnicity is an act of will, a voluntary assertion of preference for a traditional communal identity. The apparent paradox stems from the premodern, and perhaps postmodern, nature of Aristotelian structuralism, which is not determinist like that of Freud and Marx.[26]

The heavily deductive and philosophic nature of *The Rise of the Unmeltable Ethnics* may raise a practical question among scholars, What does this have to do with fact, with the documentable history of ethnic groups and consciousness in America? The answer to that question, for Novak's work as for others, would require a vast sifting of available documents and lead to a work far longer than his. Absent that formidable task, reactions are likely to be molded by the observer's own frame of reference. Realists, like Barbara Ballis Lal, might well classify Novak as a purveyor of false consciousness. But this judgment rests on a reductive theory of motives that belittles human needs for meaning, membership, and self-respect. From a more cultural perspective, *The Rise of the Unmeltable Ethnics* is a crucial document of modern American culture, embodying the rebirth of ethnic sentiment in response to two aspects of the 1960s: new, more radical challenges to what had been seen as social universals, and the indictment of America as the embodiment of evil among educated people around the world. For the purpose of this essay, Novak's work also affords the most direct and fully developed example of a structural account of ethnicity, which turned inside out the standard assumptions of older American writing. The transformation delineated here, itself highly selective and simplified, may serve also to illustrate a major change in the thought of American intellectuals over the last half-century: a re-

Europeanization of concepts and view-points that has made the older progressive tradition seem distant and vacuous.

NOTES

1. The approach used here is set forth more fully in Fred Matthews, " 'Hobbesian Populism': Interpretive Paradigms and Moral Vision in Recent American Historiography," *Journal of American History* 72 (June 1985):92–115.

2. On early American sociology, see Fred Matthews, *Quest for an American Sociology: Robert E. Park and the Chicago School* (Montreal: McGill-Queen's University Press, 1977), pp. 35–56, 94–105, 121–74; Charles Horton Cooley, *Social Process* (New York: Scribners, 1918), p. 28, n28.

3. On the kinship between romanticism and James's pragmatism, see Jacques Barzun, "William James as Artist," *New Republic* 108 (February 15, 1943):218–20. The radically relativist implication of process theory was held in check by the historical theory of progress that rationalized it until the 1940s; but it later led to such radical concepts as the labelling theory of deviance. See Fred Matthews, "Ontology and Chicago Sociology," *Philosophy of the Social Sciences* 15 (June 1985):197–203. The most searching conceptual analysis of the Chicago School is in Norbert Wiley, "Early American Sociology and *The Polish Peasant*," *Sociological Theory* 4 (Spring 1986):20–40.

4. On Wirth, see Fred Matthews, "Louis Wirth and American Ethnic Studies: The Worldview of Enlightened Assimilationism, 1925–1950," in *The Jews of North America*, ed. Moses Rischin (Detroit: Wayne State University Press, 1987); William C. Smith, *Americans in Process: A Study of Our Citizens of Oriental Ancestry* (New York: Arno, 1970; orig. pub. 1937); *Americans in the Making: The Natural History of the Assimilation of Immigrants* (New York: D. Appleton Century, 1939), esp. pp. xii, 114–27.

5. Carl Wittke, *We Who Built America: The Saga of the Immigrant* (Cleveland: Western Reserve Press, 1939), p. 362.

6. Wittke, *We Who Built*, p. xiii.

7. Peter Kivisto, "Hansen's Classic Essay After a Half-Century," in Marcus Lee Hansen, "The Problem of the Third Generation Immigrant," republication of the 1937 address with introductions by Kivisto and Oscar Handlin (Rock Island: Swenson Swedish Immigration Research Center and Augustana College Library, 1987), pp. 6–7.

8. Hansen, "The Problem of the Third Generation," pp. 16–17; Robert E. Park, "Assimilation, Social," in *Encyclopedia of the Social Sciences*, vol. 1, ed. Edwin R. A. Seligman and Alvin Johnson (New York: Macmillan, 1930), pp. 281–83.

9. Hansen, "The Problem of the Third Generation," pp. 17–18; Marcus Lee Hansen, *The Atlantic Migration, 1607–1860: A History of the Continuing Settlement of the United States*, ed. Arthur M. Schlesinger (Cambridge: Harvard University Press, 1940), esp. pp. 9–13, although p. 3 anticipates Handlin's portrait of village community; Hansen, *The Immigrant in American History*,

ed. Arthur M. Schlesinger (Cambridge: Harvard University Press, 1940), esp.
pp. 8–15, 24–7, 129–33. For James on progress, see Matthews, *Quest*, p. 32.

10. Oscar Handlin, *The Uprooted: The Epic Story of the Great Migrations that Made the American People*, 2d ed. (Boston: Little, Brown, 1973).
Two titles on a large shelf include Terry A. Cooney, *The Rise of the New York Intellectuals: Partisan Review and Its Circle 1934–1945* (Madison: University of Wisconsin Press, 1986) and Alan M. Wald, *The New York Intellectuals: The Rise and Decline of the Anti-Stalinist Left from the 1930s to the 1980s* (Chapel Hill: University of North Carolina Press, 1987). An attempt to summarize this literature is in Fred Matthews, "Role Models?," *Canadian Review of American Studies*, in press.

11. Handlin, *The Uprooted*, pp. 302–3 for encounters with theory; quotations from 1951 text (unchanged in 1973 edition): pp. 7, 94, 4–5, 5, 103–4, 104, in sequence; Robert A. Nisbet, *The Sociological Tradition* (New York: Basic Books, 1966), esp. pp. 47–106. On Niebuhr, see Richard Wightman Fox, *Reinhold Niebuhr: A Biography* (New York: Pantheon, 1985).

12. Handlin, *The Uprooted*, p. 303. This was a response to the valuable essay by Maldwyn A. Jones, "Oscar Handlin," in *Pastmasters: Some Essays on American Historians*, ed. Marcus Cunliffe and Robin Winks (New York: Harper, 1969), esp. pp. 240–45.

13. On Durkheim, see Nisbet, *The Sociological Tradition*, pp. 82–97, esp. pp. 83, 85. Nisbet sees in Durkheim a crucial shift from earlier users of the same broad conceptualization: he saw that no stability would be possible in modern society unless critical elements of traditional community, like the family, survived.

14. Ibid., p. 71; Erich Fromm, *Escape from Freedom* (New York: Farrar and Rinehart, 1941).

15. Handlin, *The Uprooted*, pp. 307, 332 (afterword to 1951 edition); Handlin in 1973 notes the problems raised by the representativeness of imaginative fictional accounts; Ole Rolvaag, *Giants in the Earth: A Saga of the Prairie* (New York: Harper, 1927); Pietro Di Donato, *Christ in Concrete* (Indianapolis: Bobbs Merrill, 1939), pp. 297–301.

16. On Hofstadter and the break with tradition, see Fred Matthews, "Historians and the Eclipse of Civil Religion," *Historical Reflections/Reflexions Historiques* 10 (Summer 1983):245–63.

17. Richard Hofstadter, "West of Ellis Island," *Partisan Review* 17, no. 2 (1952):252–56; quotations, pp. 252, 255, 256.

18. Handlin, *The Uprooted*, p. 277 (added 1973). For the 1951 Conclusion, pp. 268–73.

19. Andrew F. Rolle, *The Immigrant Upraised: Italian Adventurers and Colonists in an Expanding America* (Norman: University of Oklahoma Press, 1968); *American Italians: Their History and Culture* (Belmont: Wadsworth, 1972); Humbert S. Nelli, *From Immigrants to Ethnics: The Italian Americans* (New York: Oxford University Press, 1983); Philip Taylor, *The Distant Magnet: European Emigration to the U.S.A.* (New York: Harper, 1971).

20. This interpretation is not stated elsewhere to my knowledge, but the single thinker who comes closest to embodying and unifying all these influ-

ences was Handlin's senior colleague at Harvard, Talcott Parsons. See Parsons, *The Structure of Social Action* (Glencoe: Free Press, 1949; orig. pub. 1937); and Talcott Parsons, *The Social System* (New York: Free Press of Glencoe, 1954).

21. Barbara Ballis Lal, "Perspectives on Ethnicity: Old Wine in New Bottles," *Ethnic and Racial Studies* 6 (April 1983):154–73, quotations pp. 154, 168; Elizabeth Ewen, *Immigrant Women in the Land of the Dollar: Life and Culture on the Lower East Side 1890–1915* (New York: Monthly Review Press, 1985), p. 268.

22. Gabriel Kolko, *Main Currents in Modern American History* (New York: Pantheon 1976), pp. 68–69, 99, 97, 95–96.

23. Handlin, *The Uprooted*, p. 277.

24. Quentin Anderson, *The Imperial Self* (New York: Alfred A. Knopf, 1971); D. H. Lawrence, *Studies in Classic American Literature* (New York: T. Seltzer, 1923); Richard Slotkin, *Regeneration Through Violence: The Mythology of the American Frontier 1600–1860* (Middletown: Wesleyan University Press, 1973); Michael Paul Rogin, *Fathers and Children: Andrew Jackson and the Subjugation of the American Indian* (New York: Alfred A. Knopf, 1975).

25. Novak's most searching indictment of secular, humanist America is in *The Experience of Nothingness* (New York: Harper, 1970). An earlier, more balanced treatment of the native philosophical tradition is his introduction to *American Philosophy and the Future: Essays for a New Generation* (New York: Scribners, 1968), pp. 1–20, which includes a striking critical metaphor of human relations in America as an endless cocktail party. Novak's later views are in *Freedom with Justice: Catholic Social Thought and Liberal Institutions* (New York: Harper, 1984); and *Confessions of a Catholic* (New York: Harper, 1983). That Novak's structuralist ethics are shared by many non-Catholics is suggested by the popularity of Allan Bloom's *The Closing of the American Mind* (New York: Simon and Schuster, 1987).

26. Michael Novak, *The Rise of the Unmeltable Ethnics: Politics and Culture in the Seventies* (New York: Macmillan, 1972). A more detailed comment is in Fred Matthews, "Cultural Pluralism in Context," *Journal of Ethnic Studies* 12 (Summer 1984):63–78.

APPENDIX

MARCUS LEE HANSEN

The Problem of the
Third Generation Immigrant

[Delivered to the Augustana Historical Society, Rock Island, Ill., May 15 1937.]

By long established custom whoever speaks of immigration must refer to it as a "problem." It was a problem to the first English pioneers in the New World scattered up and down the Atlantic coast. Whenever a vessel anchored in the James River and few score weary and emaciated gentlemen, worn out by three months upon the Atlantic, stumbled up the bank, the veterans who had survived Nature's rigorous "seasoning" looked at one another in despair and asked: "Who is to feed them? Who is to teach them to fight the Indians, or grow tobacco, or clear the marshy lands and build a home in the malaria-infested swamps? These immigrants certainly are a problem." And three hundred years later when in the course of a summer more than a million Europeans walked down the gangplanks of the ocean Greyhounds into the large reception halls built to receive them, government officials, social workers, journalists said: "How are these people from the peasant farms of the Mediterranean going to adjust themselves to the routine of mines and industries, and how are they going to live in a country where the language is strange, and how are they, former subjects of monarchs and lords, going to partake in the business of governing themselves? These immigrants certainly are a problem."

They certainly were. The adventurers (call them colonists or immigrants) who transferred civilization across the Atlantic numbered more than forty million souls. Every one of them was a problem to his family and himself, to the officials and landlords from whom he parted to the officials and landlords whom he joined. On every mile of the journey, on land and on sea, they caused concern to someone. The public authorities at the ports of embarkation sighed the traditional sigh of relief when the emigrant vessel was warped away from the dock and stood out to the open sea carrying the bewildered persons who for a week or more had wandered about the streets; the captain of that vessel was happy when the last of his passengers who had complained of everything from food to weather said good-bye—often with a clenched fist; and the officers of New York and Baltimore were no less happy when the newly-arrived American set out for the West. How much of a problem the forty-million actually were will not be known until their history is written with realism as well as sympathy.

The problem of the immigrant was not solved, it disappeared. Foreign-born to the number of almost fifteen million are still part of the American population, but they are no longer immigrants. By one adjustment after the other they have accommodated themselves and reconciled themselves to the surrounding world of society, and when they became what the natives called "Americanized" (which was often nothing but a treaty of peace with society) they ceased to be a problem. This was the normal evolution of an individual, but as long as the group classified as immigrants was being constantly recruited by the continual influx of Europeans the problem remained. The quota law of 1924 erected the first dam against the current and the depression of 1929 cut off the stream entirely. Statistics reveal what has happened. During the year ended June 30, 1936, there were admitted as immigrants only 36,329 aliens. During the same period 35,817 aliens left the United States for permanent residence abroad—a net gain of only 512. But this was the first year since 1931 that there had been any gain at all. The great historic westward tide of Europeans has come to an end and there is no indication in American conditions or sentiment that it will ever be revived.

Thus there has been removed from the pages of magazines, from the debates in Congress and from the thought of social workers the well-known expression: the problem of the immigrant. Its going has foreshadowed the disappearance of a related matter of concern which was almost as troublsome as the first, a rather uncertain worry which was called "the problem of the second generation."

The sons and the daughters of the immigrants were really in a most uncomfortable position. They were subjected to the criticism and taunts of the native Americans and to the criticism and taunts of their elders as well. All who exercised any authority over them found fault with the response. Too often in the schoolroom the Yankee school-mistress regarded them as mere dullards hardly worthy of her valuable attention. Thus neglected they strayed about the streets where the truant officer picked them up and reported them as incorrigible. The delinquency of the second generation was talked about so incessantly that finally little Fritz and little Hans became convinced that they were not like the children from the other side of the tracks. They were not slow in comprehending the source of all their woes: it lay in the strange dualism into which they had been born.

Life at home was hardly more pleasant. Whereas in the schoolroom they were too foreign, at home they were too American. Even the immigrant father who compromised most willingly in adjusting his outside affairs to the realities that surrounded him insisted that family life, at least, should retain the pattern that he had known as a boy. Language, religion, customs and parental authority were not to be modified simply because the home had been moved four or five thousand miles to the westward. When the sons and daughter refused to conform, their action was considered a rebellion of ungrateful children for whom so many advantages had been provided. The gap between the two generations was widened and the family spirit was embittered by repeated misunderstanding. How to inhabit two worlds at the same time was the problem of the second generation.

That problem was solved by escape. As soon as he was free economically, an independence that usually came several years before he was free legally, the son struck out for himself. He wanted to forget everything: the foreign language that left an unmistakable trace in his English speech, the religion that continually recalled childhood struggles, the family customs that should have been the happiest of all memories. He wanted to be away from all physical reminders of early days, in an environment so different, so American, that all associates naturally assumed that he was as American as they. This picture has been deliberately overdrawn, but who will deny that the second generation wanted to forget, and even when the ties of family affection were strong, wanted to lose as many of the evidences of foreign origin as they could shuffle off?

Most easy to lose was that which, if retained, might have meant the most to the civilization of the American republic. The immigrant brought with him European culture. This does not mean that the man who wielded the pickaxe was really a Michaelangelo or that the one who took to house painting was in fact an unrecognized Rembrandt. They brought a popular though uncritical appreciation of art and music; they felt at home in an environment where such aspects of culture were taken for granted and (what is not to be overlooked in any consideration of the development of American life) they did not subscribe to the prevailing American sentiment that it was not quite moral for a strong, able-bodied man to earn his living by playing a fiddle. If they did not come in loaded down with culture, at least they were plentifully supplied with the seeds of culture that, scattered in a fertile soil, could flourish mightily.

The soil was not fertile. Americans of the nineteenth century were not entirely unfriendly to a little art now and then if it were limited to the front parlor and restricted to the women. Even a man might play a little, sing a little and paint a little if he did it in a straightforward, wholesome way and for relaxation only. But these foreigners, most of whom had been in Paris and set up what they called a studio where they dawdled away the hours, day and night, were not to be trusted. Let them earn their living by doing a man's work instead of singing arias at the meetings of the woman's club in the middle of the afternoon or giving piano lessons to the young girls, thereby taking away the source of livelihood from the village spinster who also gave lessons and willingly sang for nothing. The second generation was entirely aware of the contempt in which such activities were held and they hastened to prove that they knew nothing about casts, symphonies or canvas. Nothing was more Yankee than a Yankeeized person of foreign descent.

The leaders among the native proclaimed loudly: It is wonderful how these young people catch the spirit of American institutions. The leaders among the foreign-born sighed and said to themselves: This apostasy means nothing good. It is not good for the sons and daughters who give up a heritage richer than farm acres and city lots; it is not good for this uncouth pioneer nation which has spent its time chopping down trees and rolling stones and has never learned how the genius of one might brighten the life of many and satisfy some human longings that corn bread and apple pie can never appease. Blind, stupid Americans, they said, the one nation of the globe which has had offered to it the rich gifts that every people of Europe brought and laid at its feet and it spurned them all. The immigrants, perhaps, may be excused. Their thoughts and efforts were taken up with material cares and they were naturally under some suspicion. But nothing can absolve the traitors of the second generation who deliberately threw away what had been preserved in the home. When they are gone all the hope will be lost and the immigration of the nineteenth century will have contributed nothing to the development of America but what came out of the strong muscles of a few million patient plodders.

These pessimists were wrong. All had not been lost. After the second generation comes the third and with the third appears a new force and a new opportunity which, if recognized in time, can not only do a good job of salvaging but probably can accomplish more than either the first or the second could ever have achieved.

Anyone who has the courage to codify the laws of history must include what can be designated "the principle of third generation interest." The principle is applicable in all fields of historical study. It explains the recurrence of movements that seemingly are dead; it is a factor that should be kept in mind particularly in literary or cultural history; it makes it possible for the present to know something about the future.

The theory is derived from the almost universal phenomenon that what the son wishes to forget the grandson wishes to remember. The tendency might be illustrated by a hundred examples. The case of the Civil War might be cited. The Southerners who survived the four years of that struggle never forgot. In politics and in conversation the "lost cause" was an endless theme. Those who listened became weary and the sons of the Confederate veterans were among them. *That* second generation made little effort to justify the action of their fathers. Their expressed opinion was that, after all, the result was inevitable and undoubtedly for the best. These sons went North and won success in every field of business and in every branch of learning. But now the grandsons of the Confederates rule in the place of the sons and there is no apologizing for the events of 1861; instead there is a belligerency that asserts the moral and constitutional justice of their grandfathers' policy. The South has been revived. Its history is taught with a fervid patriotism in the universities and schools. Recently there has been formed the Southern Historical Association as an evidence of the growing interest. The great novel of the Civil War and Reconstruction era was not written by one who had participated in the events or witnessed the scenes. It did not come from the pen of one who had listened to father's reminiscences. *Gone With the Wind* was written by a granddaughter of the Confederacy, in the year 1936, approximately sixty years after the period with which it dealt had come to an end.

Immigration not only has its history, it has its historiography. The writing of descriptions of that great epic movement began almost as early as the movement itself. Every immigrant letter written from new shores was history, very personal and very uncritical. Every sheaf of reminiscences written by one of the participants in his later years was also history, a little more uncritical. There was much to be recounted and since sons would not listen the grayheaded participants got together and, organized as pioneer societies, they told one another of the glorious deeds that they had seen and sometimes performed and listened to the reading of the obituaries of the giants that had fallen. When the last of them had joined his ancestors the pioneer society automatically disbanded leaving behind as the first chapter of immigrant historiography a conglomerate mass of literature, much and often most of it useless. All of it seemed useless to the son who cleared out his father's desk and resolved not to waste any of his time on such pointless pursuits.

As a broad generalization it may be said that the second generation is not interested in and does not write any history. That is just another aspect of their policy of forgetting. Then, however, appears the "third generation." They have no reason to feel any inferiority when they look about them. They are American born. Their speech is the same as that of those with whom they associate. Their material wealth is the average possession of the typical citizen. When anyone speaks to him about immigrants he always makes it clear that he has in mind the more recent hordes that have been pouring through the gates and suggestion that the onrush should be stemmed is usually prefaced with the remark that recent immigrants are not so desirable as the pioneers that arrived in earlier times. It is in an attitude of pride that the substantial landowner or merchant looks about him and says: "This prosperity is our achievement, that of myself and of my fathers; it is a sign of the hardy stock from which we have sprung; who where they and why did they come?" And so their curiosity is projected back into the family beginnings. Those who are acquainted with the universities of the Middle West, where a large proportion of the students are grandchildren and great-grandchildren of the nineteenth century immigrants, can sense this attitude of inquiry and can not escape the feeling of pride in which they study the history and culture of the nations from which their ancestors came.

To show how universal this spirit has been we can retrace some periodic resurgences of national spirit and relate them to the time of immigration. There were Irishmen in America before the Revolution but there is no reason to question the generalization that until 1840 two-thirds of the emigrants from Ireland were the so-called Scotch-Irish. In the 1830's their influx was particularly large; in fact, the great proportion of Ulstermen who came to America arrived in the course of that decade. Sixty years later (at the time of the third generation) a renaissance of Scotch-Irish sentiment in the United States was strikingly apparent. Local societies were formed that met in monthly or quarterly conclave to sing the praises of their forebears and to glory in the achievements of the Presbyterian Church. Beginning in 1889 and continuing for more than a decade representatives of these societies met in an annual national meeting called a "Scotch-Irish Congress." Then the movement lost its impetus. Leaders died or took up other activities; members refrained from paying dues; attendance at sessions dwindled. After 1903 no more Scotch-Irish congresses were held.

We can pass to another example. The large German immigration reached its crest in the late 1840's and early 1850's. A little over a half a century later, in the first decade of the twentieth century, a breeze of historical interest stirred the German-American community.

One of the number was moved to offer a prize for the best historical discussion of the contribution of the German element to American life. Not only the prize-winning work (the well-known volume by A. B. Faust) but many of the manuscripts that had been submitted in the competition were published, forming a library of German-American activity in many fields. Several local and state historical societies were formed and the study of German literature in universities and schools enjoyed an amazing popularity that later observers could ascribe only to the propaganda of an intriguing nation. The Theodore Roosevelt Professorship established at the University of Berlin in 1907 was an expression of the same revival. The war naturally put an end to this activity and obscured much of the valuable work that the investigators had performed.

The auspices under which we have met this evening suggest the next example to be cited. The large Scandinavian immigration began in the 1850's and after the interruption of the Civil War reached its culmination in the 1880's. True to expectations we find that at present the most lively interest in history of this nature is exhibited in Scandinavian circles in America. Among Scandinavians, Norwegians were pioneers and in historical research they are also a step in advance. The Swedes came a little later and an intelligent prophet of that period looking forward to the cultural development of the nationality in their new home would have said: "About 1930 a historical society will be formed." It was. In June, 1930, the Augustana Historical Society was organized among the members of the Augustana Synod which so faithfully represents the more than a million people of Swedish descent who are citizens of the American republic. And now, having consumed half of the time allotted me in an introduction which is half of the paper, I come to the topic of the evening, a subject which will be interpreted in the light of the foregoing remarks. It reads: The problem of the third generation immigrant.

As problems go it is not one to cause worry or to be shunned. It has none of the bitterness or heart-breaking features of its predecessors. It is welcome. In summary form it may be stated as follows: Whenever any immigrant group reaches the third generation stage in its development a spontaneous and almost irresistible impulse arises which forces the thoughts of many people of different points of view to interest themselves in that one factor which they have in common: heritage—the heritage of blood. The problem is: how can this impulse be organized and directed so that the results growing therefrom will be worthy of the high instincts from which it has sprung and a dignified tribute to the pioneers and at the same time be a contribution to the history of the United States which has received all Europeans on a basis of equality and which should record their achievements in the same spirit of impartiality.

It is hardly necessary for me to remind this gathering that the Swedish stock in America is fast approaching the third generation stage. During the decade of the eighties their coming reached its height in numbers. The census of 1930 records that of the persons born in Sweden giving the date of their arrival in the country fifty-two percent landed before 1900—and this in spite of the great mortality that the newcomers of that period have suffered. The children that crowd the Sunday school rooms of the churches of this Synod it is well known are the grandsons and granddaughters of the pioneers that built the churches; grandsons and granddaughters, I am also sure, are present in increasing numbers in the student body of this college which those same pioneers at the cost of many sacrifices, built for the sake of those who were to come after them. Among the leaders of this society are men of the first generation and of the second generation but they are the proverbial exception, or it may be better to say they are third generation in spirit. No matter how active they are in leadership the organization can succeed only if the grandchildren of the pioneers will follow.

We will assume that this will be the case; that the membership of the Augustana Historical Society will continue to increase in numbers, that the members will continue to pay their dues, that a few patrons will arise to sponsor special enterprises in research and publication. It is not my object to enlighten you on how to bring about this happy condition. We will assume that many members will carry on their own investigations, that now and then an expert can be subsidized to probe deeply into some vital aspects of Swedish-American history and that the publications will continue to be of the high standard that has already been established. My suggestions will be of a different nature and will center about another set of questions: what fields shall be investigated? Where shall the emphasis be put in research and publication? What should be the attitude in which the past, which belongs not only to the Swedes but also to the Americans, should be approached? In attempting to answer I speak with no authority except that which comes from several years of delving into the records of most of the pioneer and historical societies of America.

Everyone accepts the premise that self-laudation is not the end in view. Nevertheless it will be hard to keep out because of the human characteristic of speaking nothing but good of the men who labored hard and have now disappeared from the earthly stage. At the first meeting of the Scotch-Irish Congress the speakers presented one paper after the other which dealt with the achievements of the Ulsterman at home and abroad, during all ages and in all spheres of human effort. Finally one of the delegates arose and made a cutting remark that only a Scotch-Irishman would dare to make. While listening to the programs, he said, he had been asking himself the question: "What on earth have the rest of creation been doing for the last eighteen hundred years?" That question should be in the mind of every writer who is tempted to generalize on the contribution of ethnic groups to the development of American life.

If not to the laudation of great men to what activities should the efforts of the society be directed? Let that question first be approached by a calm realization of the fact that the society will not live forever. The time will come when membership will dwindle, when promising subjects for research will be few in number and of little popular interest. That has been the life-course of every organization of this nature. The constituency becomes gradually thinned out as the third generation merges into the fourth and the fourth shades off into the fifth. Even societies with substantial endowments have in their later years found it difficult to continue to produce work of a high scholarly quality. The final judgement rendered regarding the success or failure of this society as of others will rest upon the answer given to two pertinent inquires: Did they, when the time was appropriate, write the history of the special group with whom they were concerned on broad impartial lines, and did they make a permanent contribution to the meaning of American history at large? A few proposals by the following of which a satisfactory reply can be given to both of those questions are now in order.

First of all let it be remembered that the history of any immigrant stock in America is far broader than the history of the particular religious organization that was predominant in the number of communicants that it could claim. The neglect of that fact was the first error made by historical writers in America. When they set out to write the story of the settlement of Englishmen in New England they centered it all about the migration of the Puritan church and neglected a hundred other factors that surrounded the coming and establishment of the colonies on that coast. In recent years some correction has been made but the traditional emphasis has been so great that in spite of the labors of many scholars and the resources of a dozen secular institutions, the history of New England is still less satisfactory than that of any other section of the older part of the country. From such a false start may the Augustana Historical Society be preserved!

Religion must certainly be a leading theme in the program. The church was the first, the most important and the most significant institution that the immigrants established. Its policies reacted upon every other phase of their existence but in turn and, in fact, first, those other phases of their existence established the conditions under which the church was planted and grew. If one should study the agriculture, the system of land purchase, the distribution of population, the state of the roads, the circulation of books and newspapers, the development of amusements he would be in a better position to appraise the situation that the church did occupy in the life of every community. In Mr. Rolvaag's stirring novel *Giants in the Earth* no episode is presented with more effect than that which recounts the coming of the clergyman and the effect is produced not by the description of the man and his mission. It is the background of dull, material routine that has preceded that gives to the brief chapter its epic quality. History had been made before the clergyman and the church appeared and to be understood they must be placed in their proper order in the sequence of events.

Moveover, for an understanding of religious development to the formation of those churches that broke with the faith of the old country relatively more attention should be given than the number of their communicants would warrant. In no other experience was the psychology of the immigrant more clearly reflected. When they said that they passed from the old world to the new many of them meant that the world should be new in all respects. When they gave up allegiance to a government it was easy to give up allegiance to a church. The secessions from the Lutheran faith can be dealt with conveniently, quickly and without embarrassment by ascribing them to the successful methods of proselyting that the well-financed American home missionary societies employed. But the immigrant met the proselyter halfway—perhaps more than halfway—and when one knows what was going on in the mind of the person who did break away from his mother church it will be easier to understand the actions of some of those who did not break away but certainly caused frictions within the church to which they remained true and created situations that could not have arisen in the old Swedish parish from which they had recently come.

Even the study of politics is not entirely foreign to an organization which has chosen as its mission the history of the Augustana Synod. The clergymen of that Synod like the clergymen of any other religious body in the republic had no intention of destroying the fundamental separation of Church and State which the fathers of the constitution had ordained, but how they itched to go into politics! How they lived to find in every Sunday's text some idea that could be applied to the decision of that burning political issue that the men in the audience had been discussing before the services had begun and which they would surely begin to discuss again as soon as the benediction had been pronounced. There is much evidence to suggest that the immigrant church had a great influence in determining the way in which the naturalized citizen would cast his vote. But not a single study has been made of church influence in any election and the results of such a study would throw as much light upon the status of the church as it would upon the political history of that election.

The church had some competitors in the matter of interest, affection and usefulness. Whatever the difficulties that attended the founding of the pioneer congregation, that of inducing the immigrant to join was hardly existent. The immigrant was an inveterate joiner—a habit which was, without question, the result of his feeling of lonesomeness. In Europe the individual was born into many groups that he had to join in America and he entered into them rather light-heartedly hoping that from all he would derive the satisfaction that no single one could yield. When some energetic spirit said to him: Come and join this fraternal organization, he went; when the suggestion of a singing society was broached he fell in with the plan; when some one undertook to line up a shooting corps he took down his gun and practiced marksmanship. All of these pursuits weakened somewhat the hold of the church and the minister was led to adopt an uncompromising attitude toward amusements that otherwise would have been held both innocent and useful. Therefore, it can be said that without a knowledge of the social environment the policy of the church can not be understood.

If these suggestions should be followed, the product would be a history of the Swedes in America that no one could accuse of being tainted with partiality. Perhaps not all the passages would be read with a glow of pride but there would be no humiliation and the pride in the achievement of what no other ethnic group in America has been willing to do would soon overcome regrets that arose out of what truth made it necessary to say. In such an accomplishment the Augustana Historical Society would achieve all that its founders had hoped for it in the field of religious history and the incidental products would give to the world a true and inspiring picture of what the Swedish pioneers had done in the task of subduing the primitive American wilderness.

Although a historical society has justified its existence when it has faithfully recorded the experiences and achievements of the particular element in the population or the particular region in the country that it was created to serve, still unless the story that is written from these records can be made to fit in as one chapter in the larger volume that is called American history the charge of antiquarianism can hardly be escaped. Men of insight who understand that it is the ultimate fate of any national group to be amalgamated into the composite American race will be reconciled to the thought that their historical activities will in time be merged with the activities of other societies of the same nature and finally with the main line of American historiography itself. How such a merging may profoundly influence the course of all national historical writing is illustrated by reference to that one group which is the most mature among the population minorities.

The Scotch-Irish Congress during the fourteen years of its existence published ten volumes of *Proceedings*. A study of the contents of these volumes reveals the widening nature of the interests growing out of the researches. The laudatory character of the contributions to the first publication has been mentioned. Such papers are not entirely absent from the last volume but there also appear titles such as these: "Paths and Roads of our Forefathers," "The Colonial Defenses of Franklin County," "German Life and Thought in a Scotch-Irish Settlement"— substantial contributions to the pioneer history of the environment in which the group developed. It is well known that during the decade of the 1890's the character of American historical writing changed. A new emphasis appeared. Scholars looked beyond the older settlements ranged along the seaboard into the communities in the back country. A word that every schoolboy can now explain crept into the textbooks. This work and this theory now almost dominate every page in the volume. The word is "frontier" and the theory is the "frontier interpretation of American history." Older students wise in the way of the classroom have been known to pass on to the younger students this piece of practical advice: "In any examination in American history if you don't know the answer tie it up with the development of the frontier."

This new emphasis is universally credited to Professor Frederick J. Turner. However, Turner or no Turner the frontier hypothesis was bound to come and to appear in the very decade during which he wrote his famous essay. In fact, the hypothesis may be distilled from the conglomerate mass of information and theory jumbled together in the ten volumes of Scotch-Irish proceedings. It is doubtful whether the pronouncement of one man, no matter how brilliant, could have turned the course of historical writing unless it were already veering in that direction. It is quite possible that Turner who wrote in 1893 drew upon the frontier interest that the Scotch-Irish were arousing by their studies of the part that the Ulstermen took in the movement of settlement into the West. The interest that they awakened united with the scholars that Professor Turner trained to give to American history its new and significant social interpretation.

The frontier doctrine in its original narrow statement has been overdone. We are beginning to see that the Mississippi Valley was for fifty years the frontier of Europe as well as of the eastern states and that it reacted upon England, Germany and Scandinavia with a force comparable to that which it exerted upon Atlantic America. Some historians with the orthodox professional training have recognized this fact and they are attempting, in a rather clumsy way, to analyze the operation of these influences. There is, however, one omission in their training. They know nothing about the hundreds of immigrant communities in America that formed the human connecting link between the old world and the new, nothing about the millions of personal contacts that brought humble public opinion on both sides of the Atlantic so close together.

The next stage in American historical writing will concern itself with this widened outlook. Herein lies not only the great opportunity but also the great obligation of the third generation historical activity. It also can provide the atmosphere; it alone can uncover the sources; it alone can interpret the mentality of the millions of persons who had not entirely ceased to be Europeans and had not yet become accepted Americans. The problem of the third generation immigrant is to undertake the job that has been assigned and to perform it well.

The close of the discourse may very properly be a warning. It can be assumed too readily that the history of migration can not be anything but a desirable influence. That is not necessarily the case. Prejudice and super-nationalism may be the product. Societies organized with the laudable intention of commemorating the deeds of which any people should be proud may fall into the hands of those who will use them for instruments of propaganda. Instead of a world covered with a network of associations which will foster an appreciation of the best that each nation has produced, we may find international societies for the promotion of hatred and intolerance. Historians must recognize an obligation to guide the national curiosity to know the past along those lines which will serve the good of all.

If told as it transpired, the epic of migration can add an ideal to take the place of one of the many that recent decades have shattered. For it is a simple story of how troubled men, by courage and action, overcame their difficulties, and how people of different tongues and varied culture have managed to live together in peace.

MARCUS LEE HANSEN

Who Shall
Inherit America?

[Delivered to the National Conference of Social Work, Indianapolis, May 25, 1937.]

"Who shall inherit America?" This is not a new question in American history. It was asked by Englishmen, Frenchmen and Spaniards in the Eighteenth Century and answered by a series of wars of aggrandizement. It was asked by Americans in the Nineteenth Century who were frightened, almost terrified, by the crowds of invading aliens, those whom they described as "the ragged regiments of Europe," who disembarked upon their shores. It is asked today, not in a spirit of aggrandizement or fear; rather, in a spirit of hope.

Once immigration was the problem of the social worker, of the police officer, of the political leader. Now it is the problem of the historian. For three hundred years the European invasion of America continued. All told about forty millions of adventurers (some of them called colonists and others immigrants) crossed the Atlantic to establish themselves on new shores. Irrespective of into how many volumes and series the history of the United States will run in future millenniums, the coming of these pioneers will always constitute Chapter One of Volume One. The historian of every phase of American life, in his search for origins, will retrace a course back to these people and he will find in their character and motives, the institutions that they brought with them, the environment in which they settled, the explanation of many subsequent developments. Therefore it is essential that now when according to every indication the great historic westward tide has come to a final end, the history of that movement be written. It is the problem of the historian to record with sympathy but with realism the epic of the world's greatest migration. To accomplish that task, while memory is fresh and documents still preserved, is the most challenging duty now facing American historians.

This afternoon, however, the part assigned to the historian on the program does not call for what he would willingly present: a summary of what immigration has meant to American life in the past. On the contrary, he is invited to turn from a look backward to a look forward and to discuss the subject: what the history of immigration suggests in answer to the inquiry "Who shall inherit America?"

At once the objection is heard: if the history of immigration suggests anything it proves that there is nothing to discuss; that question is settled; America will not be the heritage of the immigrants; in spite of the tens of millions that have arrived the country still belongs to the native born. In a political sense this is true. During the romantic 1830's many German minds were busy with thoughts of peopling a state in the Mississippi Valley with Germans and when the inevitable break-up of the American union took place these inhabitants would hand the area over to some German state as a colony. But that prospect disappeared with all other romantic dreams of the decade. In 1847 many New Englanders believed that Boston, at least, would become annexed to Ireland. Whatever annexation that did follow was in the reverse direction. The ties that bound immigrant communities in the new world with the countries of birth were many but none of them were political.

Whenever the newcomer in his dejected moments sighed for the "old country" his homesick thoughts ignored politics and centered about the customs, interests and pleasures that are grouped in the word "culture." Until then he had probably not realized how much of contentment in his old life had been drawn from the environment that European civilization provided. He was not a musician nor an artist but he did have an appreciation of music and art that the Yankee lacked and no matter how small the village about which his social life had revolved some means of satisfaction existed. Public opinion assumed that it should. But how different was America—certainly, the America with which he associated! Square boxes for homes and long boxes for churches; no painting but the crude sign that swung over the tavern door; no songs but unintelligible camp meeting hymns; no music but the fiddler's string squeaking "Turkey in the Straw." What was worse than the absence of the arts was the contempt in which the native American held all accomplishments of this nature. Strong and healthy men should not be concerned with such trivialities so long as there were trees to be cut, stones to be rolled or even horses to be traded. In his effort to recreate part of what had been lost the immigrant settler could expect no cooperation or encouragement from his Yankee neighbor. Therefore, he was drawn more closely to those among his fellow countrymen who felt the same craving and together they attempted to rebuild a "little Germany," a "little Norway," a "little Italy" on western prairies or in the city wilderness. The social history of the

United States between 1830 and 1860 records the success of many of
these enterprises. Operas, theaters and orchestras appeared in half a
dozen cities; and in rural communities singing societies flourished
wherever a dozen male voices could be mustered at monthly gather-
ings. Cincinnati and St. Louis lost their American character to become
German, and in Boston and Philadelphia there were quarters that reminded observers of the lively and witty society of Dublin. In each
place newspapers were published that acted as a connecting link between the city group and their compatriots scattered in the villages
and distant farms. Most of the papers were edited by men who believed
it their mission to put some color into the drab American scene and
to hold aloft what they inevitably called the "torch" of culture. They
were aided in this endeavor by clergymen who realized that religion
was one aspect of culture and that by the preservation of language
and social ideals there was also preserved allegiance to the ancestral
faith. At the opening of the Civil War there existed in America not
only a North and a South which differed in institutions and social
beliefs but the North, in turn, contained a German-America, an Irish-
America and the germs of several more Americas each of which had
developed a distinct pattern of life which it hoped could be maintained
for posterity and influence in some degree the future development of
the growing republic.

The four years of bloody and bitter sectional conflict which destroyed the old South destroyed in a less obvious way the varied immigrant America of the North. Even on the basis of the scanty historical study that this neglected phase of American history has received
one is safe in saying that the Civil War was the dominant factor in
determining what the prevailing concept of "Americanization" should
be. It changed the ideals of the immigrant group and substituted a new
leadership. Immigrant homes were filled to overflowing with young
people when the war began. Sons joined the regiments and went to
the front not so much because of patriotism but because it was good
business: bounties and promises of land. As soon as that had happened
the home had changed. Parents spent less time in thinking about the
far-off land of their ancestors, more in considering the future of the
land of their children. Dreams of the past were less important than
the realities of the present. Sons in the army caught the spirit of nationalism. The immigrant newspapers printed less about the affairs of
the Old World in order to make room for dispatches from the battle
lines. Ministers neglected theological differences of the old country to
discuss religion as a comfort for the sorrows of the day. Editors and
clergymen who did not conform lost all influence and following. When
the war was over foreign languages and foreign customs had not dis-

appeared. But ideals had changed. All who lived in America, alien-born and native-born, were to become one people.

This ideal naturally dulled in the two decades that followed. Some of the old hopes of perpetuating nationality were revived and a new following was provided by the swelling tide of immigrants that in the 1880's swept into the country. Again alien Americans were in the process of formation, Scandinavian and Bohemian as well as German and Irish. Again catastrophe bought it all to an end, this time the catastrophe being not war but the economic distress of the 1890's. The primary concern became that of meeting the mortgage payment to prevent the loss of the homestead and those who had been engaged in industrial activities had to take to the road in search of new opportunities. Settlements were broken up by the dispersion of the population, newspapers went bankrupt and churches closed. Agitators were listened to only if they talked about free silver or monopolies.

In most communities this was the finishing blow, a blow that was the more fatal because it came at a time when the children of the immigrants had taken the place of their parents in the church pews and in the family councils. It is unnecessary in a meeting of social workers to describe the psychology of the second generation. Their motto was: Forget it all! Forget the language that had given them an accent that their schoolmates loved to mock. Forget the family and community customs that the sons of the Yankees and often the Yankees themselves had delighted to ridicule. Forget everyone and everything that antedated the moment when the foreign-born father first stepped upon American soil. Judged by all outside appearances this was the end of any influence that the great influx of the middle and latter nineteenth century could exert upon the cultural development of the United States.

It is a little too early to trace in similar fashion the evolution of the interests and emphases of those later comers who are generally classified as the "new immigrants." They brought with them an even more colorful and varied culture, one that was so vital that although the American tradition of conformity was well established before their arrival, the music and art of southern and eastern Europe flourished to an amazing degree in the mining camps and city slums where many of them were forced to seek a livelihood. Among them as among their predecessors were those who took comfort in the thought that succeeding generations of Americans would inherit some of the less material and inspiring features of the civilization that they represented and these hopes were not without some encouraging signs. But again the appearance of the second generation coincided with the existence of an abnormal situation: The World War. Little could be expected to survive the hundred percentism of that period and apparently little did.

Had the current of immigration continued to flow it might have developed that the Americanization policies of the war years had not been quite so ruthless as contemporary observers believed. Continued arrivals would have kept alive the spark that had survived the deluge of patriotism. But the immigration act of 1924 cut down the normal inflow to a tenth of its one-time volume and the depression of 1929 set under way a reverse current that carried eastward over the Atlantic a larger contingent of aliens returning to Europe than entered the United States as immigrants. Presumably some day, when more normal conditions of business and agriculture prevail, the quotas will be filled but even then the number of the arrivals will be so small in comparison with the nation's population that we can say that immigration has come to an end.

Accordingly, the present is an opportune time at which to take stock of what happened and to sit in judgement upon the policy that the nation has followed. The decision is not entirely favorable. Complete approval cannot be given. American civilization and culture were bound to be European in origin. Was it not a short-sighted view that decreed that the people who came first should have a continent reserved for the particular strain of culture that they represented? The history of civilization records the manner in which many a young nation has fallen heir to the gifts, offered by some older and often declining nation. The United States, almost alone among new nations, has had offered to it the manysided culture of a continent but in its social policy it has scorned to take any but that represented by a small part of the old world from which its people have come. Is it any wonder that for over a century observers have deplored the uniformity of the American cultural scene and have commented upon the pioneer drabness that characterizes towns and cities, men and women? It is easy to explain it (as a more orthodox historian probably would) by saying that Americans have been so busy taming a wild continent that there has been no energy or ingenuity left for other pursuits. The truth is, they made a bad blunder when consciously or unconsciously they decreed that one literature, one attitude towards the arts, one set of standards should be the basis of culture.

Judging by what has been said thus far it seems that an answer has been given to the question of the day. Just as British political theory and practice have determined American political development so American culture will be British culture but why shouldn't there have been added to its wearing qualities some of the lighter and brighter-features offered by immigrants from the Mediterranean and some of the deeper feelings brought in by immigrants from Eastern Europe? The student of the history of immigration cannot but ponder on the tragedy of lost opportunities.

However, the student of the history of immigration learns to his surprise that in these matters opportunity knocks more than once. When he turns from the role of historian to the role of prophet he foresees that the second knocking will soon be heard and the response to this second appeal will give the final answer to the question: Who will inherit America, culturally speaking?

We now enter upon a realm of historical research that has been little explored. How to appraise that elusive body of public opinion known as the "popular mind" is not part of an historian's formal training. There are no established canons of judgement that he can apply. Nevertheless variations in public attention can be followed even when they cannot be measured and one of them can be formulated as the "principle of third generation interest."

This principle is derived from the generalization that usually father and son are not interested in the same things and do not have the same point of view. The participants in any great historic event or development never tire of talking about what they saw and what their place was as a participant. Their sons, however, tire of listening and are as anxious to forget as their parents are to remember. This principle may be applied in almost any field of activity in which the public has at some time been concerned. Little historical writing regarding an event is done by the sons of those who are the actors therein. In conversation they are usually apologists for what their immediate forebears had done. For many reasons the second generation immigrants are especially forgetful and apologetic and it is during the period of their sway numerically and otherwise, that the heroic aspects of modern migration are overlooked.

But after the second generation comes the third and, again, the father-son reversal is evident. History is usually written by the third generation following an event. The grandsons of immigrants are those who want to know all about the beginning of the American branch of the family. They do not have the same reasons or complexes that encouraged the second to make a complete break. They are as American as any of their neighbors. There is no accent in speech caused by the intermingling of two tongues. No feeling of inferiority troubles them in the presence of persons of Mayflower or Knickerbocker descent. They have a healthy curiosity to know something of the family saga. But after the name of the grandfather has been acquired and his brothers arranged in the proper sequence, then the mind goes on to ask:

where was he from? What manner of person was he in distant Europe? What kind of country was it from which he came?

To be proud of blood and descent is one of the most common of human desires. Pride is easily extended from a person to a country and a wanderer in the field of genealogy often strays in the field of history. He is proud of his grandfather but just as proud of the civilization that he represented and whereas his grandfather cannot be recalled to life while the civilization can the former is often forgotten in the awakened interest in the latter. A trip back to the ancestral village often reveals that the home has disappeared and with it all objects of personal interest. But new scenes and strange customs are viewed sympathetically and vivid impressions are left upon the mind of one who is American in birth, reactions and influence.

Such developments multiplied several million times are now transpiring or about to take place. A large proportion of the American people is just entering the third generation stage and the many contacts that they will establish with popular culture abroad will constitute the new opportunity that is to knock. In a recognition of this fact and by a skillful handling of the situation there may be selected from the revived interest those features of cultural life that should be added to the heritage of America.

The most obvious aspect is found in the writing of history. The books are beginning to appear. They bear titles reading: "The contribution of such and such a nationality to American development"; "Great Americans of such and such birth." Amateur historians and racketeering publishers combine to draw up a volume of biographies of insignificant people and pawn it off upon the eager purchaser as a history of that group in American life. Other productions that have involved some research lose all credibility by proceeding, like politicians the morning after election, to "claim everything." A serious attendant at a session of the Scotch-Irish Congress forty years ago arose at the close of a program that had dealt with Scotch-Irish achievements and said that although he was happy to hear of these accomplishments, he could not help but wonder what the rest of creation had been doing for the past eighteen hundred years. History can mean much in awakening the pride that will foster the revival but it must be honorable and reasonable history, the product of research, not of patriotism.

If the job should be turned over to the professional historians they would in time bring out a series of monographs with footnotes and documents, volumes that would satisfy the most critical reviewer. But the volumes would very seldom be taken down from the library shelf and little contained in their pages would pass over into the textbooks on American history. Let the monographs be written. They are essential for any understanding of what actually happened but their publication should be only the first step in this phase of national education.

Vast endowments exist in America for the purpose of discovering and revealing the origins of ancient empires. Universities that will not spend a cent to send a man to the second-hand store around the corner in search of documents and relics that will explain and illustrate the growth of American civilization will finance at the cost of tens of thousands of dollars an expedition to dig up a mound a third of the way round the world and they will account the expenditure a successful investment if the archaeologist comes back with some bits of broken pottery and clay tablets with half legible inscriptions. Stately palaces have been constructed to display the findings and by every device known to the artist and exhibitor educate the public strolling through the corridors into the mysteries of Near Eastern civilization.

There should be some institution rich in funds and staffed by men of learning and ingenuity who consider it the greatest of all callings to let the American people know something about the thirty or forty nationalities that contributed blood, ideas and labor to the founding of the nation during the first three hundred years of its existence. The story of the immigration and settlement of each of these groups could be graphically presented to leave an unforgettable impression upon even the most casual visitors. No person who completed a tour of the exhibits would ever consider the United States exclusively a Yankee nation and nine out of every ten would ask: why is it that we took so little from those who had so much to offer? The unanswered question would leave him more favorably disposed towards many people and customs that he hitherto ignored.

If, however, the world waits for philanthropic millionaires to chart the course of progress, progress will be slow and perhaps too slow to make use of the awakened curiosity of the third generation. It could be far better and of far more influence to have a thousand enterprises springing up from the people than one being forced down from a patron. The beginnings for such a movement already exist. There is hardly a community in the country that does not possess a public library and most of those libraries are now directed by persons who understand that their building can serve many purposes besides the housing of books. Each can be the collector of an historical exhibit that will reflect the cultural background of the people that first settled the surrounding countryside. Should some forward-looking librarian undertake to fill the hall cases with pioneer articles, prayer books and guide books printed in some foreign tongue, needle work and utensils unknown to the native homestead, some worthy citizen might object especially if it involved the removal of relics of the Revolution or Civil

War. But the incident in itself could be the occasion for a lesson on national culture and might spur the representatives of other groups into an effort to secure their proper share of recognition. If, on every hand, the impressionable mind of the youth of the country were reminded of the multiple origin of the American people, all presented in a truthful, dignified and tolerant way, little by little, daily life would select what it found useful or pleasant from the gifts that were still available and that a previous generation had blindly refused.

Not only does the third generation seek to establish relations with the culture of the past through history, it also approaches sympathetically their remote cousins who still live in the country of origin. "Hands across the seas" is the phrase that expresses this sentiment when an Englishman in America thinks well of an Englishman who remained at home. The Atlantic is, in fact, spanned with a network of entangled hands reaching out from remote districts of Europe to clasp those that are extended from remote prairie farms of the West. The descendants of emigrants from almost every province in Norway are organized into societies (some thirty of them all told) each of which keeps alive the feelings that tie families together and fosters the exchange of information by letter, and of personal visits by travel. No visit is complete without a souvenir and each souvenir is a reminder of something different.

Societies of this nature are generally of spontaneous origin and development. They have appeared to fill a need and if left alone they will satisfy these needs and others that will be the outgrowth of success. But, unfortunately, they are not going to be let alone. In a world full of rampant nationalism which is constantly seeking justification in the eyes of people of other countries every organization that extends over an international boundary is too effective an instrument of propaganda to escape untouched. It would not be difficult to illustrate this tragedy by reference to specific societies that have ceased to be the cultural links that their founders planned that they should be and have become violent partisans of some political regime. At one time they were promising signs of the internationalization of culture; now they cannot be trusted any more than a subsidized press and subsidized agitators. The revival of immigrant culture must be wholly an American effort.

The history of anything is justified only on the basis of the long view that it provides. The historian is interested in the millions of immigrants of the past hundred years not so much in their capacity as bewildered peasants in search of work and land as in their unconscious character as the carrier of culture from an old world to a new. While recognizing that they caused social difficulties, that their political ideals and practices were not always on the highest plane, that there were times when the country would have been better off without them, he views them and their mistakes sympathetically. He also understands that their real influence in cultural development begins only when most observers say that it has come to an end. Within the next generation the United States will decide what it wants to accept and what it wants to reject. That is the next problem of immigration that the nation must solve.

Contributors to This Volume

THOMAS ARCHDEACON is professor of history at the University of Wisconsin at Madison. He is the author of two books about New York City (*New York City, 1664–1710: Conquest and Change* and *New York: The Centennial Years, 1676–1976*); a synthesis of American immigration history, *Becoming American: An Ethnic History*; and also many articles on immigration history.

H. ARNOLD BARTON is professor of history at Southern Illinois University. He is the author of many books and articles on Swedish immigration to North America, as well as general Scandinavian history, including *Letters from the Promised Land*, *The Search for Ancestors: A Swedish-American Family Saga*, and *Scandinavia During the Revolutionary Era*. He is also the editor of the *Swedish-American Historical Quarterly*.

DAG BLANCK is director of the Swenson Swedish Immigration Research Center at Augustana College in Rock Island, Illinois. He has written about Swedish immigration to the United States, and is the co-editor of *Scandinavia Overseas: Patterns of Cultural Transformation in North America and Australia*.

NATHAN GLAZER is professor of education and sociology at Harvard University. He is the author of numerous books and articles, including two works with Daniel Patrick Moynihan, *Beyond the Melting Pot: The Negroes, Puerto Ricans, Jews, Italians, and Irish of New York City* and *Ethnicity: Theory and Experience*. Included among his recent publications is a volume of essays, *Ethnic Dilemmas*. As editor of *Commentary* magazine, Glazer was responsible for republishing Hansen's essay in 1952.

PHILIP GLEASON is professor of history at Notre Dame University. He is the author of *The Conservative Reformers: German-American Catholics and the Social Order*, *Contemporary Catholicism in the United States*, *Keeping the Faith: American Catholicism Past and Present*, and articles on the concept of the melting pot. He also wrote the essay "American Identity and Americanization" in the *Harvard Encyclopedia of American Ethnic Groups*.

VICTOR GREENE is professor of history at the University of Wisconsin at Milwaukee. He is the author of *The Slavic Community on Strike: Immigrant Labor in Pennsylvania Anthracite*, *For God and Country: The Rise of Polish and Lithuanian Ethnic Consciousness in America 1860–1910*, and *American Immigrant Leaders: Marginality and Identity*. Greene is a past president of the Immigration History Society.

JOHN HIGHAM is John Martin Vincent Professor of History at Johns Hopkins University. He is the author of the classic work in American immigration history, *Strangers in the Land: Patterns of American Nativism 1860–1925*, and *Send These to Me: Immigrants in Urban America*. In addition, he has written extensively in American intellectual history and American historiography.

PETER KIVISTO is associate professor of sociology at Augustana College. He has written on Finnish immigration to North America, including several articles and the book *Immigrant Socialist in the United States: The Case of the Finns and the Left*. He is also the editor of *The Ethnic Enigma: The Salience of Ethnicity for European-Origin Groups*.

STANFORD LYMAN is Distinguished Professor of Social Science at Florida Atlantic University. He is the author of *Chinese Americans, Asians in North America, Blacks in American Sociological Thought, Chinatown and Little Tokyo*, and *American Sociology*.

FRED MATTHEWS is professor of history and humanities at York University in Toronto. His publications include *Quest for an American Sociology: Robert E. Park and the Chicago School*. He has also written articles on ethnic theory.

MOSES RISCHIN is professor of history at San Francisco State University. He is the author of *The Promised City: New York's Jews 1870–1914, The Jews of the West*, and *Grandma Never Lived in America: The New Journalism of Abraham Cahan*. Rischin wrote an article on Marcus Lee Hansen that appeared in the 1979 festschrift to Oscar Handlin.

Index